WAR IN KANAWHA COUNTY: PROTEST IN 1974

Author

Don Means

Co-Author

Judson Means

Gotham Books

30 N Gould St.
Ste. 20820, Sheridan, WY 82801
https://gothambooksinc.com/

Phone: 1 (307) 464-7800

Published by Gotham Books (June 20, 2023)

ISBN: 979-8-88775-332-4 (H)
ISBN: 979-8-88775-330-0 (P)
ISBN: 979-8-88775-331-7 (E)

TABLE OF CONTENS

Introduction....iii
CHAPTER 1 The Protest Begins....1
CHAPTER 2 The Storm Brews....10
CHAPTER 3 The School Board's Solution....19
Chapter 4 Trials and Tribulations....30
Chapter 5 Court Order Cripples Protest....45
Chapter 6 The Calm Before the Storm....66
Chapter 7 Friendships....70
Chapter 8 The Die Is Cast....81
Chapter 9 Meeting at Watt Powell Ballpark....104
Chapter 10 Three Leaders....115
Chapter 11 Anson's Pastor....125
Chapter 12 The Alliance is Born!....146
Chapter 13 The Alliance Office Opens....156
Chapter 14 The Allies....165
Chapter 15 Is Victory Worth It?....174
Chapter 16 The Alliance Grows....181
Chapter 17 Horan's Headquarters....196
Chapter 18 Battleground....224
Chapter 19 The Alliance Struggles On....229
Chapter 20 The Alliance's Slate....241
Chapter 21 School Board Bombed....246
Chapter 22 Failed Plans....249
Chapter 23 Interview with CBS....261
Chapter 24 The Old Irishman....267
Chapter 25 Steps Taken Against the School Board....276

Chapter 26 Strange Happenings 283
Chapter 27 School Bus Attacked 289
Chapter 28 Media Blitz 292
Chapter 29 The School Board Is Arrested 298
Chapter 30 Enlightenment 302
Chapter 31 Underwood Attacked 311
Chapter 32 KKK Enters the War 315
Chapter 33 The Big March 320
In Conclusion 325

This book is not intended as a vendetta, personal or otherwise. It is intended to neither flatter nor offend. It is intended only to present the actual happenings the way the author saw them unfold, as accurately and objectively as he is capable of presenting them. What the author does hope to do is to reach good people who are unaware of what is taking place, so they will use this book like a magnet to draw the people of understanding out of the masses.

The author of this book has no grandiose dreams of convincing everybody that the information contained in these pages is true, and that the philosophy that has been foisted upon our children and our nation is genuine. After all, Christ himself and the Bible have been around a long time, and they haven't convinced everybody.

This book is dedicated to all that sacrificed so much during the protest against the books.

Introduction

Concord Bridge would have remained just a structure for carrying horses and buggies across a stream, its name being known only by the inhabitants of the territory within one day's ride, had not a shot been fired there that was "heard 'round the world."

Similarly, Pearl Harbor was a name familiar to naval personnel and geography teachers only, until a swarm of Japanese warplanes brought it into world focus.

The name "Kanawha" is derived from a Native American tribe that once made its home in the valley, the "Cohnowas." Kanawha County lay at the bottom of the well of obscurity, totally unknown outside the hills of West Virginia, until Alice Moore discovered a "plan" in the textbooks of the local public schools, one that was contrary to her Christian convictions, causing her to give a *shout* heard 'round the world. Within weeks after the first day of school that year, Kanawha County became a household name across the nation ... and a familiar one around the world. (While she was in Russia on a tour two years later, people in Moscow asked an acquaintance of mine, who travels extensively, for details of what had taken place in Kanawha County.) The author of this book was interviewed for Japanese television. Reporters from all over the world poured into Charleston, the county seat of Kanawha. They came from France, Japan, Canada, and other countries.

Everybody across the nation and around the world was asking these questions: "What is going on in the hills of West Virginia?" "What touched off this War in Kanawha County?" "Where will it end?"

The author will answer these questions and more in this book. Although written in novel form, it is factual. It is not a story based on truth but on the actual happenings as he lived them, not merely as an eyewitness but as a participant in a key role, instrumental in causing many of the major events to happen.

The fictional names of Jim Farley and Roger and Carol Banks are the only deviations from truth in the manuscript as it is presently written. The author felt this was necessary to allow him the freedom to tell the story, verbatim, as it actually happened, without being accused of bragging about his major part in the issue.

Jim Farley was born and raised in the hills surrounding Kanawha County. Having little formal education, he wanted better for his children. He viewed working hard to earn the money to send them to the best academic facilities as the way to achieve this. Like most parents, he trusted the educators, without reserve, to teach his children what he wanted them to learn; they were the professionals and symbolized advancement, a brighter future, enlightenment, and everything else that was good for his children, who were second only to his God, in his fundamentalist viewpoint stemming from his Bible Belt heritage.

When Alice Moore began the furor, Jim was skeptical—after all, "The Establishment" knew best. He examined the books in question. They were a little strange to him, but he attributed this to the progressive education he had heard so much about. It had been a long time since he dropped out of school, and a lot had changed. He slipped back into his comfortable rut.

On the eve of the opening day of school, he attended a rally held by the protestors of the books. He heard a bizarre tape playing, extolling killing, which was part of the "instructional" materials to be used in school. He was appalled by this but was still unimpressed by the caliber of the protestors.

On the first morning of school, picket lines were formed, not only around the schools but also at coal mines, factories, grocery warehouses, and the like, closing them all down. Pandemonium reigned. Jim called the teacher of his little girl who was in the third grade and asked that her books be sent home for examination.

He went through them once and saw nothing disturbing. A second time brought one story to his attention. Suddenly, a plan leaped out at him from the pages of the seemingly innocuous third-grade reader, scaring him to death. (Nicholas Von Hoffman was to write of the same plan in the July 21, 1975, issue of the *Washington Post*: "What these people"—referring to the publishers of the books—"are selling is a depraved egalitarianism in which children are turned into atomized pumpkin people.")

Jim, in his naivety and with his fundamentalist Bible Belt convictions intact and healthy, crashed head-on into the philosophy of humanism. He groped frantically for solutions through various channels—the school superintendent, the media, and the law—to no avail. He joined the fight in earnest. The ensuing battle makes for a gripping, absorbing story; embodies every human emotion; and has all the elements of sensationalism, but it can be told as a documentary. It is true.

The issue dealt with in this book is as current as today's headlines. Hardly a week goes by without its being explored: *The Phil Donahue Show*, November 1981; *Reader's Digest* (quoting James Michener), October 1981; *60 Minutes*, October 1981; *CBS Special*, September 1981; and I could go on and on.

This is largely because of the War in Kanawha County, the battles waged there, and the shock wave that Jim was describing when he told Mick Staton (now a U.S. congressional representative from West Virginia), "We'll pick this country up by the corner and shake it like a sheet." And shake it they did.

Although he always stopped just short of actually breaking the law, Jim played both sides of the street. He formed an organization of business and professional people to combat the textbooks, while he simultaneously attended a clandestine meeting to plot the arrest of the school board (totally unknown to his associates in the Alliance). His background as a demolitions expert makes the reader wonder about the dynamiting of the schools and the school board building itself. His expertise as a deer hunter and the required skill with high-powered rifles come to mind when school buses and state police cruisers were shot at. One man was shot through the heart, but Jim was never suspected of this deed since the culprit was apprehended. His dirt-poor origins, combined with his rapport with the elite of Kanawha Valley, allowed him to weave in and out of both sides of the conflict with ease. His "street protestor" compadres were usually aware of his role in the business and professional community segment of the war, but his moderate associates in that austere category would have been appalled at his involvement in the cloak-and-dagger activities of the back rooms and alleyways, had they known.

Although the War in Kanawha County spanned only a few short months before it was over, many world factions were involved—the Ku Klux Klan, The John Birch Society, the World Council of Churches, National Endowment for the Arts, both leading political parties of the United States, and the Communist Party. (One protestor was approached by members of the Communist Party.)

This book brings out many of the facts the media didn't uncover. The author was personally acquainted with all the major figures in the war and was in contact with them at the time of this writing. He also had in his possession all the personal papers and media reports of Alice Moore, plus the books themselves, and last but not least, Larry Freeman's personal copy of the review committee's report on the textbooks.)

Kanawha County was polarized by the conflict over the textbooks. It was not a class war as stated by the image so vigorously perpetrated by the liberal media, which presented it as a protest of the working class, of snake-handling fundamentalists, ignorant and fearful of change, but rather a conflict of philosophies. Admittedly, the more sophisticated of the elite, initially having only the media's version with which to judge the situation predictably aligned themselves with the "educrats." An educrat is defined as combining the Latin part of educator with the Greek part of bureaucrat. But once they were acquainted with the facts (and this acquaintance was the primary purpose of Jim's forming an alliance of business and professional people). Professional people who were against the books objected even more strongly to the contents of the books than the street protestors did (although their protest took a more moderate format) because, due to their greater depth of perception, they saw visions of future ramifications obscure to the working class.

At the height of the battle, people from all classes, financial and intellectual, were protesting vigorously (each in his own way) the usage of these textbooks. Doctors, lawyers, bankers, industrialists, schoolteachers, educators, and millionaires alike joined forces in whatever way they could to stem the tide of objectionable material and methods being used in the school system they were paying for. (Bob Dornan, now a U.S. congressman from California, and Mick Staton, the U.S. congressman from West Virginia, were two of the men who fought side by side with Jim in the battle. Both agreed to the use of their real names in this book.)

Alice Moore sounded the alarm, similar to Paul Revere crying out his warning of danger that resulted the Boston Tea Party; as the media portrayed: it was also more than that. (Eventually, a segment of the protestors, not unlike the Pilgrims, pulled out of the public educational system, symbolic of England, to form a new land of hope in Christian schools, symbolic of the New World of the United States.)

The miners, a singular breed, the backbone of West Virginia's leading industry, "King Coal," took the hard-line approach. They closed down everything in sight, beginning with the coal mines themselves. They then moved on to grocery warehouses (Kroger), thereby cutting the mainline of the food supply into the valley; chemical plants; construction jobs (curbing the valley's growth); trucking firms, cutting off other vital supplies; and even closed down the entire public transit system at one point, in a "to the death" attitude in the defense of their convictions. The author witnessed foodstuffs and canned goods being collected to keep the miners and their families from starving while they stayed away from their jobs to wage the war.

The fires of rebellion were fanned, massive rallies were held, the tempo of emotion stepped up, and there were protest marches with enough people taking part to encircle the city. Then the real violence erupted, with a man shot through the heart, the dynamiting of schools and the school board building, and the shooting of school buses and state police cruisers, to say nothing of countless fights and beatings.

Secret meetings were held between prominent politicians

and street protestors; strange alliances were formed between unlikely forces; rifts occurred between labor and management in business; factions were formed in churches; and families were split, brother against brother—all because of the controversial textbooks. Silhouetted against the midnight sky, against the picturesque mountains surrounding a once-peaceful valley, a fiery cross was burned by hooded members of the Ku Klux Klan.

To answer the question of L. T. Anderson, the leading liberal columnist of the local newspaper, in a 1974 article, his latest exercise in derision of Alice Moore—"Who is left to fight the textbooks?"—the protestors, as one voice, would answer, "The whole world, L. T. ... the whole world."

CHAPTER 1
The Protest Begins

Jim Farley lived on the other side of life, which in the Kanawha Valley, meant the other side of Charleston, and up on the hill. South Hills, as it was called, may not have had 90 percent of all the money of the valley to be enjoyed by the 5 percent of the valley's population that lived there, but they worked hard to convince the rest of the world that they did. Many people called it "Snob Hill."

Jim didn't live amongst the elite, nor was he wealthy by any means; rather, he lived on the fringe of the most exclusive subdivision and made a good living in the small business he had started.

The modest home he had built with his own hands was situated on part of what had originally been the farm of his grandfather, a proud though dirt-poor individualist of pioneer stock, who was extremely covetous of his land.

Before the Civil War, the land and the people of western Virginia had always been different. East of the mountains was a country of vast plantations, a slave state whose people were largely of English ancestry. There the political power of Virginia resided, and there the legislature spent the public's money for schools, roads, and other internal improvements. West of the Appalachian ridges was a land of small hill-country farms tended by non-slave-owning individualists of Scotch-Irish, German, Welsh, and English descent. Jim Farley was truly an original West Virginia hillbilly, having a mixture of all the above-mentioned blood coursing through his veins.

The focus of these counties was to the north and west, away from the slave-dominated society of Tidewater, Virginia. For years, there had been talk of separating from Virginia, of forming a new state. But the U.S. Constitution forbids formation of a state without the consent of the mother state, and Virginia would never give up the western counties. Then the nation plunged into civil war. Virginia left the Union, but the Northwest refused to follow. Delegates from western Virginia declared state offices vacated by Virginia secession and created a "Restored Government of Virginia," which was loyal to the Union. This government gave its consent to the creation of West Virginia, and the constitutional requirement was met. West Virginia—"Child of the Civil War"—joined the Union as the thirty-fifth state on June 20, 1863.

Jim's grandfather and the sovereign state of West Virginia were of the same age, thirty-six years old, when he bought his farm in 1899, in one of the counties described above. It was eventually called Kanawha County, named after a tribe of Native Americans who had once lived there.

In the old days, there had been three farms on this particular ridge, his grandfather's being one of the three. It had been divided among his children and their children and so on, and never was a piece of it sold to an outsider.

The other two farms were a different story, however, and some of the more moneyed of the elite had acquired several tracts and built themselves elegant estates, thus infiltrating the bastion of the poor.

Jim was eating supper one evening, several months before the dynamiting of Point Lick, when Eloise George, whom he had known all his life, brought a petition to his house, asking Jim and his wife, June, to sign it.

Eloise was distraught, telling them of the terrible things in the textbooks that the school board was trying to put in their schools. While she went into the details, Jim listened patiently, not really interested; he clucked his tongue and shook his head.

He signed the petition with proper indignation and felt good about doing his civic duty. He had a daughter, Kelly, in the third grade of the public school system.

Eloise left after a brief personal visit, and Jim thought the matter was taken care of. He dismissed it from his mind.

He was a dedicated father and went to all the school's functions, including the PTA meetings. He, like most other parents there, did not get involved in the meetings. They all shared the same naive, nostalgic concept of the educational process. They had grown up in the little red schoolhouse era, when a schoolteacher was in third place insofar as power, prestige, and respect, preceded only by God and parents.

Several weeks passed, and Jim gave no more thought to the petition, textbooks, or much of anything other than his business.

Next, his sister-in-law came to their house to tell them more about the books. She said Alice Moore, the only female member of the school board, was showing them in several places around the valley that day, and she gave them the different locations and times that the books would be at each place. She described some of the things that she had read in the books at one of the showings that morning and said that she was horrified. Not only four-letter words but also they compare myths to Bible stories.

"Jim, I know it sounds incredible and even ridiculous, but I swear it's true. I don't blame you if you don't believe it. You should go and see for yourself."

Jim didn't want to admit it to her, but he figured she was being somewhat of an alarmist and considered passing it off. But he was a dedicated family man and loved his daughter very much; he was concerned about her so he decided to check it out.

"I've got to go to work for awhile," he told his wife. "You get ready while I'm gone, and we'll try to make the showing at Cross Lanes at four thirty."

They arrived at the little church to find that the books were being shown a little early. Jim went to the table where they were displayed. He leafed through them briefly, noting several places that had been marked. (He learned later that Alice Moore herself had done all the marking, since at that point, she was waging pretty much a one-woman battle.)

The time came for Mrs. Moore to speak, and all the people sat down to listen, including Jim and June. Mrs. Moore introduced herself, and then she introduced the tall white-haired man with her as Matthew Kinsolving. He looked to Jim like a cross between a dandy and a gigolo, and Jim looked at the attractive Alice Moore a little more closely, a wry thought beginning to form in his mind. He was skeptical of this whole thing, and without realizing it, he had already formed an opinion, maybe even a conclusion. Now he was only trying to explain that conclusion to himself and everybody else.

Alice Moore lectured briefly, decrying the lack of traditional teachings in the classroom of such subjects as grammar, giving examples of the new methods, and went to other subjects. She then granted a question-and-answer session.

Jim was unimpressed by the substance of the lecture or of the speakers themselves, telling June as they drove away, "I think she's just looking for a little notoriety and an excuse to go gallivanting around with her boyfriend."

Then you don't see anything wrong with the books?" June asked. She always depended on Jim for this sort of thing because even though she had three more years of formal education than he did, she knew his experience and scope of understanding were superior to hers.

"Ah, I saw errors in grammar in them and some things I disagree with, and some things that just didn't make any sense ... but nothing to burn the little red schoolhouse down over."

She relaxed with a sigh, and that closed the matter as far as they both were concerned. When they got home, he ate a bite of supper and went back to work, wanting to catch up on things that he had neglected in order to go to the showing.

One Sunday afternoon a few weeks later, he was lazily reading that day's paper and came across a full-page ad, startling in its composition. It contained excerpts that he found hard to believe had come from schoolbooks and announced a meeting, or rally, as they were to become in the fight ahead, with Marvin Horan listed as the featured speaker and Concerned Parents as the sponsor.

Jim held the paper in both hands on the kitchen table, gazing off into space in deep thoughts. I'm a concerned parent; maybe we should go. He felt a little resentful at having his only day of rest interrupted and dreaded the thought of going out, especially at seven thirty in the evening, the time listed in the ad for the meeting. It was the day before the fall term of school started.

Reluctantly, he turned to his wife and said, "Get ready. I think we should go see what this is all about," showing her the ad. She glanced at it briefly, looked at him perplexedly, and went to get dressed.

They started to pull off the expressway onto Campbell's Creek Drive and had to wait in line. Cars were backed up for a mile and a half at the entrance. "Well, it gives me a good feeling to see this many parents who care about their kids," said Jim. "It surprises me."

At last, they made it across the expressway and started up the road into Campbell's Creek. The cars were bumper to bumper, moving slowly the three miles to the baseball field where the meeting was to be held.

They finally found a place to park, and Jim locked the car after they got out, hoping they would have enough gas to get to a service station. He'd noticed that the gas was low when they left home but figured they had enough for the drive, and he hated to stop for gas when he was tired and in a hurry. He hadn't counted on the traffic holding them up so long, using up a goodly portion of the gas to keep the heater going. The fall chill was already in the air, even though it was only September 5.

They walked across the grass field toward a wooden stand, where a man was speaking into a handheld microphone, his voice blaring from several loudspeakers placed about the field. They shouldered their way through the crowd, getting as close as they could without being rude, and then stood listening.

The man on the platform interrupted his own flowing rhetoric to introduce himself as Marvin Horan to any latecomers, and then he went on with his talk, stopping to play a tape that he identified as part of the material that was being used in their schools to educate.

Jim looked around at the crowd, and what a crowd it was. A

sea of people covered the ball field, spilling out into the road on either side and even over the creek bank, doing their best to stay out of the water but determined to take part in whatever was going on. Most of them were milling around trying to find out where the central platform was (Jim saw several more scattered around the field), but the ones nearest him were attentively waiting to hear the tape that Marvin had mentioned.

As he looked them over, Jim thought to himself that they weren't exactly the elite of South Hills. Coarsely dressed, their clothes smacked of discount houses and bargain basements, typical of the coal miners and the "creekers," as some outsiders called them. The natives considered the term creekers to be derogatory and were ready to fight at being called that.

Regardless of their places of residence, they were all obviously of the working class, the less-educated people of Kanawha County. Most had quit school before the tenth grade to go to work in the mines or to perform some other manual job to help feed their families. Jim himself had not finished the seventh grade for the same reason, but he felt out of place here. Although his formal education was slight, less even than some of these people, he had a sharp mind, with the absorbing qualities of a sponge, and an insatiable thirst for knowledge.

He keenly observed all the people with whom he came into contact. He chose to emulate the more sophisticated and better-educated ones with whom he dealt with in his business.

His attention returned to the speaker's stand when he heard a low, throaty male voice that resounded from the loudspeakers, rolling out over the crowd like subdued thunder. The voice sounded like something out of a horror movie, dripping with the macabre, and it was using the word kill quite frequently, rolling the word lovingly over its tongue like a child with a lollipop.

The sound itself attracted Jim's attention first, and then he started listening to the words. "Our whole society is geared for killing," the voice said. "The people who we send to kill are treated as heroes when they return, and we applaud their killing. Why is it wrong to kill? It is not wrong; it is the most noble of expression to kill."

There was much more to the tape, but Jim didn't listen. He had heard enough. His skin crawled. He was looking at Marvin Horan, who was watching the faces of the crowd, gauging their reactions to the tape.

This was the first time Jim had ever seen Marvin, and he worked his way closer to the stand to get a better look. He felt that since Marvin was the proclaimed leader of all this, perhaps he could gain some perception by evaluating him, which would allow him to measure the validity of the protestors' claims. He saw nothing in the rest of the crowd to encourage him to take up the banner.

Marvin was of medium height and build. He had brown wavy hair and was dressed in a mediocre suit, light brown in color. He had a pleasant face and nervous, piercing eyes that were now darting from face to face in the crowd. His look of intelligence superseded that of the rest of the crowd.

Jim was impressed—but not enough to override his feelings about the other people or the lameness of the accusations. He remembered the newspaper article he had read, without its registering until now; it said that this was all "a hullabaloo over nothing, caused by uneducated people that were ignorant to new techniques and were frightened by change."

Except for the tape and the striking personality of Marvin Horan, he could find little to argue with in that assessment. He reminded himself that there were all kinds of would-be leaders around, looking for causes and crowds to lead, some of them radicals. Maybe this man was one of them.

He left the stand and started mingling with the crowd for a closer look at the masses. He couldn't believe his eyes when he saw Carol Banks, looking as out of place as a tulip in a barnyard, milling amongst the people. Carol was the wife of Roger Banks, the vice president of the bank he dealt with, and he knew them both well. She was smartly dressed, as always, her expensive, colorful outfit standing out as starkly as blood on snow in contrast to the rest. Carol saw him, and when they got close enough, they smiled at each other and engaged in some small talk, neither asking what the other was doing there. She was clearly as surprised to see him there as he was to see her.

Jim just assumed that she had come out of curiosity since she lived on the main road, just a couple of miles above the mouth of the hollow. She'd probably seen all the cars going in on her way home and decided to see what was going on. He accepted this explanation in his own mind as she disappeared back into the crowd.

He went back to where his wife was waiting for him and said, "Let's go before this breaks up or we'll spend half the night fighting this traffic out of here." There was only one way in and one way out, a narrow two-lane asphalt road.

They reached their car, and Jim started it up, remembering the low fuel. He hoped they had enough to make it back to the main road. There were no gas stations on Campbell's Creek.

His hope was short-lived; the car began to sputter before they were halfway down the ball field to the paved road. He pulled off the dirt road so that he wouldn't block the other cars if their owners decided to leave early. The engine sputtered once more and died.

"Now what do we do?" asked his wife.

"Surely, somebody in this crowd has a siphon hose," he said. He opened the door and got out to see if he could find one.

After asking several people with no luck (he figured that some of them had one but didn't want to miss any of the tape that was being played again), one of them told him that a man standing next to the speaker's platform lived nearby, and that he might have one.

After Jim went to him and explained the problem, the man said he had a siphon in his garage. He then made his way through the crowd with Jim following him.

When the crowd was far enough behind them to hear each other over the noise, Jim said, "What do you think about everything that's going on here?"

The man didn't break his stride or look around when he answered. "I think we're headed for a lot of trouble. These people aren't going to stand for their kids being fed this garbage."

Jim hesitated and then asked, "How do you feel about the books?"

He felt as if the man were giving him an appraising look, although his head had not turned. Finally, the man spoke. "Well, I tell you, some of the people running this meeting brought some of them to show me, and I ain't slept good since."

"Are they really that bad?"

"They're worse. You have to see 'em to believe 'em, and then you don't believe it. Some people say the Communists are behind it. I don't know who's behind, it but I do know it scares me to death."

Jim felt a somber mood drop over the two of them like a blanket. They were at the garage now, and he was surprised when the man started siphoning gas into a five-gallon can from a snow-white Lincoln parked there. It seemed to be so out of place.

They took the gas back to Jim's car, poured it into his tank, and he asked the man how much he owed him.

"Ah, don't worry about it," the man said, waving a hand. "You might come on me someday in the same shape."

"What about the can?" he asked.

"Just drop it off at the corner of my garage," answered the man over his shoulder as he faded back into the crowd.

The next morning, all hell broke loose. Marvin Horan had organized a countywide boycott of the schools. The mothers of the children being held out of school carried signs in picket lines outside the school buildings. There had been several clashes between the pickets and the teachers and parents. A few arrests had been made.

The miners, traditionally strikers, were closing mines down left and right in sympathy with the boycott. Many fights had broken out between strikers and non-strikers. Pandemonium reigned throughout the valley.

Jim kept Kelly home that day.

CHAPTER 2

The Storm Brews

Jim was up early the next morning, listening to the news. The television, the radio, and the morning paper were all full of what was happening in the valley because of the uproar in the public schools.

He decided to find out for himself what was in the particular books his daughter was studying. He called her teacher at her school as soon as it was open and asked if he could drop by to pick up the books and bring them home to examine them.

"You most certainly can, Mr. Farley," said Mrs. Holbrook, the teacher. "I hope every parent will be as thorough as you and interested to see for themselves. Then they will see that all this is over nothing." Jim thanked her and hung up.

"I'll be right back," he told June as he left to go get the books.

When he returned with them, three altogether (they were the ones in her grade that were under fire), he started skimming through them, not seeing much to get excited about.

He was about to settle back comfortably in his old position on the books, but then he decided to take one more look. One short story caught his attention. He read it again, carefully this time.

It was the story of "Androcles and the Lion" from *Aesop's Fables.* (Those few who are not familiar with the story can easily obtain a copy of it at any library so space needn't be taken up here with the story itself—but rather how it was handled.)

At the top of the page, in bold type, was the heading FABLE, making it clear that the whole story was untrue. Here the emphasis was important, the constant hammering that the entire contents were make-believe.

At the top of the next page, in bold type, he found the label

MYTH. Then, alongside the story itself, in columns at each edge of the page, he found this list of suggestions for the children:

> 1. Pretend that instead of pulling the thorn out of the lion's paw, Androcles gets up and runs. What could happen next?
>
> 2. Pretend that after Androcles pulls out the thorn, the lion turns on Androcles and says, "Thanks. Now, since I'm hungry, I'll eat you." What could happen?
>
> 3. Pretend that in the arena Androcles recognizes the lion, but the lion does not recognize Androcles. What could happen?
>
> 4. Pretend that the emperor is angry when the lion does not kill Androcles. What could happen?

Jim looked up from the book to reflect on what he had read so far. Instead of showing children that kindness was rewarded by kindness, as the original story portrayed, weren't these questions suggesting to children instead that if you were kind to others, they would kick you in the teeth for your pains. In other words, you weren't too swift if you thought kindness paid off.

Then he read the fifth and final item in this particular list:

> 5. You could ask if anyone knows and wants to tell the story of "Daniel in the Lions' Den." If it is told in any detail, you could then discuss any similarities between that story and "Androcles and the Lion."

At this correlation between Androcles and the fable, and Daniel from the Bible, which Christians believed to be true, he looked again at the first four questions and suddenly noticed that they all began with the word "pretend." Wouldn't that, coupled with the heading MYTH, drive the point home that this was all make-believe, including the story of Daniel? It piqued his curiosity, so he turned the page, found another list similar to the first, and read further:

> talking about the story:
>
> Objectives: (1) to discuss the characters; (2) to discuss the actions; (3) to discuss the reality of the story.
>
> As usual, discussion questions are intended to stimulate discussion, not to test comprehension. Show the pupils that

differences of opinion will be accepted, even expected; at the same time, of course, one must be willing to have others question his opinions and to defend them by reference to the text or by a reasoned argument. The following questions, then, are intended to stimulate discussion; there may be other questions that you and the pupils will want to ask.

1. Do you think a real lion would go to a man to have a thorn taken out of his paw? Why or why not?

2. Do you think a real lion, if he hadn't eaten for three days, would remember Androcles and not eat him?

3. If a story like this could not really happen, why do people like it?

He went over the story the third time, this time studying it—taking it apart—rather than just reading it.

The preoccupation with the words "myth" and "pretend," coupled with the word "reality" in parentheses, definitely made it clear that the whole thing was untrue. Of course, "Androcles and the Lion" was untrue. It was a fable from Aesop. But "Daniel in the Lions' Den" was another matter. Why would they integrate the two stories under the same heading and in the same context? Would this not plant in the impressionable mind of a nine-year-old that Daniel was in the same category as Androcles, making it untrue or just a downright lie? This disturbed him.

He thumbed through some more pages until he came to another lesson plan called "Telling Your Own Myth." He read this one carefully the first time. Here was another set of lists like the ones in "Androcles," only longer, more pointed, and definitely more similar to the Bible. (These will be itemized in detail later.)

Perhaps without close scrutiny of "Androcles,", he never would have noticed the second story.

There must be more, he thought. There were many more. He went through the remainder of the book, this time in the "proper" slant. The thread of the theme set by the two above articles was woven throughout, in varying degrees of potency. He reached for the fourth-grade reader that he had asked for just in case. Kelly would be studying that one next year.

He began to search, and he began to find more and more and more.

He stared out the window, not seeing the flaming reds and the subtle yellows of the trees' autumn beauty. His mind was intensely focused on the insidious plan that had leapt out at him from the seemingly innocuous third- and fourth-grade readers that he held in his hands.

He was appalled, his basically religious mind repudiating the concept he had found there. The cleverness of the plan overwhelmed him; he recognized that a tremendous amount of planning, time, and effort had gone into the organizing and executing of it. It was brilliant, a masterpiece of double meaning. It reminded him of the advertisements that were placed on panels that swiveled. When they were in one position, the eye saw one picture; slant them slightly and a totally different picture emerged.

You had to look at the plan in the books in just the right slant to see it, but once you got the slant, the whole theme throughout the book was unmistakable ... and frightening.

Jim could easily see where a young, impressionable mind such as Kelly's, which was submitted or exposed to these books by an authority figure that she had been told to respect, could come away totally doubting the Bible. Children would begin to see the holy writings as just another fable. The parallel in each was too incredibly close to be accidental; they were deliberately placed there. But by whom ... and for what purpose?

That last thought sent a chill through Jim, and he felt as someone had just walked across his grave. The enormity of it boggled his mind. Who? he kept asking himself. The anonymity of the perpetrators made it that much eerier.

Jim pulled his thoughts together for another close examination of the books, hoping against hope that he had been mistaken. After searching the books once more, he had to admit to himself that there was no mistaking it: the plan was there, and it was intentional.

He stared out the window again, watching the brilliant colors of the sunset fade into the bleak drabness of the evening, then finally the blackness of night. It seemed to him that the changing scene was caused by the emotions he felt.

Jim paced the floor nervously, like a caged animal. He felt caged, boxed in by intangible bars of frustration. He didn't know what to do, where to start, but he knew had to do something.

He hadn't slept all night, the horror of it keeping him awake. He glanced at the clock hanging on the wall: 4:37. It was too early for any of the school or school board offices to be open. Then he got an idea. Maybe he should alert the news media. He was a believer of the thesis that if you threw enough rocks, eventually you were bound to hit something.

He started with the newspaper, knowing that they would have someone there all night. "Charleston Newspapers," droned a male voice. (The two leading papers had merged but operated separately, under the same ownership.)

"I'm calling in reference to something that I thought would be of interest to you," Jim said, trying hard to keep his voice calm. "I'm sure that you're aware of the problems that are surfacing in our school system." Jim didn't wait for an answer. "I've just come across a chilling revelation in my daughter's third-level reader, and I think you'll agree, when you hear me out, that the public should be informed about what their children are being taught."

The man on the other end listened courteously while Jim told him all the facts and then thanked him in a mechanical voice, saying they would check into the matter.

Jim knew by the tone in the voice that that's as far as it would ever go. He was certain that the man would forget the whole thing as soon as he hung up the phone. He felt frustrated.

He picked up the phone again and dialed the number of the TV station, which he had written down with the newspaper office number. The routine was a repetition of the one with the newspaper office; only the voice had changed.

Jim slammed the phone down in anger. The commotion brought his wife stumbling down the stairs, rubbing the sleep out of her eyes.

"What in the world is going on?" she asked.

Jim glanced at her and continued his nervous pacing back and forth. "What's wrong with those people?" he asked. "Has the whole world gone crazy?"

"What people? What are you talking about?" she asked indignantly.

Jim explained about the books, his calls to the media, and the total disinterest they showed. She sat down on the arm of the couch and stared across the room.

Jim suddenly stopped his pacing and grabbed the phone again. "Now who are you calling?" she asked.

"The head man himself," he answered. "If you want to get something done, start at the top, go to the source."

He asked the information operator for the school superintendent's phone number. He dialed it, and it was busy. He waited for a bit and dialed again—still busy. After five futile tries, he finally got an answer on the sixth attempt.

"Dr. Underwood's office," a secretary's voice answered.

"May I speak to Dr. Underwood? This is James Farley calling."

"Dr. Underwood is on another line. Would you care to hold?"

"Yes, I would."

Jim paced nervously, trailing the telephone cord behind him. In his urgency, it seemed like forever since the woman had put him on hold, and he was about to hang up when he heard the voice.

"Dr. Underwood."

"Dr. Underwood, my name is James Farley, and I want to assure you that I'm not a radical and I'm not a nut," Jim said quickly, thinking of some of the people he had seen firsthand and read comments about in the paper. "I am a father of a nine-year-old girl who's in the third grade, and I have done some research on her school books myself. I'm appalled at what I found."

He went on to explain specifics, and then the superintendent said, "Mr. Farley, I don't believe you're a radical ... and certainly not a nut. You sound intelligent enough. I can assure you that everything is being done to guarantee your daughter and all the children in the public school system a quality education." The man went on and on with reassurances and explanations—without providing anything concrete.

Finally, exasperated, Jim asked directly, "Dr. Underwood, have you read these books?"

"Well, no, I haven't, but competent, qualified people whom I trust have."

"Well, Doctor, somebody slipped up. These books are atrocious." The anger was clear in Jim's voice.

There was a pause on the other end. Then the superintendent said wearily, "Mr. Farley, I'm asking a panel of ministers to examine these books today, and I'll abide by their judgment."

A feeling of relief swept over Jim. "Well, that's the best news I've heard since this whole mess started. Doctor, I want to compliment you. That's an excellent idea."

"Thank you, Mr. Farley."

"I'm sure that once a group of ministers see what I did; this whole matter will be resolved." Jim hung up, relieved and satisfied. He couldn't wait to hear the report of the ministers.

That evening, he sat on the edge of his chair, eager for the local news. When it finally came on, he settled back with the certainty that as soon as the ministers gave their report, the outcome was a foregone conclusion. They would deplore the abhorrent content of the textbooks and insist that they be taken immediately out of the schools, finally settling the matter.

He listened intently as the moderator introduced the panel, slyly smiling to himself as he waited for their irate outpouring of indignation to begin.

His smile began to fade as he heard the introductions: Dr. So-and-So from the prestigious Lutheran cathedral, Bishop So-and-So from the district office of the Methodist church, and last but not least, two liberal reverend So-and-Sos from St. Luke's

Episcopalian church.

Jim's smile had turned to a frown midway through the names, and now he was livid with anger. The superintendent had sounded so reassuring that morning about the panel being the solution that he had fallen for it. The smooth, trained voice of the good doctor telling him about the ministers left no reason to doubt. Now he realized that he had been duped, and he wondered how many other people had swallowed it.

The panel was cleverly packed with the liberal "educated elite" of the larger churches. One of them was James Lewis, the rector of St. John's Episcopal Church. Rector Lewis was the most outspoken leader of the opposition, the book advocates, and he seemed to have the full approval of the church. He also supported abortion strongly and, later on, made an unsuccessful attempt at having a haven for gays in the church basement.

There was no representation whatsoever of the fundamentalist churches opposing the books. Jim doubted very much if the good ministers on the panel had taken the time required to research the books thoroughly enough to discover the "plan."

He knew they had to be basing their opinions on the media reports because it took weeks to go through the 164 books in question and these men had only been appointed this morning. That was what made the books so infuriatingly frustrating. On casual examination, they appeared so innocent, and even with close scrutiny, the items in question were scattered throughout the books so brilliantly that it took dedicated readers hours, even days, of searching to find anything wrong. But students being led methodically through them would gradually have their perspectives slanted so subtly that they themselves wouldn't be aware of the change. Once they were reading them in the proper slant, that's all they would see. This would be "the plan."

The diabolical brilliance of the method was what scared Jim the most. This told him that someone very powerful, with unlimited resources, finances, and brainpower was behind the plan— and with a definite purpose to it all.

He didn't like to point his finger at Communism. That

automatically branded you a radical, even a nut. He thought of some of the pitifully ignorant people he had personally encountered. Protesting the books, they'd say lamely, "It's Communism."

CHAPTER 3
The School Board's Solution

The introduction of the panel was complete, and the moderator began his questioning. "Father Caan, what is your opinion of these books?"

"I see them as a marked improvement over the methods that have been used in the past. They replace the formally dull routine of the student with an exciting, stimulating curriculum that makes the student want to read more. He can't wait to get to the next page to see what new and fresh event will be waiting for him."

"What about the alleged profanity and four-letter words?"

"The student is going to learn these anyway, so why not expose him to it in a controlled environment?"

"Do you see the books as anti-American?"

Caan smiled. "Only a paranoid person would view them in that light."

(Jim thought of the rule in the Communist Manifesto, loosely translated: "Infiltrate the churches; turn them into social clubs, making them ineffectual as religious vehicles.")

"Do you see them as anti-God or anti-Christian?"

Caan smiled again. "I don't see them as dealing with religion in any light." His smile broadened meaningfully. "Teaching religion in school is specifically forbidden by the Supreme Court ruling."

The moderator asked different but similar questions of the other members of the panel, and then he came to the big one. "Gentlemen, is there a consensus among you about these books as a whole?"

The panel members looked at each other, held a brief, hushed discussion, and then Caan answered. "I think we can say there is. We all agree that these books in general are a big step in progress and definitely should be returned to the classroom immediately."

The reporter thanked the panel. The interview ended, and the camera stopped.

Bill Seaman, the president of the Kanawha County PTA, stood before the panel of ministers and reverends with notes in his hands. They included questions he wanted to ask these men, as well as substantiating evidence from the books. This part was never televised.

Seaman's physical characteristics made it difficult for him to project a positive, imposing image, but he was trying to do just that. He was a slight man, to say the least, with thin hair since youth—not balding, just thin, wavy hair. His voice matched his hair, further hampered by a near lisp that made it sound as if someone were standing in front of him with a dill pickle in plain view, causing an excess of saliva flow. Add a few freckles to this, and it was an effort to appear authoritative.

Still, he pulled himself to his full height, and drawing his features into the sternest expression he could command, he spoke, directing his first question to Father Caan.

"Mr. Caan, do you find the phrase *f– you* offensive?" Seaman was going for the shock effect, certain that he would see the faces of the panel turn white and their eyes widen in disbelief. They smiled blandly.

"It depends on what context it is used in," was Caan's answer.

I couldn't imagine any context in which this phrase would be acceptable to a Christian leader. And Seaman looked as if he had just slammed a door, waiting in keen anticipation for the loud bang when it hit, only to discover it had a hydraulic stop attached. He was nonplussed. Then he became furious, agitated.

Trying to calm himself, Seaman asked, "What about the words *godd–* and *son of a b––*? How do you feel about those? By the way, the word *godd–* was used forty-nine times in just one of the books, Mr. Caan."

Caan remarked flippantly that he hadn't bothered to count them and said, "Mr. Seaman, I think you and your people are overreacting to this situation because it is new and strange to you. You're reading all sorts of connotations into it because you don't understand it. We're in a new era, and we need new philosophies to keep pace with that era, including in education."

Seaman was flabbergasted but recovered enough to ask, "Where do you think these 'new philosophies' are coming from, Mr. Caan?"

Caan smiled tolerantly, and the other members of the panel followed suit. "If you're implying what I think you are, Mr. Seaman, I will say I have never looked under my bed for Communists," he said condescendingly.

Seaman was tempted to ask, "How about in your bed?" but restrained himself. He didn't know which infuriated him the most—Caan's answer, the condescending tone, or the benign glee shown by all members of the panel.

He visibly struggled for composure. He stared at the floor in concentration, trembling slightly. When he felt himself in control again, at least partially, he looked up and resumed, striving to keep his voice calm.

"Mr. Caan, let's go to another aspect of these books, or 'the philosophy,' as you put it, in them. There is a lesson plan in the third-grade D. C. Heath Communicating English Series called 'Telling Your Own Myth.' In this story, these questions are asked:

1. Why do men have pain?

2. Why do men have different skin colors?

3. Why do so many animals like to eat meat?

"Then it goes on to say," continued Seaman, still reading from the actual book, 'Myths are ways of answering questions like these. The answers may not be real, but they are fun. They are an interesting part of our imaginary world.

"'One way to make up a myth is to think of a question like one of these. Suppose your question is "Why do men have pain?" Now, imagine a time when man did not have pain. Pretend that the first men on earth went around without ever feeling pain. Next imagine that some kind of God walked among men and something happened. Maybe a man did something bad or made a bad mistake. Because of this, the god punished men, giving them pain for the rest of their days.'"

Seaman paused and looked up at the panel, directing his primary attention and his question to Caan. "Mr. Caan, does the picture drawn by these questions sound familiar to you?" Caan shrugged sarcastically and smiled blandly but did not answer.

Seaman gave him a disgusted look and continued, "Doesn't that sound an awful lot like the Genesis version of creation of man and the story of Adam and Eve?" Again, Caan shrugged and smiled. Seaman's face was becoming red from anger, but he forced himself to remain calm and continued. "If you're not convinced yet, Mr. Caan, maybe this will do it. Some more of the questions follow:

1. Why do men grow old?

2. Why do men tell lies?

3. Why don't all men speak the same language?

"All these questions, Mr. Caan, are followed by a picture underneath that shows animals of different varieties, giving one the feeling that he is looking at a cutaway section of Noah's Ark. I won't ask you anymore for admission of what this article reminds you of, but we both know that it is blatantly intended to be a direct analogy to a composite of events taken directly from the Bible. They combine bits and pieces from the relation of the Creation, including Adam and Eve, the Tower of Babel, and Noah's Ark under the heading of 'Myth,' making it clear and emphasizing that they are 'not real,' but rather a part of our 'imaginary world,' and that although they are untrue, they can be 'fun.'

"Now, I ask you a direct question, Mr. Caan. Do you think, from a Christian standpoint, that this is a healthy 'philosophy' to be teaching children in the third grade?"

Caan's expression this time was more than condescending; it was aloof and superior. "Children play out everything, including

God."

"Then you admit that these questions and this story do obviously come straight from the Bible?" asked Seaman. Caan shrugged but did not answer. Seaman looked at him incredulously. "Mr. Caan, don't you think that it would be more reverent to teach children that you don't 'play with God'?"

"Mr. Seaman, these books represent a philosophy that I feel very good about." This remark was not made by Caan but by the man sitting next to him, James Lewis, the rector of St. John's Episcopal Church. It was one of the more prosperous churches in Charleston.

After this response, the panel was dismissed.

Jim Farley had known that this was where the real opposition was going to come from.

James Lewis had the face of a perverted angel. He was suave, debonair, and as smooth as oil being poured from a greased jar of wax. An articulate man, he had done his homework and was dedicated to his precepts, whatever they were. He was also one of several key proponents of the books that Bill Russell named later in a letter to the editor, which Jim talked him out of printing. No one bothered anymore to designate them as "textbooks." They were simply "the books," and everyone knew what you were talking about.

The letter asked some pointed questions that could have only one answer. The answer to all of the questions was obvious: someone had sent all these people, including Lewis, into Kanawha County on a mission.

Bill didn't come right out and say it, but he left little doubt that his idea of that "someone" was without a doubt the Communist Party. Jim wouldn't go that far in his guesses, but he did promise himself that he was going to check into Lewis's background.

One thing he did know: Lewis was in favor of everything that he was against. The books were the first. Lewis was quoted in the newspaper as saying, "These books represent a philosophy that I feel very good about." (One has to wonder at this point if Lewis was aware of the secular humanist doctrine permeating these books.) When Jim read Lewis's book *West Virginia Pilgrim*, he understood why.

With an awareness that I'm exposing myself to the battle-weary accusation of quoting out of context, herein are some of the items covered in the book written by this Episcopal priest.

The whole thing, really, consists of nothing but inane unconnected ramblings, interspersed with irreverent and sometimes derisive comments about God, Christ, and the Bible in general.

It sounded as if Lewis was either educated from "the books," or that he wrote them. He shows a definite preoccupation with anything that is vulgar, profane, racy, or just plain in poor taste.

The longest connected story (as mentioned said, the book consists of a bunch of unconnected ramblings) that I read dealt with Lewis's adventure as a cleaner of urinals. Yep, you heard me right. Cleaner of urinals. He goes into great detail, which should titillate everyone who reads this literary masterpiece. He meticulously describes the all-important placement of the little deodorizer cake under the lip of the urinal (or commode; he never did quite clarify that point), only to have his arduous and noble efforts defeated by "a drunk coming in immediately after and unloading an hour's worth of draft beer."

In an effort to expose the filth in Jim Lewis's book, Bill Russell and I purchased a full-page ad quoting some excerpts from *West Virginia Pilgrim.* Some of the literary gems are as follows:

"Two dogs copulating on the school lawn as I watched from my classroom window; why do we humans hide the most beautiful act."

"That friggin' parole board had better come through this time." (This is in reference to a female friend of his, in jail on charges that he never did specify.)

"Screwing around was what he liked best."

His version of Christ's resurrection from the tomb: "jack-in-the-box."

On politics: "God, what a mess in Washington. The political

scene looks more and more like a stagnant pool with each newscast."

Describing the reason that a married acquaintance of his had fights with his wife (the scene begins in the couple's bed): "He set the fuse by laying his hand on the large shock of brown hair between her legs."

He makes it clear that he agrees with the attitude of some people regarding rape: "If it's inevitable, might as well relax and enjoy it."

The critic, commentator, or whoever that was supposed to have reviewed his book said, "In Jim Lewis's book, even the trivial took on significance."

If it had not been for the trivial, Jim Lewis would not have had a book.

A few weeks later, Jim Lewis attended a meeting where a bill in legislature was being debated. It was to allow information between a school counselor and a student to come under the same heading of privileged information as the lawyer-client relationship. (Nice blanket of secrecy to peddle anything you wanted, huh?) Lewis was in favor of the bill.

Jim Farley thought of the many characters portrayed on television, such as the fictional Captain Flagg on *M*A*S*H*, his favorite television program. Flagg was an overzealous patriot, going around all the units in Korea, ferreting out the "commies," a one-man eradicating squad of "the pinko plague." Flagg blamed everything on the Communists.

The kooky character in the adult animated cartoon series *Wait Till Your Father Gets Home* was Flagg's civilian counterpart, running up and down the neighborhood that he lived in with a civil defense hard hat on his head, yelling that the Communist attack was upon them. He always carried a flashlight, poking into every dark corner, seeking out "the pinko." Everything that he couldn't explain with his feeble brain, he blamed on "the commies" and, like Flagg, was constantly making a nuisance of himself. They were both ludicrous, shunned by the people around them. Even pitied by some.

Then there was the movie *Tail Gunner Joe*, supposedly telling the true story of Senator Joseph McCarthy's rise to power and the subsequent Communist purge. The movie began with McCarthy, slovenly dressed, driving a chicken truck down a dirt road in his home state of Wisconsin and addle-headedly driving it into a ditch. He got out of the truck, looked at the chickens scattered all over, and mumbled that he was going to find another line of work. So he decided to be a senator.

When he had taken care of that small detail and had become one, he was sitting in a restaurant in Washington one evening boring some acquaintances when he blandly decided that the way to gain recognition was to rout out "commies," even if you had to invent them. He set about his task, gained much notoriety, and then went to the South Pacific during the Second World War. While visiting one of the army air bases there, he impulsively climbed into the tail gunner's seat in a fighter plane parked on the field, much to the consternation of the objecting officers. With army personnel wringing their hands, McCarthy proceeded to grab the machine gun and irresponsibly shot up the tops of the surrounding palm trees, swinging the chattering machine gun back and forth, all the while grinning fiendishly, and thereby earning the nickname for the title of the movie: *Tail Gunner Joe*.

No, Jim thought, I don't want to be typecast with people like that by pointing a finger at Communism. He wondered who would have the power, the money and the motive to instigate such a massive and clever plan as the one that he had discovered in these textbooks.

Jim went to his job the next morning and tried his best to work, but he couldn't concentrate on what he was doing. The contents of the books kept buzzing around in his head—why and who is behind these books, and what to do about them. What can I do? Wondered Jim.

Finally, he gave it up, saying to the man working with him, "I'll be back as soon as I can." He'd decided to go back and talk to Mrs. Meadows, Kelly's principal, mostly for lack of a better idea at the moment. He stopped at a pay phone to call her first and make an appointment. She was waiting for him when he got there, and he walked into the room and sat down.

He wasted no time with small talk but got right into the matter. "What, exactly, is your opinion of these books, Mrs. Meadows?"

She was a matronly woman with nearly a lifetime of teaching behind her. She looked at Jim, concern showing clearly in her face, obviously trying to choose the right words to answer his question.

"Mr. Farley, I've been a schoolteacher all my adult life. The pay is not all that good, but I thought I could help children." She glanced sadly down at her hands, which she was rubbing nervously together. "I only have two more years until I can retire. But if these books are what you and the other people say they are, I'll resign my position before I will allow them to be taught in my school! I promise you that."

"Have you read the books?" asked Jim.

"No, I'm afraid I haven't, but I certainly intend to."

Jim started to explain to her what to look for and where to find it but decided against it. He would rather she find it on her own.

"Mrs. Meadows, I think you mean what you say, and if enough people like you will take a stand, we can beat this thing."

She smiled weakly, and he saw the sincerity in her eyes as they shook hands. Jim left, feeling much better.

He looked around at the suburban countryside that he was driving through, remembering when he had played there as a boy. There were few houses then, only woods, meadows, and grapevine swings. It was a happy time, a carefree time that was going to last forever. Guidelines then were clear and concrete. Good was good, and bad was bad. There were never any clouds of doubt over the schools or teachers, only over whether the more mischievous pupils were going to play hooky and ramble over the hills in search of adventure in the swimming holes of Davis Creek.

Now there were prestigious estates and houses choking back

the wilderness that he once considered his own domain. Suddenly, he felt crowded, suffocated, as Daniel Boone must have felt when he saw the smoke of his neighbor's chimney over the next hill.

He thought of the simplicity and reverence of religion in those days. God was real and always there, and the Bible was true and the mainstay of their lives. Jim had never made a commitment to God or Christianity, but he had deep religious convictions.

He shuddered at the picture conjured up in his mind of what it would be like a generation from now if these books were allowed to undermine the Bible, the belief in God, and all respect for authority. Ministers would be mocked, and churches would be forced to close their doors; and without their calming influence, there would be chaos. They had to be stopped ... but how?

Dropping down from the hills surrounding Charleston on the winding road, Jim looked at the beautiful valley of Kanawha. It lay between two mountain ranges, with the Kanawha River going right down the middle, dividing the flat bottomland of the valley in half.

The city of Charleston occupied the central portion, with smaller towns in the narrower parts of the valley in either direction, both up and down the river. Houses were sprinkled on each side, as if the magic wand of the good fairy had done the sprinkling. He had flown over it once, and it had reminded him of a miniature model town out of Disneyland, with the tiny winding roads connecting the houses to each other and to the city.

The beauty of this scene had always taken his breath away, and today it was especially beautiful and peaceful looking. Bathed in the warn autumn sun, its rays causing the river to sparkle as it wound its lazy way through it all, it looked like the valley of peace itself. It was hard to believe that the turmoil that seethed up and down its full length was real. But he knew it was there. That seemed to be the only thing on people's minds wherever he went these days. The newspapers hardly had room for anything else; the television kept a running account, as did the radio. He kept the radio in his car on constantly, keeping up on the happenings.

The valley was as divided by the books as it was by the river. The controversy had turned neighbor against neighbor, friend against friend, and in some cases, brother against brother. It had split churches, political factions, labor against management—generally fragmenting the county the way a dynamite blast fractured stone, which he had seen so many times.

CHAPTER 4
Trials and Tribulations

Jim had mixed feelings as he walked toward the milling crowd of people covering the playground across from the school board building. He had heard of the gathering and decided to come, again for lack of a better plan. This was not his way of dealing with a controversy, but for the time being, he had no other plan, and he had to do something.

As he got closer, he could tell that they were pretty much the same people, or at least the same type of people, that he had seen at the first rally. One knotted group was standing facing the school board building, looking intently at the door of the building as if waiting for something or someone to appear there. The rest were wandering back and forth across the field of the playground, some listlessly, some angrily. Jim could tell that all the protestors were being sure not to stand directly on the School Board's property. Jim walked up to the edge of the group looking across the street and became part of it as unobtrusively as he could.

Someone started singing a hymn, low at first, then others joined in, and the singing got louder. Miners could be seen throughout the crowd, their grim faces and hard hats contrasting with the soft reverence of the melancholy hymn singers.

It was a crowd motley in temperament. The hymn singers were like frightened children, certain in the knowledge that their Father would right this terrible wrong. The miners were eager for a more direct approach, ready to use any method necessary: picket lines, fists, or poleaxes.

"We're gonna give 'em one more hour, then we're movin'," Jim heard a miner say, recognizing him as the father of one of the boys on his Little League team that he coached. His angry scowl made his words quite clear. The mood of the miners was getting uglier by the minute. They were a singular breed and quick to fight any intruder upon their rights.

There had been a lot of talk about the people who were in the meeting with the school board. Marvin Horan was the key negotiator for the protesters, trying to get the board to take the books out of the classroom. Alice Moore, the Joan of Arc of the protest, was supposed to arrive shortly. Jim had just learned of the meeting, and now he understood why the people in the knotted group were staring at the door. They were waiting anxiously for a decision about the meeting.

"There's Marvin," someone said, and a hush fell over the crowd. All eyes turned toward the doorway of the school board building.

Marvin came out and raised his hands to subdue the cheer that had started to ripple though the crowd. "Don't cheer yet, folks. It's not finished" he shouted.

A groan of dismay rumbled through the crowd, and two miners started out of the park, one of them yelling, "Well, that's it!"

"Hold on a minute," said Marvin. "Let's not go off half-cocked either. Let's give 'em a little more time. I think we're gonna get what we want. Dr. Underwood has said some encouraging things, but he wants time to talk it over with his people."

"How long are we supposed to wait, Marvin?" asked an angry miner. "We've been here over half a day now."

Marvin appraised the miner carefully, then said, "I know you're getting tired, boys, but let's give 'em thirty minutes more." Marvin's tone, as always, was diplomatic but decisive and firm.

The miner glanced around at his compadres and then grumbled, "All right, Marvin, thirty minutes—but not a second more."

Marvin smiled, waved a hand in gratitude, and disappeared back into the building.

The crowd became sullen, bunching off into little groups, each one hashing over its own solution to the problem. Murmuring voices could be heard from all corners.

Suddenly, there was a ripple of excitement through the crowd, and someone yelled, "Here comes Alice Moore." A light-colored sedan came into view, pulling around the corner. The crowd surged toward it as one body, like drones flocking around the queen bee.

The car pulled up to the front of the school board building, and Alice Moore got out, walked up the steps, and turned to face the crowd. A loud cheer went up from the crowd, vibrating the windows of the old building. The crowd paid homage to her as they would have the queen, submitting themselves to her will as though they were her subjects.

She smiled down at them with that sweet smile that would infuriate the opposition in the fight to come, the same sweet smile that would cause some enemy reporter to sardonically dub her "Sweet Alice."

Jim looked at her in a completely different light from the first time he had seen her, which was at the book showing. Looking beyond her attractiveness, he saw the woman that she really was—intelligent, sincere, and dedicated—and he was to learn later that she had a razor-sharp wit, tempered with an iron will and determination. He promised himself silently that someday he would apologize for his first impression of her.

After waving for silence for several minutes, Alice finally got the crowd to hold the applause. "Thank you from the bottom of my heart," she said with warm emotion. "You are the salt of the earth. I don't know what I would have done these past weeks were it not for all of you. I was warned not to come here today because of threats that I have received and possible violence, but I told them that was silly. These are my people. I have nothing to fear."

The approving applause was thunderous. A queen never had more loyal or revering subjects, yet they embraced her in a very human way.

The ovation for Alice Moore was still at its peak when the door behind her opened and Marvin Horan appeared. He walked up beside Alice and stood smiling appreciatively until the cheering stopped.

The crowd grew quiet and anxious, looking expectantly at Marvin.

Marvin was a spellbinder with a crowd, leading one as the maestro directs a symphony orchestra. He waited, smiling for exactly the right effect, and then said, "Folks, we've won." A loud but brief cheer went up. The crowd was too anxious to hear what Marvin had to say to cheer too long.

"I have in my hand," said Marvin, holding up a paper, "a copy of an agreement between us and the school board, which I have just signed. The agreement states that we will call off the boycott."

A protest of rage drowned him out. "No, No!"

Marvin finally got them quiet again. "Listen to me," he said in that gentle but commanding tone. "In addition to calling off the boycott, we call off the strikes. In other words, we cease all our activities against the public school system, and they have agreed to pull the books out of the classrooms for thirty days for what they call a 'cooling-off period.' They will appoint a panel of parents to review the books."

Jim thought with disgust of the "panel of ministers," and he wasn't the only one apparently because disbelief was written on all the faces in his range of vision as they shouted their disagreement with what Marvin had done.

Alice Moore, "the queen," stepped to the forefront and held out both hands, palms down for silence. When it finally came, she said, "What Marvin has done is a great victory." Her voice was filled with assurance that the people would agree with her; these were "her people." But even a queen can be wrong. The crowd roared with fury, becoming agitated, some angrily shaking their fists at the speaker's stand.

Alice Moore was visibly shaken; the sweet smile was replaced with a hurt frown as she struggled to regain her composure. Momentary fear flickered in her eyes. Loyal subjects had been known to turn into a vengeful mob. Even a faithful dog could turn on its master.

But she was a woman with a strong will, and she finally got them to listen, saying with conviction in her voice, "This is far more than I dared hope for when I first began all this."

Jim considered the last part of that sentence, and his insight into this remarkable woman began, his admiration growing. It was a masterstroke of subtlety, gently reminding the crowd that *she* was the one who had started all this. Two months before, she was the only one who ever knew about it. Jim thought of his first impression of her with guilt. He now understood what it must have been like in the beginning for her, seeing this horrible thing happening, knowing what it would do to her and her family. He thought of the long hours, countless hours, that it must have taken her to read the 164 books. Then to search for and mark the villainous passages ... It was a monumental job to say the least.

But then, when all that was finished, the real job would begin: trying to get skeptics like him to see what she had seen.

"The most I ever expected to come out of our efforts," Alice continued, deftly putting her arms around the crowd, was to have the parents alerted to what these books contained, and maybe, just maybe, to have the school board review them. I never dreamed that they would remove them from the classroom."

The crowd listened sullenly, some of the miners looking down at the ground, shaking their heads disgustedly, and it was clear that they could see all their efforts going down the drain. Miners' hard hats were profuse in the crowd, their owners wearing them to show solidarity, like badges of honor or possibly combat helmets. As of right now, mines were almost at a standstill, coal production was nil across the state, and they knew that when the precious "black gold" stopped, West Virginia stopped. But they also knew that once the picket lines were taken off the mines, and the boycott of the schools ended, they would be hard to reinstate at the end of the thirty-day period. The impetus would be lost; the parents' anger would subside. The board had named it appropriately: "cooling off."

The miners had been without paydays for six weeks now, and

some of them were hurting for money. They couldn't afford much more time off. Presently, they were so mad about the books that they would go hungry to fight them ... but a month from now? They all knew, especially the school board, that a week now was worth six weeks a month from now.

Jim felt defeated. The rest of the people must have shared the feeling, because they left the playground without purpose, unhurried, as if there were no place to go and nothing to do.

Jim got in his car, pulling it out into the traffic, not yet deciding which way to point it. He felt empty. None of the options that he ran through his mind held any appeal. He drove to his job, not wanting to go home. He didn't want to be alone with his thoughts. He just didn't want to think anymore, about anything, especially the books.

He finished the day numbly, like a mechanical man. The only emotion he experienced was being glad when the day ended.

When the paper came the next morning, he read the headline: textbook battle comes to an end. The accompanying article quoted Marvin Horan as saying, "There ain't gonna be no picket lines nowhere." Jim felt bitter about how the papers always seemed to go out of their way to make the protesters sound as illiterate as possible. From his past experience of being interviewed for a couple of different things, he knew that the papers almost never quoted a person verbatim; why did they tone the language of the advocates up and the protesters down?

The next several days were anticlimactically calm and uneventful. Jim wondered about the parents who were supposed to review the books. Members of the school board were now selecting the panel. Each member of the five-member board was allowed to choose three parents for the review. The process took about four days, with the media announcing each new selection.

He didn't recognize any of the names, but before this was over, he would know them all, well. Indeed, they would in effect become a family.

The mood of the valley seemed to mirror his own. Everybody seemed to be in limbo, yet there was the unmistakable feeling of an impending storm. It was like being in the eye of a hurricane after passing through one side of the storm. Rough as it was, there was the expectancy of passing through the calm into the storm on the other side of the eye and the foreboding that it was going to be of much greater intensity.

As the list of review members grew, so did everyone's anger and frustration. It was obvious what was happening. Alice Moore's candidates were the only hope that the protesters had. The other board members were packing the review board with liberals who were in favor of every innovation from the new math to the new morality. Their only criteria for selection seemed to be that it was new. Nothing else mattered.

And Alice's little group was greatly outnumbered.

The valley was like a big simmering kettle. The agreement signed by Marvin had put the lid on it temporarily, and half the valley was trying to turn the fires up, while the other half was trying to put them out altogether. The feelings hadn't changed—just subdued. If someone could fan the fires higher, the pot would come to a boil and blow the lid off.

But there was no one to fan it. With Marvin out, the protesters had no leader. No one seemed to know what to do.

The next Monday morning, Jim heard that a group of protesters was going to meet outside the governor's office at the state capitol. They were hoping to encourage him to take some kind of executive action, having heard that he was—in spirit, at least—in sympathy with them.

When Jim arrived, there were about three hundred people milling around aimlessly on the huge concrete walk outside the governor's office. There seemed to be no direction to the crowd and no one to guide it. After about an hour of nonproductive waiting, everyone looking at each other for suggestions, a man suddenly stepped up on one of the brick planters. The planter was about twenty inches high, so it put the man in clear view of everyone there. When he was sure he had everyone's attention, he said, "I'll be your spokesman, if you want me." The crowd cheered, even before anyone took a good look at him, and a new leader was born. At this point, the protestors would have accepted anyone to take the lead.

ANTITEXTERS AT STATEHOUSE

Jim looked the man over. He looked like a leader, dressed in an attractive tan business suit. He had a friendly, pleasant-looking, rotund face; clear blue eyes; and a full head of light brown, almost-blond, hair.

The soprano voice didn't quite fit the body it emanated from—large but not fat; maybe a little plump.

"My name is Ezra Graley," said the voice with a backwoods-ish drawl. "If you folks want me to suggest what we ought to do, I will." The crowd gave an affirmative yell, and he went on. "Well, it's obvious that we ain't gonna git to see hide nor hair of the governor, so we're wastin' our time here. Whatta you say we go down to the school board and let 'em know what we think of their agreement?"

Another roar of approval went up from the crowd. Graley stepped down from the planter and strode authoritatively out of the capitol grounds, toward the street, people trailing behind like the body of a serpent following its head.

Jim was about halfway back in the crowd as it made its way down Washington Street, the main thoroughfare going through the middle of Charleston, parallel with the river. The line had finally made it around the corner and was now stretched out straight, reaching almost three full blocks, about twelve abreast.

He suddenly got an idea and, totally foreign to his usual behavior, broke from the crowd and headed for its leader. There was some construction work going on, and he found himself running up and over a large mound of dirt that had been excavated and piled up. (He later saw a picture of himself on the mound in a national magazine.)

He rounded the lead marchers full tilt and headed for Graley just as they reached sight of the corner of the street that the school board office was on. He ran up to him, panting for breath. They were total strangers at the time.

"Look, I've got an idea," he said.

Graley gave him an aloof sidelong glance. He was clearly the leader today. "What's that?" he asked.

Jim was still breathing hard, almost running to keep up with the long-legged stride of the man he was talking to. "If you take these people to the school board, all you're going to accomplish is more of the same that you did on Friday. The people in the board building already know that we're out here. Why not lead them straight through town and let the whole world know what's going on?"

Graley shook his head with resolve. "Nope, we're going to the school board.

"But you may not have this opportunity again."

"We'll have it."

"But not this many people."

"We'll have more next time." And with that, Graley reached the corner and turned onto Elizabeth Street, the serpentine body trailing obediently behind him.

Jim felt like a person riding the merry-go-round for the first and last time in his life, a rider who had just missed the brass ring. The frustration welled up in him like a groundswell. He dropped back into the crowd and stayed there as they went on to the school board building. But his heart wasn't in it.

Like a Mexican general at the Alamo, Graley marched his newfound followers onto the playground across from the school board offices and then turned to face the building. He watched a moment and then turned back to the crowd.

"You folks stay here. I'm going in to talk to Underwood."

He strode across the street as if about to take care of the whole problem and disappeared into the building. Several police cars had pulled up on the side street, and city and state policemen had drifted up to the front of the building and fanned out, their backs to the building, watching the crowd.

A short, skinny man dressed in a bargain house suit detached himself from the crowd of protestors. He walked across the street and up the school board office building steps with four followers.

The steps leading to the building went up from two sides, parallel to the sidewalk, meeting at a landing in the middle, with the main entrance opening onto the landing.

The group, led by the skinny man, stopped on the landing and turned to face the crowd. The little man spoke, and the voice coming out from under the black mustache this time did match the body it came from.

"Folks, anytime I'm troubled, I get a lot of comfort from the old hymns. How about singing 'Power in the Blood'?" He started the hymn with his four companions on the landing backing him up. Some of the people across the street joined in.

Avis Hill had made his somewhat unheralded climb to leadership in the controversy. He was the skinny little man leading the hymns. This made "the three leaders" complete.

They were singing the third hymn when Graley appeared in the doorway and walked out onto the landing. The singing stopped and Graley spoke.

"Folks, I've been talking to Mr. Underwood, and he says he'll help us work this thing out." Then he mustered every attempt he could at sounding masterful. "Believe me, we got our message across."

"Hah," came the reply from a lone voice across the street, sounding as loud as thunder in the silence. Every police officer turned to look straight at Jim, and he couldn't believe he had done that. All the pent-up frustrations had come out in the one shout.

The officers stared at him for a long time, and he had the chilling feeling that he was on his way to jail. He thought the officers would never stop staring, but finally they relaxed and looked away. Jim sighed with relief.

The meeting didn't formally end this time. It just sort of dissolved, and everybody went home.

Two days had passed since the fruitless rally at the board with Ezra Graley and Avis Hill, without much happening. Then Russell Skiles, a paint contractor he knew, and had come across at several of the meetings, called him one evening and told him that Marvin was having a rally at Watt Powell Ballpark at seven thirty. Russell asked if he wanted to go, and Jim told him that he would be there.

The park was dark when he got there, and he wondered if Russell might have had the wrong information. Then he pulled into the parking lot and saw that it contained a large number of cars and trucks, some of which were becoming familiar to him. He was seeing them at all the rallies and gatherings.

He had come alone this time, his wife electing to stay at home, so he searched Russell out for company. He found him at the gate entrance, waiting with the rest of the people there for someone to open the gate.

"Russ, are you sure there's going to be a rally?" Jim asked after they had waited for more than a half hour.

"Well, that's the word I got," answered Russell.

"What's it all about? I thought Marvin was out of it."

"That's what I thought too," said Russ. "From what the papers said, he's restrained from any active role in the fight. I don't know what he's got in mind."

Just then, the field lights nearest the stands came on, illuminating the speaker's podium near the dugout in front of the stands, the passageway beyond the gate where they stood, and part of the group standing there. The gate opened.

Jim and Russell flowed into the park with the rest of the people and found a seat in the bleachers. The lights were directed primarily toward the field, so they had to grope along, feeling their way.

The crowd looked pitifully small in the huge bleachers, filling only one little corner. Jim estimated that a little over two hundred were there.

"Not many people, is it?" commented Russ.

"Well, no, but it was called on very short notice and depended on word of mouth. There were no announcements, and I wouldn't have known about it if you hadn't called me."

"Well, that's true," said Russ.

They stopped talking, as though they had run out of

something to say, and sat there in silence. There was a strange mood over the park. Jim couldn't quite put his finger on it. There was the steady drone of voices in the semidarkness of the bleachers, but the tempo wasn't normal. Instead of the usual up-and-down sound of individual voices involved in one conversation, it was a steady, mournful, almost-bizarre groan—like a wounded giant of a monster emitting the sound from his single throat. It reminded him of some of the movies that he had seen about zombies and secret cults having their religious rituals with hooded participants.

There was an ethereal quality to it all, and this set the stage for the sudden appearance of a long figure stepping out of nowhere and into the shock of the bright spotlight. The effect was dramatic.

The figure was Marvin Horan, looking pale and frightened. He was dressed in casual wear this time. The white shirt opened at the throat beneath the light jacket. His complexion looked white as snow, his eyes like two burnt holes in a sheet.

"People ... I have been deceived." The voice was haunting, hollow. It was not the voice that Jim had heard on other occasions. The authority of it was gone, and it lacked the firm, decisive tone of old. It was now the simple, plaintive sound of a wounded animal begging for relief or death.

An ominous expectancy hung over the crowd like a shroud. The silence was so complete that it caused a buzzing in one's ears. The pause was interminable.

"I have failed you," the haunting voice started again. There was still no sound from the bleachers. "People, I have failed you. You trusted me, and I let you down." Puzzlement and curiosity could be felt building in the crowd of shadowy figures. "The only reason I have asked you to come here tonight is to explain why I failed ... and to ask your forgiveness." The crowd was starting to stir. Marvin paused, turning his head back and forth slowly, panning the bleachers.

"I made the unforgivable mistake of thinking the people who are pushing these terrible books were trustworthy, and that they would keep their word. They are not, and they will not."

The voice blaring from the loudspeakers started to climb out of the swamps of despair, searching for middle ground, and it sounded a bit more solid.

"If those people had kept their word, we would have cause to rejoice. They led me to believe that the parents that would be selected for the review committee would be from our midst, representative of us. We all know now that this is not the case."

A roar of anger went up from the crowd, now come to life. Marvin seemed to note with satisfaction that the roar was directed not at him but at the opposition. He continued, his voice stronger.

"They have deceived me, and if they will deceive us once, they will do it again."

Jim noted the "us," his admiration growing for this master speaker and spellbinder. He was glad Marvin was on their side. The people in the crowd came to their feet this time, venting their anger and frustration toward the enemy, and at the same time embracing the man that their anger had been directed at just a few short days ago.

Marvin went on to explain the options open to them, saying that he wouldn't expect them to exhibit the same confidence in him that they had prior to the signing of the agreement. The crowd disagreed heartily with this.

A puzzled look crossed Marvin's face, and he appeared to be surprised but pleased at the crowd's reaction. A faint smile flickered across his face. Jim wondered if it was genuine or part of the staging of a natural showman.

"I wouldn't blame you if you never trusted my judgment again."

"Anybody can make a mistake, Marvin!" someone yelled, and a loud agreement came from the crowd.

The people had been tuned like a violin, and now they vibrantly played the concert. "We want Marvin, we want Marvin, we want Marvin ..."

Marvin's voice was choked with genuine emotion as he said, "God bless you. You are the finest people on earth. God bless you."

"Tell us what you want us to do, Marvin," a single voice cried out.

"Yeah, what do you want us to do?" the crowd chorused.

Marvin looked back and forth across the bleachers. "At this point, I can only suggest because I'm bound by the agreement that I signed." The crowd started to protest, and he raised his hands to cut it short. "Regardless of the lack of integrity shown by the other side, that does not release us from our Christian principles. After all, that's what this whole thing is all about, and if we destroy the very principles that we are fighting for in the fight itself, what have we gained?"

The people, seeming to know that he was right, smothered their objections to listen further.

Marvin's voice had regained its old confident ring. "Until the thirty days agreed to in the document have passed and the results of the screening panel are in, I will have to stay on the sideline. I cannot take an active part. I'm committed to that by signing the agreement. But I can suggest and advise."

"Tell us what to do, Marvin," the crowd implored.

"Folks, I came here tonight for the sole purpose of asking your forgiveness. I am completely unprepared to give you a direction; I just don't have any plans available right now." His voice was raised to a climax on the last sentence, and smiling broadly, he said, "But I'll sure go home and start making some."

Maybe there were only two hundred people there, but it sounded as if a thousand voices roared their approval and encouragement.

Jim wondered if the sleepy valley around them heard the roar of the wounded animal that was licking its wounds and rebuilding its strength for the next round of the fight.

CHAPTER 5
Court Order Cripples Protest

The next few days were a mishmash of nothings—a little bickering amongst the protesters themselves and a false report or two of strikes, fights, and what have you. The review committee was making slow progress, also with bickering and disagreements. Factions were being divided into liberals and conservatives.

Jim saw several filmed sessions on the news as they did their work in one of the elementary schools in the evening. Mick Staton, the spokesperson for the conservative group, had expressed dissatisfaction at the way things were going. The morning paper and the six o'clock news were what everybody in the valley lived for these days.

The protestors were getting impatient for action, and Jim was no different. His brother-in-law, a miner, had become involved, independent of Jim. Jim got so fidgety for lack of something to do that he had gone to his house one evening just to talk about what was going on. While he was there, another miner that worked with his brother-in-law came up and excitedly told him, "There is a meeting at the Kroger store in Kanawha City," a suburb of Charleston. He asked him if he wanted to go. Eager for anything at this point, Jim said yes.

They all climbed into the miner's car and started down the road into Davis Creek., a suburb of Charleston. It was almost midnight and as dark as the inside of a coal mine. The two miner's talked among themselves about their jobs. Jim, having little in common with them, kept to his own thoughts, wondering why they were calling a rally this time of night, especially at the Kroger warehouse.

The car pulled up the winding road out of Davis Creek, over the hill, and dropped down into Kanawha City. As soon as they pulled up across the road from the warehouse, Jim saw a long line of cars strung up and down the highway, parked on either side of the main thoroughfare on this side of the river.

Many men were straggling up and down the road in front of the warehouse. He thought the whole thing was a little peculiar, the time and place, but so many bizarre things had happened since this thing started that the unthinkable was normal. Everything had taken on the air of a cross between a melodramatic spy movie and science fiction.

They got out of the car and walked toward a knotted group of men directly in front of the building. Two men were talking, while the others looked on.

"Look, we've got to get these trucks with their loads out of here. Otherwise, there's going to be a lot of empty stores tomorrow and a lot of hungry people," said the Kroger spokesperson.

"That's too bad, old buddy," snarled a big miner, clearly distinguished by his hard hat. "These trucks ain't goin' nowhere."

The other man glared at him, clearly aware of all the other miners around him, and then said through gritted teeth, "We'll see about that." He turned on his heel and headed for the truck that was first in line, waiting to leave the terminal.

He disappeared into the cab, and the big truck roared to life. As this was going on, several of the pickets left in a run. The tractor-trailer lurched forward, snarling as it came, gaining momentum toward the picket line. It had almost reached the end of the driveway, where the pavement flared out to give it plenty of room to escape, when two cars careened into the driveway. They approached it from opposite sides, and Jim thought they were going to collide head-on. They screeched to a stop just in time, throwing dust everywhere. The huge truck was almost on top of them when its air brakes brought it to a lurching stop.

Jim felt as though a thousand cold pins were pricking his skin when he realized what he was in the middle of. What he had thought was going to be a peaceful rally, with him sitting anonymously in the crow while someone else did the speaking, had suddenly turned into a picket line. The potential for violence turned his blood to ice water. He had said many times, "Some people are born cowards; not me; I work at it."

He didn't know which bothered him the most, the danger of being involved in what could develop in form of conflict fostered by the workers ... or the prospect of being arrested and taken to jail.

This was totally new and foreign to him, and the suddenness with which he had been thrust into it stunned him, which was not exactly what he had in mind when he decided to do something about the books. This was interfering with people's livelihood, their means of feeding their families. Besides, Kroger was a powerful company, and that driver was big and looked mean.

Jim slid away from the confrontation that was about to happen. He was edging his way toward the car that had brought him here. He was almost there when three flashing red lights, coming up the road fast, signaled the arrival of the state police. Weaving their way around the parked cars, they slid to a stop just a few feet away from the two groups of men heading for each other.

Doors flew open on both sides of the cruisers, and officers piled out, armed with riot guns and billy clubs. They looked ten feet tall. They fanned out, almost surrounding the group of men, guns held ready. "All right, boys, I'm not even going to ask who started this or what it's all about," said the leader." I'll just simply count to ten, and any warm body left in my field of vision is going to jail, clear?"

It was plenty clear; the men wasted no time in heading for their respective cars or workplaces. By the time the state trooper got to eight, he and his squad were all alone in the parking lot.

From there on in, Jim promised himself, he would find out a little more about the meetings before committing himself.

The next morning, he was up early. He paced back and forth, trying to clear his mind and think of some productive direction to take. Last night's boondoggle was not the way. His experience with life had taught him that the first law of physics held true in almost everything: for every action, there is a reaction. The more force the protestors exerted, the more force the establishment would use to stop it. He knew that the fundamentalist leaders of the protest felt God was on their side and they were facing the establishment as David had faced Goliath. But his secular mind demanded a more logical plan of action.

He stopped his pacing long enough to pour himself another cup of coffee and light another cigarette. A gulp of the hot, black coffee was followed by a deep drag from the cigarette, flooding his being with their nerve-tightening drugs, bringing his senses to full alert.

Fight fire with fire! It hit him like a Mack truck. Of course. Why hadn't he seen it before? The "plan" was devious, subtle, a war of words. This war was far more devastating than a nuclear war, although slower. In the end, with its far-reaching effects, it was much more effective. Control the minds of one complete generation and the world is yours.

Violence was the weapon to use in a nuclear war—but this was not a nuclear war; this was a war of words. The only weapon that would win it was words. Turn their own words against them, like deflecting a bullet back on the person firing it. Violence would be necessary to keep the fires of rebellion burning and to assure holding world attention. And last but not least (in his mind, he smiled grimly at this), violence would be the very diversionary tactic used against the opponents that they had counted on so heavily to work for them.

He became excited as the possibilities unfolded. His mind, honed to a fine point by the caffeine and nicotine, darted here and then there, turning over rocks, finding clues, and formulating a plan—a "plan" of their own.

The books! He needed the books! Especially the third- and fourth-grade readers. Those were the two where he had seen the "plan" so clearly. He had no doubt that he could take those two lone books and convince any person with any reasonable measure of intelligence that the plan was real. Whether or not that particular person admitted it openly was another matter, but he or she would see it.

Without thinking, he had sent his daughter's books, with the revelatory evidence, back to school with her. Now, with his desperation mounting, he wished that for just once in his life, he would have put priority and common sense over principle. He was too hung up on principle. It would have been easy to have pretended they were lost, misplaced, stolen, or whatever, and kept them. But he hadn't kept them, and now he had no books.

He cursed himself for his principles. Casey Stengel was right! Nice guys finish last.

He had to get those two books. But how? Where? Where would he even start to look? He began running the list of names through his mind like a movie reel of the people he had met, read about, or even heard about since this thing had begun.

Suddenly, one name shined though like the North Star. Ginny Cracraft. He heard it almost everywhere he went in connection with the textbooks. She was mentioned by people from all aspects of the fight and from all levels of strata. Her name in this war was like the name of Davy Crockett at the Alamo (or Betsy Ross in the Revolution, if you prefer the same gender). It was used as a battle cry.

Jim had never met her personally, but he had heard that she was instrumental in getting Alice Moore elected to the school board. A book called *The Child Seducers*, by John Steinbacher, had been written about conditions in the schools, and Ginny was one of the characters. He figured this accounted for a lot of her charismatic mystique. She would be the most likely, except for Alice Moore herself, to know where he could get his hands on the books.

At this point, he had not attempted to contact Alice. He knew the whole world was clamoring to talk to her, and he figured she would be more unattainable than the president. A nobody like him wouldn't stand a chance of reaching her. Later, when he got the idea for the Alliance, he told June, "Alice Moore has such a crowd around her that I wouldn't stand a prayer of getting to her. But with this organization formed, she'll come to me."

He looked up Ginny's phone number and dialed it. Miraculously, the phone rang. His heart pounded.

"Hello."

"Mrs. Cracraft?"

"Yes."

"My name is Jim Farley. You don't know me, but from what I've head, we're on the same side in the textbook issue."

There was a long pause at the other end. He was getting used to this. Everybody was suspicious of everybody.

"Well, I hope so. What can I do for you?"

"I'd like to do my part in stopping these books, but I need two of the books themselves to do it. I was hoping that you could help me locate and obtain them."

"I have all kinds of excerpts that you are welcome to."

He hesitated, not wanting to offend her. "Well, I appreciate that, Mrs. Cracraft, but I'm afraid that excerpts won't do the job I have in mind. I'll just be accused of quoting out of context, as so many other people already have been. No, I'm afraid that I need the actual books."

There was a long pause. He wondered if she was trying to think of someone who would have the books or groping for words to tell him to get lost. Finally, she said, in a voice that was hard to put a face to, "I know of a couple of possibilities." He relaxed. She was going to help.

"One is a woman in St. Albans. A Mrs. Mabscott. I heard that she had some of the books." She gave him the full name and address, which he wrote down. "Then there is a man by the name of Glen Roberts, who I know has the two that you're looking for." He detected a slight change in her voice inflection and wondered about it. "I don't know if Glen will let you have them or not. He's pretty fired up about fighting them himself."

"Could I impose on you enough to ask if you would call him and ask?"

Another pause, then, "Sure, I don't mind."

"I hate to appear pushy, but could you possibly call him now and call me back?"

"I'd be glad to except I talked to Glen yesterday, and he was leaving town for a couple of days. I'll be happy to call him as soon as he gets back."

His heart dropped over the delay, but it couldn't be helped. "Okay, I'd appreciate it if you would. I'll wait a couple of days, and if I haven't heard from you, I'll assume that you've talked to him and take a run by. In the meantime, I'll try to go by Mrs. Mabscott's and see what she has. By the way, do you know her?"

"No, but she knows me."

"Would you mind calling her and let her know I'm coming?"

"I'd be glad to."

He thanked her and hung up in jubilation. The books were within his grasp. He thought of Ginny Cracraft and her willingness to cooperate. He liked her already and had a feeling that they would be working together before this thing was over. He headed for St. Albans.

"Mrs. Mabscott?" The woman who answered the door just a crack looked up at him curiously. She was short but broad.

"Yes?"

"I'm Jim Farley. I believe Ginny Cracraft called to tell you I was coming to pick up some books you were willing to lend me." He had learned that jumping to conclusions for other people sometimes pushed them over on the right side if they happened to be on the fence.

The woman's eyes showed expression for the first time. "Come in, come in." She opened the door wider to allow him entry. She had the books ready for him in a neat stack on a coffee table. She began a chattering harangue about all the filth and perversion in them, and he listened as patiently as he could. He had heard this so many times before that he was finding it harder and harder to be patient. As soon as he could, without offending her, he cut the conversation short and was preparing to leave when she said, "My son has an appointment this evening in Madison to show these books so he will pick them up at your house on his way."

He pulled his car away from the curb and drove around the corner, out of sight of the house. He pulled into the first place he could find to park. Excitedly, his hands trembling with haste, he flipped through the pages of the books, searching for the villainous passages. Dull, innocuous reading matter was all that met his eyes. Frustration, all too familiar now, began to well up in him, causing more shaking. Each was feeding on the other.

Angrily, he threw the books on the seat of the car and slammed it in forward gear. That was the infuriating thing about these books. The "plan" was scattered through them so diversely that even when you had the right one and knew what you were looking for, it still was like looking for a needle in a haystack. The faster you tried to find it, the longer it took. He vented his anger on the accelerator, and the car skidded around the corner and onto the main drive back home.

The minute he got in the door, he sat down and, calmly this time, began at page one. Patiently, though the patience was forced, he leafed through the pages, one by one. None of the books were the all important third - and fourth-grade readers, but he hoped to be able to find something that he could use.

When he did finally find a lesson worthy of attention, he tried to think of someplace he could find a copier at this time of evening. It was after eight, and all the places he knew of would be closed. Desperation brought a thought to mind. It was a long shot, but it just might work. He would do anything to get copies of some of these pages before he had to give the books back. He grabbed his coat and headed for the nearby drugstore. It sold film and would still be open.

When he returned with the film, he got out his Polaroid camera and loaded it. He aimed it at the first page he wanted to copy. The resulting picture was fuzzy. He tried again with the same result. He frantically went through all six rolls of film that he had bought. Nothing. Not one legible word. He slammed the film to the floor. Why? Why couldn't he find some way to get some copies? So near, yet so far. He clenched his fists in frustration.

The knock on the door irritated him further. He angrily jerked it open, revealing a young man in his early twenties. "Are you Mr. Farley?"

"Yes, I am," answered Jim, not too kindly.

"I'm Charles Mabscott, and I'm here to pick up the books that belong to my mother."

"She just loaned them to me a few hours ago."

"I know, but I've got to have them now."

"Look, I've got to get some copies of them made."

"Hey, man, I've got to have them now. I've got an appointment to show them to some important people in Madison an hour from now, and it takes that long to drive over there."

Jim stomped angrily back into the room, grabbed the books, and shoved them into the man's arms. "If you're representative of the kind of people that I'm going to be fighting this thing with, I'd just as soon not do it. Take your books and get out of here." He slammed the door. (Jim was to learn later that frustration and desperation would cause people to do strange things, he among them). He stomped around the house in disgust, trying to vent his frustration. What in God's name am I doing in this mess? He asked himself. I should be out drinking booze and chasing women like every "well adjusted, mature male" that our society considers "normal" nowadays.

He stopped his pacing. Why is that the norm now? How long has the influence of these books been around? Oh, c'mon, Jim, he chided himself. You are becoming paranoid. He threw his arms up in exasperation and went to bed.

The next morning, he started the cycle again, with the coffee and cigarettes as stimulants. His thoughts of last night returned. Maybe he should just forget this whole thing and go about his business. But then the spectra of this nation marching in lockstep toward the precipice of atheism swirled in his mind, injecting ice water into his veins. He could see his little world in the corner of that nation being trampled under that lockstep. His Bible Belt reflexes began to quiver anew.

He stopped his habitual pacing, filled his thermos with

steaming black coffee, and headed for his car. Glen Roberts should be expecting him by now.

Roberts was a man in his middle or late fifties. The modest home he lived in would have given most people a presumed opinion, but Jim had seen too many people affected by too many circumstances to jump to conclusions.

"How long have you been aware of what's going on?" Roberts asked.

"In the schools, you mean?"

"Well, that's part of it, of course, but there's much more to it." Jim looked at him curiously.

Roberts continued without seeming to notice. "I've devoted a large portion of my life to fighting this thing. I've followed it for years, gathering information wherever I could." He leaned closer, as though someone might overhear. "Have you ever heard of the Triple T program?"

Jim admitted he hadn't.

"Its official title is Training the Trainers of Teachers. A woman named Loretta Moore"—Jim was to come to know her better—"smuggled some of the classified material out of the capitol."

Jim marveled at his openness. For all Roberts knew, he could be working as a spy for the other side, and the information they were discussing could put Loretta Moore in prison.

"I have some of it here," he said, handing Jim some papers. "Take it with you, and when you have time, study it carefully. Briefly, it is a program designed to brainwash the teachers of the public school system to teach this propaganda."

Roberts was becoming emotional as he talked. He went on, explaining generally, with occasional specifics, about how this had been going on since the advent of John Dewey. Dewey is known as the father of progressive education. The term "progressive" was designed purposefully to connote improvement and denote, definitely, advancement. After all, what loving parent does not want better for his child?

"But this soul-withering garbage is not advancement; it's regression of the worst kind. It will wipe all morals from the soul and erase all guidelines of principle from the blackboard of the mind."

He leaned forward, clenching his fist for emphasis.

Jim was shaken by the vehemence in his voice and the fanatical, almost maniacal expression on his contorted face as he rasped out, "I watch with hatred as those vile ... unspeakable ... mad dogs of South Hills do their evil work—while they peddle their perverted propaganda." His eyes were glazed with fury and hatred. Spittle frothed at the corners of his moustache.

My God, thought Jim. Is this what fighting these books do to you? Am I looking at myself a few years from now? He wondered if his own dedication had already turned into obsession. For the first time, he felt doubts about the worthiness of the struggle. Which was worse, the poison or the cure?

He shook himself from his stunned silence to clear his throat nervously, and then he said, "I'm sorry to have to cut this short, but I have an appointment. Would it be possible to take these two books with me?"

Roberts was breathing heavily from the emotions he had just vented. It took a while for him to regain his composure. Finally, he said, "Of course. Take what you need and keep them as long as it's necessary to do the job. Good luck to you, Mr. Farley." With that, he saw Jim to the door. Jim left as hurriedly as possible without being obvious.

He was relieved to be out of that house and on his way home to sanity. When he got there, he decided to call John Wilsher, who was a member of the parents' review committee of the textbooks.

"Hello?"

"Is John there?" asked Jim.

"This is John."

"Is this John Sr. or John Jr.? Is John Sr. there?"

"Yes, just a minute. May I ask who's calling?"

"Jim Farley."

There was a long pause.

"Dad asked if he could call you back; he's busy having a garage sale. He said he has the books together."

"Yes, that will be fine."

He hung up the phone in disbelief. The world was on the brink of Armageddon, and John was having a garage sale, while the books that could save it were lying in his basement.

The next morning, Russ called to ask if he had heard about the gathering of the protestors at the school board building. Jim reminded himself of his promise not to get involved in anything illegal.

"Russ, didn't Judge Goad's court order specifically prohibit more than five people gathering on school property at one time?" After his encounter with Glen Roberts and Mabscott, he was less than enthusiastic.

"Well, yeah, it did," said Russ.

"You know there's gonna be more there than that. We could all go to jail." There was a long pause at the other end.

They were talking about the announcement in the headlines of yesterday's paper of the court order handed down by Judge John Goad. It was directed at preventing a crowd of protestors from getting together for any reason on school property. This would cut the effectiveness of the picket lines around the schools, prevent buses from being hampered as they left the garages, and stop the pressure being applied to the school board by the demonstrators gathering on the playground in front of the school board building. In effect, it would cripple the protest. Or so they thought.

"Jim, I've got to do something ... and what else is there?"

Jim didn't answer for a minute. He couldn't think of anything to say. He understood Russ's feelings of frustration; they mirrored his own.

"Russ, I don't know, but I don't want to be a martyr going to jail. I'm not the type. Besides, I don't see what purpose it will serve."

"Maybe if enough people show up, it won't be possible to take us all to jail. Jim, if we let 'em get this over on us, we're whipped."

Jim thought a minute and knew he was right. Desperation got the better of his judgment. "All right, Russ, I'll meet you there in an hour."

He started to hang up and then said, "Russ, wait a minute. Just for a little insurance, you call everybody that you can think of, and I'll do the same. If we're gonna rely on numbers for safety, let's get all we can out there."

Jim called his cousin, brother-in-law (who was already planning to go, being a miner), and everybody else that he could get hold of and asked them to come to the rally. Then he left for the school board location alone.

When he got within two blocks of the school board building, he saw the crowd. It was medium in size and growing. He walked past his brother-in-law's pickup parked at the curb.

Jim got closer and cautiously peered around the parked vehicles at the crowd, searching for the police. So far, they weren't there.

Maybe the court order was only a threat, he thought, intended as a scare tactic. Maybe the powers that be knew that it was unenforceable. This was the beginning of irrational thinking on both sides. The whole situation was unreal—so much out of the norm that logic was lost.

Jim walked closer and saw Russ and several other people he knew; he felt a little bolder.

There were no hymns this time, only silent staring at the school board building, with occasional hushed conversations. Again, miners' hard hats were profuse in the crowd. He recognized several of them, including his brother-in-law.

"Graley's inside talking to 'em. Have you noticed something, Jim? Jim looked around but couldn't quite get the point of the question.

"What do you mean?"

"There's not a black face in the crowd." Jim looked around again, more carefully this time.

"You're right. I wonder why?" His brother-in-law shrugged.

The miners were the only ones who had any faith in Graley's capabilities as a leader. The people who followed him here from the capitol two days before had done it only because he had offered the symbol of a leader. They lacked any other at the time.

But this gave Graley the feeling of leadership, convincing him that he was a leader.

Jim summed up his own feelings toward the minister later by saying, "Graley's got a heart as big as all outdoors. He's all heart ... no head ... all heart."

But his influence with the miners was tremendous, not only because he spoke their language, as Marvin did, but also because he happened to be blood related to half of them. Especially the miners in Lincoln County, the outback neighbor of Kanawha County. There was a saying among the miners in Lincoln County that if you weren't a member of the Graley clan, you had better be a "friend" of a member of the Graley clan. Ezra pastured a church there.

Jim took advantage of a lull in the conversation to survey the crowd. Apparently, it had matured in size. No newcomers had shown up for more than an hour. Jim estimated that between 350 and 500 people were milling around the playground. It was hard to tally them because of the constant movement, and besides, Jim admitted to himself that he wasn't much on judging crowds. But he did know that there was more than the handful of people allowed by Judge Goad's court order. This worried him.

There was a sudden stir in the crowd, and Jim looked toward the school board building, where the interest was directed. Graley had just emerged and walked to the edge of the landing. He waited until all attention was focused on him, and then he spoke.

"Folks, I've been talking my head off at them people in there, but they just won't listen."

A roar of anger went up from the crowd.

"That does it," shouted one of the miners. "C'mon, boys. Let's close 'em down."

He started hurriedly off the playground, followed by an eager small army of hard hat owners.

There were several large construction jobs nearby, and Jim knew that these would be their first targets. They were union jobs, and the miners knew that all unions were a brotherhood. One union membership would honor the picket line of another union, regardless of their differences in policy or philosophies. The huge jobs, crucial to the valley's growth and economy, would come to a grinding halt in minutes.

With the aggressive hostility of the miners gone, the mood of the remaining crowd became more pacifist, more religious in tone. The hymns began in a doleful baritone.

Before they left, one of the miners had told Jim that he had heard that the state police had been called out. They would be here at any time, but one of the troopers, a secret protestor himself, had passed the word along that as long as they stayed peaceful, they had nothing to fear. But above all, he'd warned, they had to stay together. Their great numbers were the only defense they had against going to jail.

The state trooper was symbolic of the protestors' unseen strength: people in key places that were unannounced but wholeheartedly with them.

About that time, a caravan of state police cars came slowly up Virginia Street and pulled into the parking lot. As the troopers began to disembark from their parked cruisers, they were unhurried, walking casually to the front of the building. It was obvious they had been instructed not to spook the crowd. Their riot guns had been discreetly left in one of the cruisers, with two troopers standing inconspicuously nearby.

Their demeanor was pleasant, almost friendly. They watched

the crowd with seemingly mild interest, appearing oblivious to the hymns. They offered no interference to the crowd in any way.

Everything was peaceful. It seemed more like an old-fashioned "all day meetin' with dinner on the ground" type of service, which the country church Jim had attended when he was a boy used to have.

The hymns went on, changing from one to another without interruption, like a medley. The time went on with nothing eventful taking place. The sun was getting higher in the sky, its rays warming the protestors and the pavement around them. The crowd was passive for the time being. Lunchtime had come and gone, and different segments of the crowd were pooling their orders for sandwiches and drinks, which individual volunteers went to fetch at the corner restaurant. Jim decided to go for his group because he wanted to be alone to think.

When he got to the little restaurant, he ordered a cup of coffee before he gave the waitress the written order for the food. He sat sipping the coffee in deep reflection.

He wondered what the outcome of the day would be. What was happening at the construction sites where the miners had gone? Why hadn't the state police troopers followed them there? (He was to learn later that this had been assigned to the sheriff's department, and many deputies were already covering the situation.) He considered the very real possibility of being arrested and hauled unceremoniously to jail, and he felt a powerful desire to walk out of the restaurant, turn left away from the school board, and get the heck out of here, leaving it all behind him. Remembering all the people who were at the school board location because he had asked them there, he ruled that out. He thought about all the people just a few blocks away, going about their business, oblivious to what was taking place here. He envied them.

The sandwiches and drinks came. He paid for them and reluctantly turned right when he left the restaurant, heading back to the crowd in front of the school board building.

There was almost a festive mood over the crowd as they ate.

A feeling of camaraderie prevailed. The hymns were continuing, different groups alternating, to allow everyone time to eat, without the singing being interrupted.

After everyone had eaten, and they all had the satisfaction of full stomachs, the crowd became more vigorous and energetic. The singing became louder and the tempo picked up. One could feel the building tension. The hymn "I Shall Not Be Moved" started, led by Graley, who was still standing on the landing above the crowd. The old favorite was turning into a battle hymn, at once stating their position and defiance. The voices singing were mixed, some with resolve and some threatening.

The crowd had been there since nine in the morning, and it was now nearing three thirty. Nothing of importance had happened, and they were getting restless. No one appeared to know what to do, an seemed reluctant to be the first to give in and leave.

Finally, the state police trooper in charge decided it was time to end it. He walked to the front of the landing, where Graley was standing, and raised his hands for silence. The singing stopped momentarily.

"We have been patient because we think you mean well, and that you believe in what you are doing. But Judge Goad's court order is specific and will be enforced. Any persons left on these premises beyond the number of five, thirty minutes from now, will be arrested and charged with contempt of court. Go home; it's all over. You can do no good here today."

"They can't take us all to jail, folks!" shouted a lone voice. "Stand your ground!" All the officers looked him over carefully, as though marking his face in their memories.

Jim had been thinking a lot about that, and the man was right. They county and the city put together didn't have the facilities to jail them all. The state used the county jail.

But what they could do—and in his opinion, what they would do—was wait them out. Wear down the less-determined ones; weed out the weak. When those people tired of it all and left, the crowd would eventually be reduced to a manageable size. Then is when the police would act.

The crowd started singing "I Shall Not Be Moved" again, more defiantly than ever. The police looked on, their pleasant, neutral expressions replaced with impatient scowls. The tension on both sides was growing.

The thought of going to jail appealed to Jim less and less. He watched as a few people here and there drifted away.

A cold chill of fear swept over him. He could almost hear the finality of the steel doors clanging behind him. The repercussions that would result from his being thrown in jail would seriously hamper the plans he was formulating in his mind.

While he had been standing there all day doing nothing, his mind had not been idle. He had watched the crowd of working middle-class people in their futile assault on the establishment. As well intended as it was, and as forceful as they knew how to be, short of violence, it was pitifully ineffective. He loved these people and had great compassion and admiration for them, but he knew that they would never get the job done this way.

He also knew that he was just another warm body here, just another face in a sea of faces. Part of him could identify with these people, the working-class part.

But then there was the other part of him. He thought of Bert Wolfe, his friend and the largest car dealer in the state. They had a good relationship. He knew Bert held his opinions in high esteem. He thought of Roger Banks, the senior vice president of the Bank of West Virginia, who was also a good friend. He ran a list through his mind of all the well-educated, influential people with whom he had a rapport. Some of them were wealthy and powerful.

A lot of them, like Bert, whose name was a household word throughout the county, he knew well enough to know that once they knew the contents of the books, they would quickly repudiate them. Others, he would have to feel out.

Jim knew that people in Bert's category were as far removed from these people here in this crowd as the North Pole from the South. He felt he was the only person in the valley who could bridge the gap. His idea was to form an organization of business and professional people. People in high places would listen to them. They could wield a power and influence that these people never could.

That's why Jim could not afford to go to jail. He knew that if he did, people of importance and prestige, people that he needed to accomplish this purpose, wouldn't come near him. They understandably did not want to be attached to the stigma of the protestors that the media was rapidly building—that of a mob of radicals, lunatics, hoodlums, and what have you.

He looked around him again, and a cold wind swept through him; his hair bristled. He turned and said, "Russ, have you noticed something?"

"What's that?" he asked casually.

"Look around you at the crowd."

Russ looked around and lost no time in getting his meaning. "The crowd is getting smaller."

"That's putting it mildly; it's almost gone."

The concern showed clearly on Russ's face. "Russ, they're going to wait until a few more are gone, then they'll haul the rest of us off to jail."

Russ asked, "What do you think we ought to do?"

"Well, I for one don't want to go to jail."

"Neither do I," said Russ.

"I don't see where it will do any good," said Jim.

Russ looked around again apprehensively. "Jim, I agree with you. You and I going to jail will serve no purpose. I think I'm going back to my job. I'll see you later." He sauntered out of the playground, walking faster as he reached the other side of the street. Jim enviously watched him go.

The crowd had diminished to less than fifty people. Jim walked over to the people he had asked to come. "Look, there's no use in you all gettin' in trouble. Why don't you leave now, while you still can?" Relief and gratitude swept their faces. He thanked them for coming, and they quietly left.

Just as Jim saw them cross the street, he heard a commotion from the landing. When he looked around, he saw Graley with his hands outstretched upward as though reaching for heaven. Tears were streaming down his cheeks. He was saying repeatedly, "I have done no wrong." The state troopers, one on each side, were pulling at him, trying to get him off the landing and to the paddy wagon that had just arrived. At last, they applied such pressure that he half walked and was half dragged to the black vehicle that would take him to jail.

This signaled the attack. Troopers moved swiftly, next arresting the man who had defiantly encouraged the crowd by telling them to hold their ground—saying that they couldn't arrest us all. No, they couldn't, thought Jim bitterly. They never intended to, just the key people to set an example, with a few of the small fish thrown in just to prove a point.

Some of them went grudgingly, kicking and holding back. Blue uniforms of the city police materialized out of nowhere to give assistance. It developed into a brawl.

News reporters and photographers from both newspapers and all three of the local TV stations were there. One photographer, a small white-haired man of approaching years, had started past Jim to get a better shot of the action at the paddy wagon. He stopped short, his camera posed halfway to shooting position. He stood beside Jim as if he were in a daze.

He watched, entranced, as the people, men and women, were dragged into the black van. "I've covered news for forty years," he mumbled, more to himself. "Wars, tyranny, cruelty, injustice. I never thought this could happen here. This is America." He said the last as though to make it true.

His camera remained transfixed, as he was. He just stood there, his eyes unbelieving, watching peaceful, hymn-singing, taxpaying American citizens being roughly dragged and pushed off to jail like war criminals. He winced when one of the protestors attempted to get away and was clubbed for his action. One of the women screamed.

Their only crime was in loving their children.

Jim had seen enough. The van was full; the police were satisfied that they had made their point. Several people on the fringes were easing toward the street. Jim unobtrusively joined them, and the group faded from the raucous scene as the sirens wailed.

CHAPTER 6

The Calm Before the Storm

In a lackluster mood, Jim searched the morning paper for something to give him direction. He was still nervous about yesterdays near disaster. The picture of Graley on the front page, holding his hands outstretched to heaven, tears streaming down his cheeks, brought back the goose pimples. Jim skipped the article under the picture, turning to the inside of the paper. There, he found an article rehashing the shooting of nearly a week before.

A picket line of protestors had been formed around the United Parcel Service terminal, effectively closing it down. No trucks were moving.

William Noel, a twenty-seven-year-old driver, showed up for work. He saw the picket line and stopped his car a hundred feet or so away. As he sat there watching, some of the protestors on the picket line spotted him and started running toward him. He reached into the glove box for the .32-caliber pistol he carried. The protestors were closing in fast.

He held the gun out the window in plain sight to frighten them into stopping. They kept coming. He fired one shot, and thirty-year-old Phillip Cochran fell, shot through the heart. A shot rang out from a blue Volkswagen.

The running protestors stopped. They stood frozen, looking into the muzzle of the .32. Noel, stunned at the result of his actions, just sat there, not knowing what to do. He soon found out when the door being jerked open on the other side of his car snapped his head in that direction. He was looking into the bore of a service revolver of the deputy sheriff holding it. He meekly laid the .32 on the seat beside him and slowly raised his hands.

Some of the protestors crowded around the fallen Cochran.

"Somebody call an ambulance!" one of them shouted. "He's still alive."

Phillip "Skip" Cochran had heard that when a person drowned, his whole life passed in front of his eyes as he went down for the last time. He didn't relive his whole life as he lay there in the grass waiting for death to come—just the last several minutes of it, trying to make sense of it.

Leaving his house for the one-block walk to work, Skip Cochran had suddenly remembered what day it was—Friday the thirteenth. He smiled inwardly. He had never considered himself a superstitious man, and besides, what could happen to a man on such a beautiful day? The sun was shining, the air was crisp, and he felt great. He had not taken part on either side of the battle raging in the valley over the textbooks, so there was no reason to worry there. He came into sight of the UPS terminal where he worked, and his pace slowed. People were all over the place.

He walked on, curious, not knowing what was going on. As he got closer to part of the main body of the crowd, someone looked up and saw him, yelling, "Go back!"

Skip stopped and hesitated. Then, when he heard a stronger warning directed at him, he turned and started back toward home as ordered. He didn't know what was going on but figured it had something to do with the textbook war. He didn't want to find out the hard way; tempers were hot, and logic was short these days.

Man Panicked, Fired Gun, Lawyer Believes

About the time he thought he had made it to safety, a car pulled past him and stopped. A hand holding a gun appeared at a window, and a voice said, "Get back or I'll shoot." Skip didn't know what to do. He had been told to go one way; now he was being told to go back. Before he had time to make up his mind, the gun roared, and he felt the air go out of one of his lungs. It didn't knock him down, and he felt no pain. He just staggered back and looked around. He saw a grassy spot nearby, stumbled to it, and lay down to die. He didn't know how long he lay there, waiting for death to come. He had accepted it as inevitable. But then he thought of his wife and children. You can't die; they need you, he thought. He started screaming for help. That was the last time he gave any thought to dying. He had to live!

CHAPTER 7

Friendships

The screaming siren and the flashing lights of the ambulance as it careened into the huge parking lot made vivid the grim reality of what was happening. It settled over the participants like an invisible fog, chilling them in the warm sun.

The ever-present black paddy wagon followed. Victim and assailant were loaded into their respective vehicles and taken away.

Jim laid the paper down, seeing vividly in his mind the scene described in the article he'd just read. It made his stomach churn; sickened him throughout.

The whole thing was getting out of hand. It was no longer a peaceful protest by loving parents; it was an all-out war. And now it was a shooting war!

His thoughts turned to the idea that had come to him yesterday at the school board fiasco. He felt certain that if he could get respected people of the business community involved, reason could be introduced into the struggle. Calmness would prevail, and the problems could be rationally discussed.

But where should he begin? He knew he would have to start at the bottom, with some of the smaller executives. Once he had enough of these to form a nucleus, he hoped to be able to attract the bigger, more influential ones. He planned to point to the smaller ones as an example to the more successful ones that nothing disastrous would befall them if they became active in the protest.

He realized that he had nothing to start with, no point of beginning, no definite plan, no definite people—save one: his good friend Bert Wolfe. His eventual goal was to persuade Bert to head up the organization he hoped to put together. But as of now, all he had was a germ of an idea, and a compelling resolve to do something about what was happening.

Jim still labored under the naive concept of Christendom that stemmed from his youth. He had always believed that good was good, bad was bad, and all churchgoers were heaven bound. He knew that Bert shared his strong religious convictions and was as devoted to his family as Jim was to his own.

He missed the article on the editorial page of the paper, which commented on "the fashionable churches of the city staying aloof from the textbook controversy." This was the launching of his education in Christendom, and he wasn't even aware of it. He would learn much in the coming months.

Jim walked into his bank that morning, feeling like a total stranger in the place that had been like a second home to him for so many years. He knew all those who had been there over six months by their first names. The kinship he felt toward all the officers of the bank made him feel as though they all belonged to the same family.

He had chosen Roger Banks as his first candidate to approach for his group. He knew Roger was a family man who loved his children, but he had no idea how he felt about the books or the protest movement.

Waiting for the customer that Roger was taking care of to leave, Jim then walked over and sat down at his desk. "Roger, how are you doin'?" he said in his usual manner of greeting.

"Oh, pretty good," Roger answered customarily. "How about yourself?"

They had some small talk about the economy, weather, construction, and so on.

Then Jim built up his nerve and asked, trying hard to sound casual, "Roger, what do you think about what's going on in the schools?"

Roger's answer took him by complete surprise. "The public school system is finished," he said with somber resignation.

Jim looked at him, astonished. "You really think so?"

"Oh, there's no doubt about it." Roger leaned closer, his tone becoming confidential. "You see, Jim, I know Alice Moore personally, and I've been getting inside information for a long time. The public education system is a mess; a disgrace."

Jim couldn't believe his luck. Here he had cautiously approached Roger, planning to sound him out to see what the possibilities would be of winning him over to his way of thinking. He'd had only a faint hope of being able to persuade him to get involved. Now here was the same Roger, telling him that he had been in on it from the start, long before Jim had become involved. What's more, he was a friend of "Joan of Arc" herself.

Jim had not come prepared for this, so he didn't broach the subject of his plan. He felt Roger would be a willing ally when the time came. He wanted to get as many people lined up as possible before disclosing his intended plan.

His next stop was the Glenn Paint Company to see its owner, Ceyphus Hill. Jim dealt there frequently, and a few days before, he had seen a flyer lying on the table there, listing some excerpts from the textbooks. An accompanying sheet of paper asked people to sign a petition against the books.

He got right into the matter with Ceyphus, who readily agreed to do anything he could to combat the books. Jim left.

At the end of the busy day, in addition to Roger and Ceyphus, he had Jack Douglas of Save Supply, the large retailer for kitchen and bathroom fixtures, and he had gone by Bert Wolfe's office, but Bert was out. He was elated at the results.

He couldn't wait to return to Bert's office to discuss making him the leader of the organization that he had decided to call "The Business and Professional People's Alliance for Better Textbooks." He admitted it was too long but could find no way to shorten it and still embody the image that he felt necessary to be effective.

The next day, he walked into Bert's office, confident of the outcome. Bert emerged from behind his desk to greet him warmly, shaking his hand. They went through the usual amenities, and then Jim asked, "How do you feel about what's going on in the valley?"

Bert looked at him guardedly. "Do you mean the textbook thing?" When Jim said yes, Bert said, clearly choosing his words carefully, "Well, I sympathize with both sides in the problems they're having."

"Have you read any of the books?"

"No, I haven't."

Jim rummaged in his briefcase, pulled out some of the excerpts, and handed them to Bert.

Bert read them and then looked at Jim, shock and disbelief in his eyes. "Jim, are you telling me this is actually in the books our children are reading?"

"Every word," said Jim. "And that's only a small sample. The worst is here," he said, handing him the third-level reader.

Bert looked through it, glancing at the passages that Jim had underlined. He looked back at Jim, his expression puzzled. Jim knew that he was expecting to see four-letter words; when he saw none, it threw him. Jim patiently led him through each passage, giving the direct parallel in the Bible that went with each.

Bert saw what he was talking about but still didn't understand the implications. "I don't understand, Jim. If this is all there is to it, why all the strikes and confrontation?"

Jim felt the all-too-familiar frustrations starting to build. "Don't you see, Bert, that if children are submitted to these books, with this comparison of the Bible in this light, by the time they reach high school, where they'll find the really raunchy stuff, they won't believe a word the Bible says. It will be just another fairy tale to them."

Jim thought he knew his old friend well, but he had to admit to himself that he couldn't tell whether the perplexed look he was now wearing was caused by the inability to grasp the plan in the books or if Bert was trying to find a tactful way to decline the anticipated request for involvement.

"Jim, let me think this over. Could you stop back in a few

days?"

Jim was disappointed. He was impatient to get started, and he had hoped to have the first official meeting of the Alliance within three days, on Saturday. Yet he knew that there was no use in pressing Bert. That was how well he did know him.

He sighed heavily, getting up to go. "Sure, I can stop back whenever it's convenient for you."

"Do that," said Bert. Jim thanked him and left.

It was raining dismally as he pulled out of the shopping center where Bert's agency was located. He passed through the stoplight and headed up Central Avenue. Two blocks up, he passed the Kanawha Valley Transit bus terminal.

The unnatural look of all the buses jamming the parking lot wove a foreboding atmosphere into his mood. The buses that normally would be hustling up and down the highways, happily carrying workers and housewives alike, were resting forlornly idle, side by side. Their drivers were refusing to budge them as long as the books were in school.

Two of the drivers were his brothers. He had talked to neither of them since this had started. There was a picket line in front of the terminal to assure that none of the "scabs" took out any of the buses. Scabs are workers that cross a picket line and continue to work when the goal of the picket line is a total work stoppage.

He slowed down, thinking he might see one of his brothers there ... but he didn't. He drove on disconsolately

Three days later, Jim walked back into Bert's office. Bert still had no inkling of Jim's real plans: asking him to head up the Alliance once it was formed.

"Hello, Jim," Bert said, his usual warm greeting, coming out from behind his desk to grasp Jim's hand. But this time something was different. A strained, standoffish feeling pervaded the room.

Jim came right to the point. He was tired of verbal fencing. "Hello, Bert. It's good to see you again. Have you thought about what we discussed the other day?"

A pained look crossed Bert's face, and he became very serious. "Yes, I have, Jim, and I'm afraid I'm going to have to decline any involvement in taking sides in this issue." He waved a hand at Jim's not-too-well-hidden look of disdain. "Now, Jim, you're going to have to try to understand. I've got people on both side of this working for me."

Yeah, and customers on both sides of it too, thought Jim disgustedly. He made no effort to hide his anger. "Bert, do you realize what's taking place in this valley? What is going to take place if this thing is not stopped? There's going to be more bloodshed; in fact, it could turn into a bloodbath before it's over."

Bert gave him a look of reprimand. "I have assurances from the right people," he said, "that the necessary steps will be taken to prevent that."

"You mean the National Guard. I know that, but how many of them can you depend on in a situation like this? How many of them are protestors themselves? Besides, I have a son and son-in-law in the Guard, and I don't want them out there shooting and being shot at. Why wait until it goes that far? There are more peaceful ways of settling this if we act quickly and decisively."

"Jim, I'm sorry. I sympathize with you, but I just can't get involved."

You mean you won't get involved, thought Jim bitterly. You're afraid of the business you might lose.

"There are, however, things that I can do. Russell Isaacs and I play tennis together." (Isaacs was the school board member who at the outset of all this called the books in question "absolutely profane" and then, for reasons of his own, did an about-face and became a staunch supporter of them.) "If you like, I'll call him right now and see what can be done. Would you like me to call him?"

"If you like," said Jim wearily.

Bert picked up the phone and began dialing.

"Russell, how are you; how's the family? Fine. Russ, about this textbook thing, exactly what is being done, and what is your position?" There was a long pause on this end while Bert listened. "Uh-huh, I see," said Bert. "Well, I can't disagree with that. Thank you, Russ. See you this afternoon? Fine."

He hung up the telephone, looking smugly at Jim. "Russell says that the school board can't back down now—that if they remove the books the people are protesting, where will they stop? Next it will be the library and *Huckleberry Finn*."

"But isn't that a two-way street, Bert?"

"What do you mean?"

"Isn't it just as reasonable to assume that if the protestors let the school board get by with putting these textbooks in our schools, that next we'll have X-rated movies in the classroom?"

A flicker of real concern crossed Bert's face, and then he regained his composure and pseudo-confidence. "Jim," he said sternly, "I think you're overreacting to this."

"Bert, one man has already been shot, no public or school buses are running, the valley is in turmoil, and industry has come to a virtual standstill. And you say I'm the one overreacting? What does it take? An all-out war? Well, that's exactly what's coming if this thing is not brought to a peaceful conclusion."

Bert looked at him, visibly trying to hide the fear in his eyes and attempting to sound confident. "Jim, we do still have law and order in this valley and the National Guard to back them up, and I'm depending on that."

Jim considered arguing further but decided against it. It was obvious that Bert wasn't going to budge. He would have to look for his president elsewhere.

Alice Moore, whom Jim still had not met at this point, had told him on the phone that an industrialist, the owner of one of the chemical plants in the valley, was trying to get a group of his contemporaries together to come out against the books. His name was Elmer Fike. Jim had to go see J. D. Landers anyway, and he figured he would know the man since they both had their places of business as well as their homes in Nitro.

He always dreaded going into J. D.'s place when he was in a

hurry. J. D. loved to talk more than anything. Jim enjoyed talking to him when he had the time, but the trouble with J. D. was he didn't care whether you had the time or not; he still loved to talk. This time it couldn't be helped. He was in a hurry, but he still had to see J. D. He braced himself and went in.

Carol Hudson, J. D.'s secretary and an avid member of the protest group, looked up from her work and smiled. "Hi, Jim, how's it going?"

"Oh, pretty good, I guess. Is J. D. around?"

"He was here just a minute ago. I think he went in the storeroom. He'll be out in a minute. Want a cup of coffee?"

"Sounds good."

Carol gave him the steaming black coffee, and he gratefully accepted it. As he was starting to sit down, J. D. came out of the back room.

He smiled broadly when he saw Jim. "Hi, Jim, glad to see you. What's going on?"

"Well, that's what I'm about to find out, I hope. J. D."

Puzzlement took second place to the excitement at seeing Jim, and both expressions flooded J. D.'s face as he motioned Jim toward his "office." Actually, it was a desk just behind the counter where Carol stood to greet the customers as they came through the door.

Jim studied him a minute, took a deep breath, and then asked bluntly, "Do you know a man named Elmer Fike?"

"Curiosity was added to J. D.'s other expressions. "Yeah, I know him. Why?"

"How well? What kind of man is he?"

"Well, he's a fighter—I do know that. He runs a chemical plant that he owns down at the lower end of town. What's your interest in Elmer?"

Jim looked down at his hands, rubbing them together. He wasn't sure just how much he should tell J. D. at this point. "Well, let's just say that I'm interested in trying to get him in the

Alliance."

J. D. looked at him curiously but seemed to resign himself to the fact that he would get no more information on the matter. He changed the particulars, but the basic subject stayed, naturally, on the protest of the books.

He began to deplore the behavior of some of the methods used on both sides in the textbook matter. Knowing that he was getting wound up for one of his long, long sessions, Jim interrupted to ask directions to Elmer's plant and left in the middle of a word, much to J. D.'s consternation.

Following the directions wasn't too difficult, and he soon found himself in front of a building with a sign declaring it to be Fike Chemical Co. When he got to the receptionist's desk just inside the main door, he asked if Mr. Fike was in. She said yes and directed him up the stairs and to the first door to his left.

He found the office door ajar and stood watching the heavy squat man working on the figures that he was bent over. Jim wondered how anybody could make a rational decision of any kind out of the chaos of paperwork piled haphazardly across the desk. It looked a foot deep. The acrid odor of the chemicals coming from the plant behind the office created a peculiar backdrop, set the illusory mood.

He waited awhile, and when he wasn't noticed, he cleared his throat.

The man looked up and said, "Come in."

"Mr. Fike?"

"What can I do for you?"

"I'm Jim Farley, and I'd like to discuss some things with you."

Elmer motioned him to a chair and sat back to give him his undivided attention.

"Mr. Fike," he began.

"Elmer," the man rumbled in a subdued voice that was somewhere between a grunt and a growl.

"Thank you, Elmer. I won't ask the obvious, of whether you're aware of what's happening in the valley over the textbooks. I won't even ask your opinion of them ... or which side of the fence you're on. I've talked with different people about you, and I think I have a pretty clear picture of you and your position."

Elmer's blue eyes, studying him from beneath thick eyebrows, kept changing from limpid pools of water to glittering blue ice and back again as the conversation progressed and topics changed.

"I've been told you're a fighter." There was no change of expression. "I was also told that you were trying to raise support from your associates to put together a group of industrialists to combat these textbooks."

Elmer shrugged, noncommittally, saying, "Oh, there's been some talk."

"Well, I've been doing more than talking," said Jim. "I already have the nucleus of an organization that will encompass the entire business community and the professional people as well."

Elmer's bushy eyebrows went up, and his ice blue eyes sparkled in anticipation and interest.

Jim explained what his idea was all about, mentioning people like Roger, who had already agreed to participate actively and were anxious to get moving. Elmer listened in silence, making no comment, facially or verbally.

Jim named all the officers that had been selected and that had accepted. He knew that Elmer hadn't escaped notice that he hadn't mentioned a president. Jim doubted that he was surprised at his next words.

"All we need is someone with drive, position, and eloquence to head it up."

Elmer was clearly pleased but hid it well. "Why don't you do it?" he asked.

"Because I don't have the stature needed for the position."

Elmer's appraising look was mixed with respect for a man who would recognize this in himself and admit it. "Aw, I don't know," Elmer said in that half-growl voice. "I've got more than I can handle already. I just don't know where I'd find the time. My wife, Frances, was putting pressure on me the other day to drop out of the legislature race because of the time it involves."

Jim was only slightly apprehensive about the outcome because he could tell that the idea intrigued Elmer, especially since the nucleus was already formed, complete with officers.

After thinking, or appearing to, for some time, he said, "All right, let me talk to Frances about it. I'll have my answer this evening. Is there a number where I can reach you around seven?"

Jim scribbled down his home phone number, gave it to him, and left with the conviction that the Alliance had its president.

CHAPTER 8

The Die Is Cast

Jim was having difficulty in separating the participants of the controversy into their proper respective strata. For this reason, he had developed the habit he was exercising now. Appraisingly, he looked over the church that housed Charley Quigley's headquarters for his new Christian school.

The school had been born of the book protest and the boycott of the public schools a few weeks before.

Since time did not permit the checking of credentials and background of each person he came into contact with, the only method he had available to him was to survey the surroundings of the person, observing his dress, speech, grammar, and so on. He knew it was a superficial and ineffectual evaluation process, but it was the best he could do under the circumstances.

He had never seen Charley, only heard and read about him, so he didn't have the slightest notion of what to expect.

He parked his car in the average parking lot and walked to the rear of the average brick church, where he had seen a smaller structure built along the lines of a dwelling. The word OFFICE was neatly lettered on the glass half of the door, so he opened it and walked in.

A slender, bespectacled man looked toward the door as he heard Jim come in. He continued talking into the telephone that he held in his hand.

Jim unobtrusively seated himself in front of the desk the man was standing behind. He tried not to listen to this end of the phone conversation, but it was difficult since the small office compelled togetherness. He was not surprised the talk was about the textbooks. It seemed that's all anybody discussed these days. Even though he was trying hard to avoid hearing the context of the conversation, he couldn't help noticing the voice itself. It was of a different quality from the three leaders. It was pleasant, even-toned, and slightly high-pitched. The vocabulary was more extensive than those of the other three.

Quigley terminated the phone conversation with some disparaging remarks about their position in the controversy and hung up the phone. He glanced at Jim across the desk, not speaking but with a question in his eyes.

"Mr. Quigley, I'm Jim Farley. I'd like to talk to you about the fight against the textbooks." Quigley nodded perfunctorily, without answering. Jim went on. "How well do you know Alice Moore?"

"That was her I was just talking to," Quigley answered. "I'm in daily contact with her." He was a man of quick physical movement. He would be sitting one minute as if he were there for the day; then he would suddenly be on his feet, heading for the filing cabinet, then back to his chair, assuming a relaxed position of permanence, shuffling papers on his desk all the while and only glancing at Jim occasionally. Jim found it hard to communicate under these circumstances. He plowed on anyway. "What would be the chances of talking her into going on television?"

Quigley glanced up from the papers he was sorting. "They won't let her have the airtime."

"What if we bought the time?"

Charley stopped shuffling the papers and looked at Jim levelly for the first time, with interest. "We don't have that kind of money."

"What if the money were made available to you?"

Charley stopped shuffling the papers and studied Jim with new interest. "If that were the case, we'd have no problem."

"Then you think you could persuade her to do it?"

"I'm sure I could."

Jim studied him for a moment and then grew extremely serious. "Mr. Quigley, as of now, I'm committing ten thousand dollars to the cause, to be used in any constructive way that's beneficial to stopping or exposing what these books contain."

Charley looked him over appraisingly and appeared to believe the sincerity he saw, accepting it as fact. "When do I get the money?"

"It will be made available to you as you need it. Preferably, the first of it will be spent on the airtime for Alice Moore. You set it up and I'll be in touch."

Jim got up to leave, indicating the meeting was at an end, not bothering to leave his telephone number. Quigley nodded vaguely and went back to his papers as Jim went out the door.

Jim pulled into Shoney's parking lot. (This restaurant was the original one that started the Shoney's chain, which spread over several states.) The lunch crowd had come and gone, so there were very few cars in the lot. Marvin Horan had agreed to meet him here to discuss how they could work together and what they could do.

The real reason for the meeting was to become acquainted and feel each other out. He looked around for the white Lincoln Mark that had become the man's trademark. It didn't belong to him. Bob Burdette, the man who had siphoned gas when Jim ran out of gas at the rally, a neighbor, owned it, but Marvin felt it improved his image and gave him more clout with the upper class. It wasn't there.

Jim wondered what kind of man he was going to be talking with shortly. Would he be reasonable? Was he as intelligent as he appeared to be at a distance? Was he genuinely concerned about the books ... or was he a crusader looking for a cause? He hoped to have the answers to these questions and more before the day was out.

A white car turning into the lot caught his eye. It was a Buick. Jim decided to drive around the lot again. It covered about half an acre, with the restaurant located in the center, so to be able to see the whole lot, one had to drive around the entire square. He completed the turn with no white Lincoln in sight.

It was forty minutes past the agreed meeting time and Jim

was getting tired of waiting. He was beginning to get the feeling that something had gone wrong.

He wondered if Marvin was testing him, like a kidnapper having the victim's relative make a dry run of delivering the ransom to a telephone booth for further instructions. The phone rings in the booth, the relative answers, and a voice tells him that he did good—no police—and to now go home and wait for the real drop.

Jim felt agitated at the thought of this. Time was precious; so little of it and so much to do. Almost two days had already been wasted trying to set up this meeting, and he resented wasting more.

He looked at his watch and saw that it was almost an hour past the agreed upon time. He started his car to head for a phone. Then he thought of the cloak-and-dagger feeling that Marvin seemed to have and decided against it. He might spook him if he called him from a phone booth; it would sound so transient. He needed something a little more solid. He turned his car up the hill toward home.

As soon as he got there, he tried to phone Marvin and got the busy signal that he expected. It seemed the whole valley was trying to get in touch with the man. He tried again ... with the same result. He was tempted to place an emergency call but was afraid to. As skittish as Marvin was, anything out of the ordinary could cause him to call off the whole thing.

After constantly dialing for almost an hour, he finally heard the phone ringing.

"Hello." Marvin's voice was casual yet guarded.

"Reverend Horan, this is Jim Farley, and I was wondering if something came up. I waited at Shoney's for an hour and decided that something must have happened." Jim kept his voice relaxed and friendly.

"I'm sorry, Mr. Farley, but I've been on the phone the whole time. Could I call you back in a few minutes? I've got one more call to make."

"Sure," said Jim, hiding the reluctance in his voice. They hung up. Jim knew he had been right; he was checking him out.

He knew he would check his phone number in the book, if he hadn't already, and then dial the number to make sure that he was who he said he was and where he said he was. He wondered if someone had observed him while he was in Shoney's lot.

The phone rang. "Mr. Farley, this is Marvin Horan. I'm ready if you are."

"I'll meet you there in twenty minutes." Jim was exultant; this time it would happen.

He was in his car and moving, hardly realizing it. The drive down the hill and working his way through traffic was vague to him. His mind was excitedly working out the details of the meeting.

This time when he pulled into the parking lot, the white Lincoln was already there. It was backed up to the fence, pointed toward the exit, with a clear path to the street, leaving the occupant with a clear view of any cars coming into the lot.

Jim pulled up beside it and parked. Marvin got out of the Lincoln and came over. He leaned down, looked in the open window, and said, "Mr. Farley?" When Jim said yes, Marvin opened the door and sat down.

Jim noted with interest that Marvin left the door open and kept one foot on the pavement. The piercing dark brown eyes looked straight into his. They didn't stare, nor did they flinch. There was an indefinable mixture of expression, but it gave the definite impression of a cat poised on the fence—neither defiant nor defensive, ready to jump either way depending on what happened next. Marvin waited for Jim to begin the conversation.

"Reverend Horan," he began.

"Marvin," the other man interrupted flatly.

"Marvin, then," Jim began again. "This is the first time you've seen me, Marvin, but I've been watching you from the crowd for so long that I feel like we've been friends for quite a while." The gaze stayed the same, no change of expression to indicate reaction. "I could take up a lot of your time telling you how much I agree with you about these books, how committed I am to stopping them, and what great lengths I'm willing to go to accomplish this, but you're not gonna believe a word of it anyway. A flicker of amused admiration flared in Marvin's eyes, momentarily losing their control of the neutral, then regaining it.

"You want proof, and I don't blame you. Many peculiar things have happened lately, to say the least. You can check me out any way you want to—any way you can think of—and keep a close eye on me at all times. That doesn't bother me; in fact, it would make me feel better, and I would advise you to do so.

"I've only been in the crowd up to this point but I've been involved in it from the night of your first rally the night before school opened. I've been watching not only you but Graley, Hill, and the rest of them as well. There's one big thing wrong. We're spending more time fighting each other than fighting the enemy. We've got to get organized." He wondered if Marvin recognized his own technique in the use of "we."

Marvin didn't make a comment or move a muscle; the gaze remained the same. "I've got some plans of my own on how I can contribute a great deal to the effort, but you have to keep it alive until I can work them out and put them into action. And to do this, you need the whole group working with you."

"Who do you mean by the whole group?" It was the first thing Marvin had said since he had said the one word to indicate what he wanted to be called. It made Jim feel better, as if it was beginning to be a two-way conversation, not just a monologue falling on deaf ears.

"I mean you, Graley, Hill, Charley Quigley, and of course, your followers."

"I can't work with Quigley," Marvin said abruptly.

The remark took Jim by complete surprise. He was annoyed. "What do you mean?" he asked, wondering about the disdain in Marvin's voice.

"That night we had the rally at Campbell's Creek, not the one you went to but the one that all the media played up, the one where somebody was supposed to have roughed up a news cameraman ... When that happened and a scuffle started to develop, I called off the rally. I made it clear that I was not going to be a party to that sort of thing and told everybody to go home. When I left the speaker's stand, Quigley jumped up on it, grabbed the microphone, and took over. I can't work with him," he repeated. "I refuse to work with him," he added.

Jim had learned a long time ago, back on the farm, that when a bull charged, you didn't stop in front of him and try to stop him by hitting him head-on. You ran with him in the direction he was going until you got a good hold on his halter. Then you gave a little jerk to change his direction. Then another little jerk until you swerved him a little. Finally, when you got him headed in the general direction you wanted him to go in, you got hold of the ring in his nose. Then you had him. Then he was your bull.

He and Marvin were both staring out of the windshield of the car, giving Marvin the impression he accepted this.

After a period of silence that lasted so long it grew awkward, Marvin started to fidget, swinging the knee that was inside the car listlessly back and forth. It seemed they had reached an impasse, that the conversation had been terminated. And Marvin obviously didn't want it to end.

Jim waited for a few more swings of the knee and then said, "Marvin, I know exactly how you feel."

Marvin brought his attention away from the windshield, returning to the noncommittal gaze of before. But it wasn't quite the same this time. The eyes showed a little more expression; they were a little less impersonal. He nodded his head several times slowly, as if they had agreed on something.

Jim went back to staring out the windshield in deep thought. Finally, still looking straight ahead, he said, "Marvin, maybe we're looking at it wrong. Did it ever occur to you that maybe Charley wasn't trying to take over and push you out?"

"What do you mean?"

"Well, maybe he was just trying to salvage what he could out of the opportunity of the rally—with all the people there. Maybe he was afraid that if they were just sent away with nothing, they wouldn't come back."

Marvin kept the level gaze directed at him for a long time and then stared out the windshield, seeming deep in thought.

At last, Jim asked him, gently, "Did you ever consider that possibility?"

"No, I didn't," answered Marvin.

Jim saw the door open just a crack and gently pressed to widen the crack. "Look at it from his point of view, Marvin. Charley is as wound up about all this as we are." (The "we" was matter-of-fact this time.) "You know the feeling of frustration that we all have ... the desperation. I know that I, for one, would grab any opportunity I could to do something that I thought would do any good. Especially if I thought that was going to be the last chance I was going to get." Jim let that sink in and then continued.

"Suppose this is the way it happened. Suppose that Charley was standing there in the crowd with the rest of them, waiting for you to tell them what to do. He's eager to get going. Maybe he didn't even see the fracas with the newsman; you said it was way back in the crowd. Charley had to be close to the stand where you were." Marvin nodded his assent.

"Okay, then, let's say he didn't see it. All he saw and all he knew was that one minute, five thousand people were waiting to get their instructions from you, and the next minute, you were telling them to go home."

Marvin mulled this over and then said, "You know, it could have happened that way. I never thought of it that way before."

Jim felt the door open wide, and he stepped boldly through. The bull was his. "Then wouldn't you say that if it had happened the way Charley saw it, that he would have saved the day?"

Marvin said thoughtfully, "Well, if it had happened that way, I guess he would have."

That's when Jim knew that he was dealing with a fair and reasonable man.

"Then will you reconsider working with him?"

"What is your idea? You said you had some plans."

Jim knew he was in control. "Marvin, you're the undisputed leader of the protestors." Marvin deftly masked the pleased look that flitted across his face. "Especially to the people in the upper part of the valley. Those people won't listen to anybody but you and they would follow you anywhere. But Graley has a certain following too—Lincoln County, for example—and Avis Hill has his little group. We need them all. And Charley Quigley has something that none of the rest of us have."

"What's that?" asked Marvin.

Jim said in a careful, well-chosen way, "Something that the other side seems to respect: a college education."

Jim knew he would have gotten a tirade of rebuttal from Graley or Hill, but this was Marvin. He looked understanding as he nodded. "Okay, so what's your plan?'

"You will be in control, along with Graley and Hill, with Charley as coordinator. If the four of you can keep the pressure on long enough, I plan to put a group together myself."

"What kind of group?"

"Marvin, I've met a lot of influential people in my business. I know the elite on a first-name basis—powerful people. I know most of the ones who would be in sympathy with our cause. I plan to get an organization of these people together to help you fight these books."

Marvin's face lit up. "How do you know that you can do it?"

"I've already approached some of them, and we are ready to start building and planning, but it's going to take time. Our group's methods will be different from yours. We can't just decide to throw up a picket line and put it into effect thirty minutes later. Our way will be slower but effective."

Marvin was no fool. He plainly saw the potential of power in Jim's plan. He became excited. "What can I do?"

"Set up a meeting with the four of us first: you, me, Avis, and

Graley. I don't care where it is; you can decide that. We four will lay the groundwork, decide how to divide the territory of leadership ... that sort of thing. Then we'll go from there."

By this time, the bull was running full tilt with him. Marvin extended an eager, friendly hand. "Mr. Farley."

"Jim," Jim interrupted.

Marvin flashed a warm smile. "Jim, I think you're one of us, and I'm looking forward to working with you. You have some good ideas. I'll set the meeting up and give you a call."

He was in!

Word of the battle in the valley was beginning to leak to other parts of the country. It went out in letters from people on both sides, then in requests for help to various organizations, and finally in news articles. The media news began with small items of interest, stuffed inside the paper on the ninth page, but then came the shooting of Cochran, followed by full-page coverage of Graley being dragged to the paddy wagon, tears streaming down his cheeks and his arms stretched toward heaven. The wire service picked up both items and Graley, looking like a governor in the photographs, became a familiar figure across the country.

Curiosity became piqued from coast to coast. Just what in the world was going on in the hills of West Virginia? "For that matter, where is West Virginia?" asked different organizations and individuals. Among these was The Heritage Foundation out of Washington. It was just what the name implied, an organization set up to protest violations of the Constitution concerning an individual's rights. The foundation sent Elmer Fike an answer to his request for assistance, telling him to expect their legal representative, James T. McKenna. Also, coming in on their own, was a husband and wife team that had dedicated their lives to combating inferior quality textbooks in the public schools, Mr. and Mrs. Mel Gabler from Longview, Texas.

Last but not least was Bob Dornan, who was later elected to the United States Congress from California in 1984. He was coming in as the representative of CDL (Citizens for Decency through Law) at the request of J. D. Landers. J. D. and Elmer were both contributors to each respective organization.

Jim paced the floor of his living room, going now and then to the door to look out at the gray fog of the morning. It would be over three hours until James McKenna's plane touched down at the airport. He was the man whom The Heritage Foundation was sending in from Washington to see what they could do to help with the textbook problem.

Jim had never heard of the foundation before yesterday, when Marvin told him about McKenna's visit. Marvin wasn't much more informed than he was; he only knew that it was some kind of organization that protected the basic rights of Americans.

Marvin had wanted Jim to go with him, Graley, and Avis Hill to meet Mr. McKenna at the airport, but Jim declined. He had tried to maintain a low profile through all this, and he intended to keep it that way.

"The three leaders," as Jim had dubbed Marvin, Avis, and Ezra, liked the spotlight and publicity. Jim did not. He knew that the airport would be swarming with reporters, both local and national. The national news ranks had been growing steadily as the protest spread over the state.

Jim glanced at his watch; it was 7:43. McKenna's plane touched down at 9:02. He planned to leave for Graley's house at about the same time the plane landed. The five of them were supposed to have a meeting there. He figured that by the time the other four got to Graley's, a forty-minute drive from the airport, the reporters would either have all they wanted or would just give it up.

It still wasn't quite nine o'clock, but Jim couldn't stand the waiting any longer. He put his jacket on and left for the drive to Nitro, where Graley lived.

Nitro got its name from its reason for being. During World War I, the U.S. government spent eighty million dollars (you can imagine the cost at today's prices) to establish a completely self-contained explosives plant and an entire town for the employees about twelve miles west of Charleston on the north bank of the Kanawha River. This installation was called Explosives Plant C, commonly known as Nitro. Twelve thousand men built it in ten months. After all this, it was in operation for just one week. That's right, one week. It opened on November 4, 1918, and closed on November 11, 1918, when the armistice was signed. The war was over, and the need for the nitrocellulose, "guncotton," no longer existed. The government was stuck with a white elephant. (Now that's unusual, isn't it?)

They proceeded to parcel it out at less than two cents on the dollar, hence the city of Nitro. In the ensuing years, seventeen chemical plants have mushroomed on the site of Explosives Plant C, including Elmer Fike's Fike Chemicals. Although the petrochemical industry was the largest, with plants strung up and down the valley, including such giants as DuPont, Carbide, Viscose, and others, other related and helpful plants began to crop up.

The industrialization of the valley, however, began long before the birth of Nitro. In 1755, Mary Ingles was captured by the Shawnee in Virginia and brought to the Kanawha Valley and was forced to make salt for the Indians. Forty-two years later, the first salt furnace was opened in the valley by Elisha Brooks. Industry in Kanawha Valley was on its way. The Kanawha River offered easy transportation for the salt and all products to come later.

From the humble salt furnace, industry in the valley grew to eventually include, in addition to the petrochemical, a huge synthetic rubber plant (built to fill the needs of government again, in World War II), a glass plant, a bottle plant, armament plant, barge companies, boiler companies, and eventually, an automobile plant.

And of course, there was the king of them all, "King Coal." These industrial installations covered the entire valley from the narrow upper reaches, where the plants eventually filled the valley floor and spilled out into the hills, clear to Point Pleasant, sixty-two miles downriver, where the Kanawha River dumped into the Ohio.

When Jim got to Nitro, he drove around looking at the house numbers until he found the right neighborhood, and then he started looking for Graley's house. It was a shabby neighborhood, and Jim silently hoped no reporters would follow them here. The image of the protestors was bad enough already. He drove down an unpaved alley that the rains of the last several days had turned to mud.

He saw a plain cinder block house with an old truck backed into the yard and an assortment of tools and material strewn around. He had heard that Graley was a small-time roofing contractor. This had to be it. He parked the car in front of an outdated garage and got out. Walking around the house to the front door (the alley approached from the back of the house), he looked out over Kanawha River.

As he knocked on the solid panel door, he didn't know exactly what to expect. The house could be full of reporters and hangers-on for all he knew. Lord knew who else might be there.

After the second knock, the door swung open. The small man who opened it looked up at him questioningly, one eye looking straight into his, the other one surveying the river, or the yard, or the sky—Jim couldn't be sure where it was looking. He finally recognized him as Avis Hill, his moustache shaved off. He had looked bigger on the landing at the school board location—more commanding and authoritatively directing the crowd in the hymns.

"I'm Jim Farley," he said. As he started to explain why he was there, Marvin's voice called out from a part of the room Jim couldn't see.

"C'mon in, Jim."

Avis backed away from the door to let him in, still looking at him suspiciously with the one eye, while the other admired the wallpaper.

Graley sat on a couch against the wall, dressed only in pants, undershirt, and slippers. He had one arm across the back of the couch and a cup of coffee in the other hand.

The three leaders knew nothing of protocol, so Marvin got up to greet him and introduce McKenna, who nodded but remained seated. Graley sat, looking on, sipping his coffee. Avis went back to his seat at the far end of the room.

It appeared as though they had already been discussing the role that McKenna's people might be playing in the matter, for they picked up where they had left off before the interruption. Jim listened as though he was totally engrossed, but he took the opportunity to look Ezra and Avis over, as well as the newcomer, McKenna. He had come to know Marvin well enough at their meeting in Shoney's parking lot.

He sat down on the couch next to Graley, whose uncombed hair added to his slovenly appearance. He looked fatter now, his stomach, encased in the undershirt, bulging over his wrinkled pants. His eyes were red and bleary. When he spoke, somehow the backwoods drawl was more pronounced now than it had been at the capitol, when he stood before the crowd in a suit.

Marvin was carrying most of their side of the conversation with McKenna, while Avis constantly interrupted with inane remarks.

McKenna kept directing his questions at Graley, even though Marvin continued to answer them. Jim couldn't quite understand his persistent interest in Graley, until he remembered the photos of Ezra on the front page, looking like a governor. Jim knew the impressive picture had gone out on the wire service. No doubt McKenna had seen it. Add that to the fact that Marvin has been out of action for the past several weeks, thought Jim, and it explains everything.

McKenna had been trying to learn more about the particulars of the fight: their position, their strength, their needs, how many people they could count on for support, etc.

Jim overrode Avis's ramblings about their grandiose worldwide backing to ask McKenna, "What would be your opinion of an organization of business and professional people coming out against the textbooks?"

McKenna gave him a hard, searching look, then answered, "Oh, well, if you could get people like bankers, lawyers, and influential businessmen to take a stand, the battle would be over."

Jim smiled to himself, thinking of Roger, Bill Hamb, and Bert Wolfe, who, respectively, matched the criteria. He was about to explain his plan for the Alliance, and how far he had already progressed, when McKenna went on. "But it's been my experience, in similar struggles across the country, that it's always been the working class that does the fighting. It's hard to get the kind of people that you're talking about to get involved."

Jim started to tell him that he already had the nucleus of such an organization started, with many more people expressing interest. He wanted to explain the rapport that he had with so many people of importance.

"I tell you who's gonna win this fight—the miners," Avis said. "That's who's gonna win this fight."

McKenna half nodded his assent but didn't quite mask his disdain at the bantam rooster voice coming from Avis.

Marvin turned to McKenna. "Mr. McKenna, just how much support can we expect from your organization?" Marvin was by far the most intelligent of the three.

McKenna eyed him warily. "Well, we will provide any legal assistance necessary, searching out different laws, defending anyone involved against the protestors in court, making sure that your constitutional rights are not violated, and so on. We also are prepared to offer certain financial assistance in other ways. I can't go into detail as to the nature or the amount right now, but it would be decided by me when the need arises."

"The miners could use some money right now," chirped Avis.

McKenna ignored the asinine statement, looking once more at Graley. "How many people do you estimate that you have control of or direct influence over?"

Graley drew himself up to his fullest and said, "Buddy, let me tell you, all the people in this valley is again' them books. Not only this county, but Boone County, Lincoln County, and the whole state."

Boone County was Graley's old stomping grounds, and Lincoln County was where he had been raised.

You just tell me how many you want and I'll git 'em." He glanced at Marvin.

McKenna winced at the all-encompassing sweep of Graley's once-again grandiose answer. McKenna knew that superlative talk was usually used to cover ineffectual fact.

Marvin spoke up. "Mr. McKenna, if we had the money to put a full-page ad in this Saturday's newspaper, I can promise you five thousand people would be in Watt Powell Ballpark the next day."

McKenna took a closer look at Marvin. This was the first tangible offer of a plan that had been made, and Marvin said it with such simple, unadorned conviction that you had to believe him. McKenna looked into Marvin's level, unflinching gaze, seeing the intelligence in the eyes.

"All right, you've got it. You draw up the ad and submit it for my approval. If it looks good, we'll go with it. The expense for the ad will be a worthwhile investment to ascertain the leader."

Marvin's expression didn't change. It was as though McKenna's answer had been a foregone conclusion to him. But Graley's face came alive with feeling, jubilation over the ad, consternation over the sudden, unexpected shift in power and decision making. After all, wasn't he the new, undisputed leader? Wasn't he the one who had led the enormous crowd out of the mighty halls of the capitol and to the school board? Wasn't he the one who had gone to jail? Wasn't this his house? Avis ranted on, and Marvin ignored them both.

Marvin's keen mind was on the plans for the coming rally and the ad. It was whirring like a fine machine on how to win the fight. Somehow, by the look on McKenna's face, it was evident that he sensed all this and knew whom he would be dealing with from now on.

Just then, the phone rang and Graley answered. He listened for a minute, nonplussed, and then started smiling broadly. "Yes, ma'am, that sure was my picture on the front page." He continued listening, and then putting his hand over the mouthpiece, he said, triumphantly, "This lady is calling all the way from Oregon. Well, thank you, ma'am. I do my best." He beamed.

He listened, then said, "Well, I tell you, ma'am, we sure could use that." Covering the mouthpiece again, he said, "She's the head of a national women's group and said they could provide us with all the money we need." McKenna shifted his position in the chair uneasily.

"Get her name and phone number," Jim said impulsively, in a low but urgent voice. Graley unconsciously nodded his head and then went on listening. McKenna stared at the ceiling.

"Well now, ma'am, that's real nice of you."

"Get her number," Jim said impatiently.

Finally, he took his pen from his pocket, found his small notebook, and thrust them under Graley's nose, saying for the third time, "Get. Her. Number."

Finally, Graley interrupted the woman and said, "Excuse me, ma'am, but could I have your name and phone number?" Jim sighed with exasperated relief. Shortly after, they all left Graley's house with the understanding that they would be meeting together again shortly.

Several days later, Jim was on his way to Campbell's Creek for the long-awaited meeting with Marvin, Graley, and Hill. He was excited, and rather than vent the feeling or suppress it, he chose to channel it into constructive thinking.

It was a beautiful sunny day, and he felt good. He was dressed in his suit, complete with tie, which had become his habit since he had begun working on the idea of the business and professional group. It was part of what he felt necessary to build an image, an image that he considered vital to their effectiveness.

As he tooled the car around the twisting curves that led off the hill, Jim's mind was racing, in character with his mood. He had seen enough of the three leaders to evaluate their traits, good and bad.

Marvin was definitely the leader, with much more basic intelligence than the other two. He also had a charisma that was unique in the sense that it worked its charm in a one-on-one situation and was equally prevalent before a large or small crowd. It made him a natural spellbinder. In a later conversation, when Jim told him that he, Jim, could do fine talking to one person at a time but was not good in front of a crowd because he had to be able to gauge the other person's reaction, Marvin explained that he got the same feedback from a crowd as he was able to read a crowd's reactions.

The odd part about it, or maybe it was typical of life, was that although Marvin was the obvious one to lead, the other two were clamoring for the top spot. They exhibited much more desire to gain recognition than Marvin did. It wasn't that Marvin didn't like the spotlight, but that he had a regal humility about him. This was just one of the characteristics that made him a natural leader.

Jim knew his biggest job would be that of a diplomat. He would have to somehow convince Graley and Hill to take secondary positions. That wouldn't be easy. If it weren't handled properly, he could lose them altogether, and he couldn't afford the loss.

He turned into the mouth of Campbell's Creek, remembering the night he and June came up here for the first rally. It seemed like a long time ago.

He felt like an outsider as he drove up the hollow, past the Jenny Lind houses, which is a small economically built house typically, built on piers of stone, block, brick or wooden posts. He knew the feeling was enhanced by his being dressed in a suit and driving his new LTD. He had literally, body and mind, stepped into the role of a successful executive for the purpose of image for the cause.

The ability to adapt himself to any level of social or intellectual climate came so naturally to Jim that he was totally unaware he had it for a long time. When he finally discovered the attribute some years back, he had put it to work quite successfully in his business and figured it would serve him well in the fight ahead.

Whenever he was with successful businessmen, he thought and talked like a successful businessman. When he was with manual laborers, such as miners, he thought and talked like a laborer.

Only this time he knew that he had to think and talk like an executive while dealing with laborers. He could do it; he knew he could. His mind flashed back to the time that he had to meet seven men from a neighborhood group concerning a single job he was doing for them. He was giving one price for the entire job and each man there would have to pay an equal share.

He had stood before all seven at the same time, knowing that each one of them was on a different social, intellectual, and educational level. He met each on his own ground, right in front of the rest; he answered their questions to their mutual satisfaction and got the job. Yeah, he could do it.

He pulled up in front of the building where they were holding the meeting. It was a small frame building that served as a union hall for the United Mine Workers of America

Marvin was standing in the doorway waiting for him. He smiled warmly as he shook Jim's hand.

He recognized the man behind Marvin as the owner of the white Lincoln. He seemed to have assumed the double role of benefactor-bodyguard for Marvin, being omnipresent.

"Jim, I'd like you to meet Bob Burdette, a very good friend of mine." Then Marvin glanced at Burdette and said, "Bob, this is Jim Farley, the man I was telling you about." They shook hands and sat down, Marvin behind a desk looking as if it belonged to him, the other two in front of the desk. They were the only three there for the time being.

Burdette was a big man with a deep, mild voice. He was laconic, preferring to keep to his own thoughts whenever permitted. You always wondered what was going on behind the gray eyes that were shielded by his glasses. Jim recognized him as the man who had siphoned gas from the white Lincoln for him that night of the first rally.

They had just started to open the conversation when an attractive young woman walked through the door. She was small but well proportioned.

The men looked up, and she blurted out, "Marvin, that phone is ringing off the hook at the house, and they all want to talk to you."

Marvin glanced at her with that lazy yet piercing look of his and abruptly began giving staccato orders.

"Call the phone company; tell them I want a phone installed in this building before the day is over, within the hour if possible. List it in the name of Concerned Parents. Make that two phones—and call Avis and Graley to see what's holding them up." He glanced around the room, "Have two tables with chairs moved into here ... and another desk. I want writing material, paper, pens, pencils ... You know the stuff. Get Graley and Hill up here."

The young woman stood nodding as if used to this. Marvin paused in his order giving and turned to Jim. "Jim, I'd like you to meet my wife."

Jim nodded to her, smiling, and said, "Mrs. Horan, I like the way your husband works."

She smiled weakly, nodded in reply, and left to do her husband's bidding.

Graley and Hill came in together. After the amenities, they all sat down, Marvin behind the desk, the rest in a semicircle in front of it. Jim and Burdette were the only two dressed in suits. This somehow gave Jim a better feeling of control. It was a symbolic illusion, but he was glad for it.

"Well, what did you have in mind?" Marvin asked, reminding Jim that this meeting was his idea.

He glanced at each of them before answering. He took a deep breath. "Each of you has been doing a good job in your own way and with your own following, but we've got a problem. We're bucking heads without meaning to. It's kind of like it says in the Bible; the left hand doesn't know what the right hand is doing."

They didn't agree, but they didn't disagree either.

"With each of you working alone, independent of the other, nobody knows what anybody else is doing or planning at any given time."

"I call Marvin and Ezra all the time," chirped Avis.

Jim hid his disgust and said, showing patience, "I'm sure you do, Avis, but sometimes one of you can't reach the other." He was making every attempt to be tactful.

"I know each of you wants to see these books thrown out of our schools as much as I do." They nodded assent. "With all of us working together, we can do it."

"Whatta ya mean, workin' together?" asked Avis suspiciously.

Jim surveyed him carefully while taking another deep breath. "Well, Avis, I mean just that. All of us should be cooperating with each other."

"We three do cooperate," snapped Avis.

"Then let's get on with our plans for the big rally coming up. And I hope it's the biggest yet."

"It will be," said Marvin quietly.

Jim glanced at him, thinking it strange how much more impact Marvin's low-key statement had than Avis's loud shouting. Superlatives seemed to lose their effectiveness for the same reason, nullified by their very force, rather than emphasized by it; shouting was lost in hoarseness. He thought of Elmer's favorite saying to illustrate his stand against something: "That's unacceptable." It mirrored the stance that leading politicians took, including the president himself. That's unacceptable. Somehow, that low-key statement, almost just the elimination of a negative, said it louder than all of Avis's blustery shouts with superlatives.

Push in one direction too hard and things seemed to go in the opposite direction. Someone once said, "Happiness is a fragile thing; try to force it and it will elude you; strive for other things and it will settle lightly on your shoulder like a butterfly."

This same rule seemed to apply to the plan in these books. The very enormity of it made it almost impossible to see. It reminded Jim of the building that housed the rockets at Cape Canaveral. It was so enormous that when the tour group he was with walked inside, everyone, including Jim, pointed cameras upward and then lowered them without a single shutter snapping. Each person realized in looking through the lens that the enormity of the building made it impossible to see. Even from the outside, the doors for the rockets to pass through were so huge that you couldn't tell they were doors until you were at least seven miles away. Standing close to them, the individual features were indistinguishable. And so it was with the plan. Try to point out its individual points and people could not see the significance of them; therefore, they did not recognize "the plan." It was frustrating.

"I've got it all figured out on how to keep order at the rally," said Avis commandingly.

"What are you talking about, Avis?" asked Jim.

"I've talked to some of the miners, and they're all for it. What we're gonna do is have our own squad to police our own ranks. The miners are gonna wear their hard hats so's everybody will know who they are and why they're there. They will take care of any disturbances and hecklers."

Jim was appalled at this, even coming from Avis. "You do that, Avis, and you're gonna start a riot."

"Just the opposite; we'll keep order. The police won't do anything to help us. People won't pay any attention to cops no more."

"Avis, you can say what you want, but those blue lights flashing on top of a police cruiser still command a lot of respect. You go through with this idea about the miners and their hard hats, and you're going to have a bloodbath. And I won't be a party to it." Jim ended his angry statement with his finger under Avis's nose. "You can count me out."

Bob Burdette hadn't spoken, but he did now. "You'd better listen to him, Avis. He makes a lot of sense."

Avis rolled his eyes around at Burdette and then looked at the floor. It was clear that he was having second thoughts about what he had originally considered a perfect idea.

Jim decided to quit while he was ahead. Nothing more could

be accomplished here today. "All right, then, let's all do what we can to get ready for the rally."

The meeting was concluded.

CHAPTER 9

Meeting at Watt Powell Ballpark

Even though they were early, Jim had to park their car almost two blocks up from the ballpark. Its sizeable parking lot was packed to overflowing. Cars and pickup trucks lined the streets in both directions.

As he walked toward the same park gate where he and Russ had waited the night Marvin called his meeting, he was struck by the antithesis. It began with the warm sun illuminating the total scene, cheerfully contrasting with the sinister coldness of that dark night.

But the stark difference was felt as he got to a position where he could see the packed ballpark. Marvin clearly had the five thousand he had promised McKenna—and more. It gladdened his heart to see the rows of people pushing over to make room for another to find a seat, and more were still streaming up the ramp.

He looked the crowd over and was gratified to see a greater percentage of well-dressed middle- and upper-class people than he had seen at any of the rallies or meetings before. Jim did not judge people or their values by their dress or educational or social level, but he knew all too well that others did, especially "the world out there." Maybe this will change the image of the protest, he thought hopefully, looking around at the TV cameras that were already set up.

This was one of the few times that his wife and daughter accompanied him. As the three of them found seats, he noticed that this time the park hummed happily, and Jim's feelings joined the mood of the crowd. He felt as if they had climbed a mountain and was now on the sunny side of the peak. From here on in, it would all be downhill.

He could just see the TV cameras whirring, recording the massive crowd—the well-dressed, well-behaved crowd—for the entire world to see. Without a doubt, they would see for themselves that this was more than an uprising of rednecks objecting because of ignorance. Maybe his idea for the Alliance would be unnecessary now. Surely the world would get the message once they saw the results of the filmed events here today when they were flashed coast to coast on people's TV screens.

His jubilant hope was short-lived. He watched with eager anticipation as a national news team, complete with camera, looked over the crowd, obviously looking for a person to interview.

He couldn't believe his eyes when the crew brushed past several extremely well-dressed people and tapped on the shoulder of the seediest-looking character he had ever seen, beckoning him to step out into the aisle.

The creep did so, grinning idiotically through tobacco-stained teeth, the few he had left. His jaw bulged with its present chew, the juice trickling through his scraggly beard. Many of the protestors carried signs, no worse than any political convention, but the cameraman made sure that they got a shot of the one hanging around his neck. It read CASTRO-ATE UNDERWOOD. (His name was Kenny Ferrell, and he was later charged with a threat to kill the president; he was found to have a mental problem.)

Jim felt as if he had been soaring through the air on a trapeze and then suddenly hit a solid cliff. He seethed with fury and frustration. Why did the reporters do this if they really did want to report the news without bias? Why didn't they at least pan the crowd, or better still, why didn't they interview an intelligent member of the well-dressed upper class, which was in plentiful supply here? Why? Unless they deliberately wanted to give a slanted version to the world?

While the reporters were still interviewing people in the stands, Marvin Horan walked out of the dugout and onto the field.

He made his way up the steps to the speaker's platform, his

stride bouncy. The crowd applauded loudly. He stood there smiling, waiting for the applause to end. "Welcome, ladies and gentlemen, to the kickoff rally of the new phase in the fight to save our children." The crowd went wild.

Marvin smiled broadly during the entire ovation. When it finally subsided, he continued. "Thank you all for coming. We have a big day planned for you here, with some very important guest speakers." The bright sunlight added an air of freshness to the brisk fall day.

"First, we have Lewis Harrah, the pastor of the North Charleston Church of Jesus Christ. We have Mr. Jim McKenna from The Heritage Foundation of Washington, D.C. We have Mr. Bob Dornan from the Decency through Law organization, from Los Angeles, California. And last but not least, we have the honor and great privilege of introducing the man-and-wife team that has devoted their life to fighting filth in textbooks. They will be our first speakers today. Ladies and gentlemen, I give you Mr. and Mrs. Mel Gabler from Texas."

The crowd cheered as a slender man emerged from the dugout and made his way to the platform, followed by a matronly, slightly plump woman.

Gabler filled in some of the background of their fifteen-year struggle against inferior quality textbooks, then got into specifics. He zeroed in on one particular article about the late Marilyn Monroe, which took up the better part of seven pages in a current history book about the United States. The name of the book is *Search for Freedom—America and Its Past.* This book was rejected by the Board of Education in Austin, Texas, on November 3, 1972. Then he turned to an article in the same book, dealing with George Washington, the father of our country. This lesson consisted of one small paragraph.

Jim wondered if the other people there were as appalled by this as he was. He wondered what our country had come to. Had the mood of the nation changed so much since he had gone to school that a celluloid sex goddess was that much more important than the man responsible for the Republic coming into being? Or was somebody trying to make it appear that way?

(Get their minds off important issues and onto trivial matters such as sex, etc.)

Hmmm, thought Jim. He was thinking of the copy of "The Dusseldorf Rules for World Conquest", which someone had given him. It was supposed to have been taken from a high-level Communist agent who had been captured in Dusseldorf, Germany. The story was, they were a top secret outline by the Communist Party, on a plan to take control of the world so subtly ("We will bury you so silently, you won't even know you're dead," Nikita Kruschev, 1959) and so gradually that the very people involved would not be aware of its happening—many of them actually becoming unwitting dupes helping carry out their own destruction.

There were those who said the document was a fake; some said it was genuine. Jim didn't know who was correct, but he did have to admit, right or wrong, fake or real, that it looked suspiciously like each rule of the ten was being implemented before his very eyes. Could this be one of them?

Gabler covered other subject matter in diverse areas, but none of it held Jim's interest. He was much too preoccupied with the magnitude of the priority of Marilyn Monroe over George Washington and the implications it connoted.

He reached down and pulled his briefcase out from under the bleacher seat. He rummaged through the reams of papers he had accumulated from various sources, dealing with the issue at hand. After several fruitless minutes of digging, he found what he was looking for: a single small sheet of paper. He slid the briefcase back under the seat and leaned back to study the sheet. The heading at the top read IT WAS PLANNED FIFTY YEARS AGO! Below is the complete copy of the pamphlet:

> If you think most of the problems that beset the world and our nation today just happened that way: if you think it is a natural trend born of the modern age. If you think it will suddenly all dissolve when we the people get tired of being bothered, then read an excerpt from a file on "Communist Rules for Revolution," published before 1919. The file was obtained by the armed forces in Dusseldorf, Germany. These

were the instructions issued to those who were to bring about world revolution:

A. Corrupt the young [get them away from religion]. Get them interested in sex. Make them superficial [destroy their ruggedness].

B. Get control of all means of publicity and thereby achieve the following:

1. Get people's mind off their government by focusing attention on athletics, sexy books and plays, and other trivialities.

2. Divide the people into hostile groups by constantly harping on controversial matters of no importance.

3. Destroy the people's faith in their natural leaders by holding the latter up to contempt, ridicule, and obloquy.

4. Always preach true democracy but seize power as fast and as ruthlessly as possible.

5. By encouraging government extravagance, destroy its credit and produce fear of inflation, rising prices and general discontent.

6. Foment unnecessary strikes in vital industries, encourage civil disorders, and foster a lenient and soft attitude on the part of the government toward such disorders.

7. By specious argument, cause the breakdown of the old moral virtues, honesty, sobriety, continence, faith in the pledged word, ruggedness.

8. Cause the registration of all firearms on some pretext with the goal to be confiscation, leaving the population helpless.

This treatise was first given public notice when it was printed in the Bartlesville, Oklahoma, *Examiner Enterprise*. Printed, but no one gave it much thought. Just fifty-one years later, those who were given the plan of attack are sure there is now another set of instructions, going on where these left off. This time, past history presents full reason to be concerned, if not completely frightened. Your enemies are patient but thorough. Your greatest enemy, however, is your disregard for the danger signs.

In his book *Masters of Deceit* (Holt, 1958), J. Edgar Hoover, the longtime director of the FBI, said of the Communists and the documents of their conspiracy, "These doctrines threatened the happiness of the community, the safety of every individual, and the continuance of every home and fireside. They would destroy the peace of the country and thrust it into a condition of anarchy and lawlessness and immorality that passes imagination. Apathy is our greatest enemy."

Amen, J. Edgar, thought Jim. Amen.

Jim stopped reading, looking out at the field in the ballpark but not really seeing it. His mind was on rule number three from the list he had just read: "Destroy the people's faith in their natural leaders by holding the latter up to contempt, ridicule, and obloquy."

What better way to help accomplish this than the humiliating measure of importance applied to George Washington as compared to Marilyn Monroe?

Jim had heard different opinions as to whether the list containing these rules was genuine or a farce. He made no judgment himself as to their authenticity. In the first place, how many diverse opinions were floating around on the authenticity of the Bible, or parts of it thereof, such as the Virgin Birth and Christ's resurrection?

Then there were the different opinions of the authenticity of the events and the way they had happened in history, in the United States and all other countries.

Whether the "rules" listed here, called "The Dusseldorf Rules for World Conquest" because they were discovered in Dusseldorf, Germany, are genuine or fake is of no consequence. What is important is that if you will take the time to look around, you'll see that every one of them is being carried out and fulfilled right before your eyes and under your nose.

Whether this is of Communist origin or not, I will not say. But ask yourself this question: if there is any country in the world,

Communist or otherwise, that wished to weaken a country in a nonviolent way (in this nuclear age, physical overthrow is not profitable due to the devastation), with the goal in mind of eventually taking that country over, can you think of a better set of rules or guidelines to accomplish that goal?

Jim turned his attention back to the speaker's stand just as Gabler wound up his part of the program and walked off the podium.[1]

Marvin stepped to the microphone. "Ladies and gentlemen ... fellow protestors," he said, "it gives me great pleasure to introduce our next speaker. Here we have a man who has been not only a television star—he was the copilot on the lead bomber of the series *Twelve O'Clock High*—but a man who also ran for the office of mayor of the city of Los Angeles on a budget of two thousand dollars and finished second in a race of thirteen candidates.

"He is now engaged in the most important job of his life, and that job is with the organization called Decency through Law. It's an organization dedicated to the attempt to get legislation passed that will improve and maintain the moral fiber of our country. Ladies and gentlemen, I consider it a great honor and privilege to present to you our prestigious fellow protestor from California, Mr. Bob Dornan."

The crowd welcomed the newcomer with a standing ovation. Most of the people there had already seen him a time or two on the local news broadcast and had been favorably impressed. Unlike Marvin and the rest of the local protestors, Bob was at home in front of the cameras. This was his element. Consequently, he was relaxed and proficient, very professional compared to the rest of them.

Dornan stepped to the microphone, dressed dramatically in a khaki African bush hunter's outfit, complete with the little shoulder straps. (He apologized later for "dressing down" for the occasion due to the primitive image he had of West Virginia and her people.)

"Thank you, Marvin, for that flattering introduction. I may

have difficulty living up to the image you just projected of me but thank you anyway." The crowd seemed to smile in approval.

He turned to the crowd. "Ladies and gentlemen, I am very happy to be in your beautiful state. This is my first visit to West Virginia, and I wish it were under different circumstances."

He panned the crowd like a matador before a bullfight, as though he were trying to evaluate the response he could expect for a good performance.

"When my good friend J. D. Landers asked me to come here to see what Decency through Law could do to help with the textbooks, my superiors were skeptical. They were reluctant to send me here to expend a lot of time and money on a few distortions in children's schoolbooks. We, after all, are in the business of fighting explicit sex being perpetrated upon our citizenry. My organization, of which my friend J. D. is a member, tries to get laws passed, tries to lobby even, if you will, to suppress the blatant avocation of homosexuality, of pornography being openly displayed on magazine racks where our children of any age have access to them. We encourage the passing of laws against obscenities in any public form. So I'm sure you can understand how my superiors felt. With all the above things flooding our country every day in an ever-increasing sea of filth, how could they possibly justify the time and expense to come here to examine a few four-letter words in textbooks? All of us know that four-letter words are going to be seen by our children sooner or later, especially in our society of today, when they are so prevalent.

"The media, I'm afraid, isn't doing you much good either." (Jim was sure this part of the program would never be seen on the six o'clock news.) "They portray West Virginia as a backward state, its inhabitants as the stereotypical tobacco-chewing hillbilly walking to his moonshine still in his bib overalls; smoking his corncob pipe, of course.

"With all this in mind, my superiors and I grudgingly gave in to J. D.'s persistent requests for assistance, and I finally boarded a plane for Charleston. On the way here, I had a lot of time to think, and quite frankly, ladies and gentlemen, I was more than a little annoyed at having to leave my family, whom I hadn't seen for several weeks, to come all the way across the country for such a trivial thing. I thought about all the hullabaloo over a few four-letter words in books, and it seemed ludicrous to me after spending the last several years swimming in the filth that inundates our nation, coast to coast. I was preparing myself more for a diplomatic mission to convince J. D. and the rest of you that you were making a mountain out of a molehill than I was for gearing up for a fight. I expected to find some bad things, of course. There had to be some fire behind all this smoke."

Dornan paused, looking the crowd over in silence. Then he spoke. "I was a skeptic too, ladies and gentlemen. Let me tell you of a little anecdote that changed my mind. As I said, J. D. Landers was the one who wanted me to come here. He also was the one who persuaded the Gablers to come. For the benefit of those of you who don't know, he runs a motel-restaurant in Hurricane, down in Teays Valley. As an added inducement to the three of us to come, J. D. made those facilities available to us free of charge.

"I was tired after my trip in here last night, so I went straight to bed. I met Mr. and Mrs. Gabler for the first time this morning at breakfast in J. D.'s restaurant. While we were eating, they kept telling me about what was in these books. I suppose my skepticism was more obvious than I realized because midway through the meal, Mel Gabler excused himself, saying he would be right back. He returned with several books he had retrieved from his room. They were some of the books that you are objecting to here. The two men at the next table, who identified themselves as local ministers, saw what we were about. They made it clear that they had not taken part in any of the protest and weren't planning to. They felt the protestors were all wrong. Nothing could be bad enough to warrant all the trouble they were causing."

He paused for effect and to collect his thoughts. "I began to read, silently at first, some of the underlined passages in the books. I was so shocked by what I saw that I began to read aloud. My voice carries rather well"—he smiled slightly—"and the ministers at the next table as well as the other people in the dining room heard me clearly. The ministers couldn't believe it.

They had to come over to our table and read it for themselves. They were appalled, as I was. The mind refuses to accept it at first. It is unbelievable that our expensive, sophisticated public educational system that we pay for could be infused with such destructive material. How did it happen? Who put it there? What is its purpose? As to how, I think I can easily explain. Our elected officials are much too busy to look into such 'trivial' matters. And besides, they trust the educators. Most of them won't believe it even when they are told about it. As to whom, I can only guess, but its ultimate purpose is clear."

He paused as if taking a deep breath. His voice has been level, moderately pitched.

"Ladies and gentlemen," he began in a low but emotional voice, "I never dreamed that I would find what I discovered in these textbooks. I expected it to be bad ... but not this bad. In all my years of fighting filth and perversion, I have never seen anything like this."

He emphasized "never" with a voice inflection that sounded as if he was gritting his teeth.

The four-letter words do not bother me that much," he continued after a brief pause. "But looking beyond that, I found an insidious"—he almost hissed the word—"plan in these books that shook my very soul. If this plan is allowed to be carried out, to do its work, I can guarantee you there will not be a church of any denomination left standing a few years down the road."

He looked around the sun-drenched stadium. "I'm sure there are some of you here who are nonmembers of any church, and maybe you think that lets you off the hook. Stop and think what this country would be like without the calming influence of the church.

"This plan and these books will undermine everything that we believe in, twisting our children's minds until you won't even recognize your own child." His voice rose. "Try to imagine, if you can, a world without morals, without principles of any kind. A world with no belief in God, no guidelines of any kind—all respect for law and law enforcement officers a thing of the past." Dornan's voice was not an emotional shout, but his handsome face was contorted in a crimson mask.

"Don't let them do this thing to your children, I beg you. Fight with any legal means available to you. Fight in any way you can, with everything you've got." The veins stood out on his neck. "People of West Virginia, don't ever give up. Fight to the end; fight until you have won!" He finished in a voice so loud that the end was lost in hoarseness.

A sudden blur of movement at the right side of the field caught Jim's eye, and when he turned to look, he saw Reverend Lewis Harrah burst from the players' dugout, run to the speaker's stand, and throw his arms around Dornan in an emotional bear hug. Harrah, who was an old-fashioned Pentecostal preacher, told Jim later that this was the only time he ever felt like hugging a Catholic, which Dornan was.

CHAPTER 10

Three Leaders

Jim stood in the shadows of the foyer leading to the one big room of the one-room schoolhouse. He could hear every word being spoken in the room without even being seen.

Graley had called this rally since it was in his home county of Lincoln, but as usual, Marvin was stealing the show unintentionally. Jim was making notes of the things being said and the many mistakes being made. The context of the talks was much the same as it was at all the rest of the rallies he had been to, and when Marvin began his fervent plea for everyone to chip in to the collection plate being passed around, he cringed. He hastily wrote, Marvin, we're going to have to stop bugging these people for money. It's going to discourage them from coming to the rallies, and we're going to lose them altogether.

"Folks, we're no longer alone in this fight," Marvin was saying now that the money had been collected. "We have powerful, influential people from South Hills on our side. We have the best lawyers in the valley with us."

Jim knew Marvin was taking his words about Bill Hamb and the others and making them sound like his own.

"We have industrialists, doctors, businessmen, bankers, and many others. Folks, this is no longer a fight of miners and illiterate preachers; we've got the educated, the socially prominent, and the financially powerful with us."

Marvin's lusty delivery and his triumphant smile at the end brought a rousing cheer from the packed room. Jim thought of the contrast between the people here, filling the little outdated frame building to overflowing, and the people of South Hills that he knew so well. The divergence culturally was analogous as the geographical contradiction.

Jim thought of the beautifully manicured lawns flowing up to the grand homes on South Hills, the ribbon-smooth streets leading from the busy mainstream of downtown Charleston to the quiet dignity of the wealthy's habitat.

How stark the comparison of the pothole-filled road that he had traveled to get to this meeting, winding its narrow way past the bleak tar-paper shacks, the dirt yards filled with castaway car parts, and the trash spilling over into the creek below. The interminable roads, or semi-paved trail ways, really, always followed the creeks. This probably came about because of the handwork, which was the only method the original builders and users had available to them. They had to take the path of least resistance, and the water always found the easiest route along the base of the hills, usually with a flat bench running parallel. The hills of West Virginia are close and steep. In some hollows, the bottomlands in between is less than the width of a football field.

These weren't bad people, most of them; they were just victims of a continuing cycle. Their forbearers were ignorant and poor, spending the bulk of their lives just keeping body and soul together for each member of their usually large families. Most made little progress toward a better life. When occasionally life became more than they could bear, they found solace either in the Bible or the bottle, depending on the individual. Some stayed with their particular choice. The ones preferring the Bible trusted the Almighty to give them a better set of circumstances in the next life; the ones choosing the bottle numbed themselves to a point of not caring about this life or the next.

Some were sporadic drinkers, easing their unbearable pain for a time; then, when the hellish sobering-up process came, they were so guilt-ridden and short of cash (having wasted a goodly portion of their meager paychecks on booze) that they worked harder and longer to compensate for both. This left little time or energy for thoughts of home beautification or better education for their children.

Many were miners, and when you spent the biggest part of your life deep in the bowels of the earth, knowing that at any given moment a post could crack, bringing the whole mountain down on you, God came simple and unvarnished; whiskey had to be straight and strong. In either case, they lived both figuratively and literally in a tunnel, with little if any light at the other end.

Their harsh lives made them singular and steadfast. Survival was their normal goal; give them a new one that they believed in, such as combating a threat to the convictions, and they would follow it to their deaths.

But in this fight, their lack of education—particularly their atrocious vocabulary—was an insurmountable handicap. After all, education was what it was all about, and how could the uneducated stand in judgment of educators? Education was the vehicle, and most people thought it ended there, seeing it as a protest by backward ignoramuses afraid of change or innovation.

The more they shouted their backwoods butchering of the King's English, the more convinced the world became that they didn't know what they were talking about. Sometimes violence was their only voice.

Jim had been studying the work-hardened faces around the room in conjunction with his thoughts. They were showing an intense interest in what Marvin was telling them, signs of new hope, or maybe the first hope they had of winning.

Marvin built them to a fever pitch, announced the next rally, and concluded the meeting.

Afterward, when everyone had moved outside, the people formed groups. Segments knotted around each of the three leaders. Jim overheard one of Graley's group saying, "We don't care what Marvin says, Ezra. We're gonna do what you tell us. We don't need a Campbell's creeker givin' us orders."

He noted that Graley wasn't very successful in hiding the pleased expression. Hillbillies were clannish my nature, and the miners were the worst.

He sauntered over toward the group knotted around Avis Hill. "Folks," Avis was saying, "what Marvin says is all fine and good, but I don't think we can depend on la-di-da highbrows on South Hills to do our work for us. I think that we've got to do it ourselves." The small group rumbled in agreement.

Jim walked away, back toward the frame building of the schoolhouse, wearing a worried look. This would never do. He had to call the three together for a talk. Three different leaders going in three different directions were tearing the movement apart, and the problem had to be resolved. The news media was having a field day over this very thing, the aspect of the controversy. Marvin was saying his good-byes and shaking the hands of the last of the people leaving. Jim waited until they were all gone and then went over.

"Marvin, we've got a bad problem."

"What's that, Jim?"

"I've been listening to all the different groups here tonight, and we've got three different leaders leading three separate protests in three different directions. It's tearing us apart. That's doing us more harm than all the other side put together."

Marvin grew thoughtful, finally answering, "Jim, you're right. I've been aware of this for a long time; there just wasn't anything I could do about it."

"Well, I've got an idea that should solve the problem if the three of you will agree. I think you will, but I don't know about the other two."

"What is it?"

Jim hedged. "I'd rather tell it to all of you at once, if that's all right with you."

Marvin gave him that searching, penetrating look that Jim had become so familiar with. Finally, he said, "Sure, Jim, if that's the way you want it."

"Thanks, Marvin; I think it would be more effective and also fairer to do it that way. Can you arrange the meeting?"

"Sure, no problem. When do you want it?"

"How about one o'clock tomorrow afternoon at Graley's house?"

Marvin appeared concerned. "Why Graley's house?"

"I figured you would already know, Marvin. You're more reasonable than the other two, to say nothing of being the strongest leader. The other two are going to be a little reluctant to agree with what I have in mind, and we don't need to make them more hostile by having the meeting in your headquarters. Graley will be the most likely to object to the idea, and he will be more relaxed and receptive in the security of his own home. Avis doesn't worry me as much, and he seems to feel right at home at Graley's. Besides, it's centrally located. Avis lives about as far north from Ezra's as you do south."

"Makes sense," said Marvin. "Okay, you've got it."

As Jim walked across Graley's yard, he wondered wondering why someone in the construction business had never gotten around to building a sidewalk of some kind. He glanced at the river, thinking that its rushing rain-swollen waters were comparable to the textbook protest. The valley had been so calm and sleepy before, and now everything was as turbulent and obscure as the muddy river rushing along with its trash tumbling about.

He knocked on the door twice before it opened. This time it was Graley's smiling face looking out at him.

"Well, hello, Jim. C'mon in." Jim walked in and saw Marvin and Avis Hill sitting around a table having coffee.

Avis gave him that cocky grin and said, "Jim, how are you?"

"Hello, Avis."

They all sat down. Avis and Ezra were talking over the top of each other, as usual, each trying to tell the other of his accomplishments.

Jim never bothered with formality with these three. Incongruous to begin with, it would have been considered pompous by all concerned. But he was cautiously tactful in a blustery fashion that was apropos.

He stepped right in, between words thrown by Avis and Ezra, both at the same time, without asking or apologizing. "Ezra, I noticed that you had quite a following at the rally last night."

Graley beamed and said, "Well, I guess them folks in Lincoln County do like me. They trust me too," he said pointedly, offering a meaningful look. "'Course, they've known me practically all my life. I'm kin to a lot of 'em."

Jim smiled inwardly, knowing that with his little nudge, Ezra had just brought into focus the image of himself as the indisputable leader. This is exactly what he wanted.

He left Ezra to bask in the glory of his own thoughts and turned to Hill. "Avis, although the people out there"—meaning Lincoln County—"grouped around Ezra, I saw that the ones from your area looked to you for guidance."

Hill's uncontrolled eye wandered nervously; his good one lit up. "There's a lot of folks that understand what I'm telling them," he said, obviously hopeful of yet a chance to be number one. This was shaping up better than Jim had dared hope.

Through all this, Marvin had sat benignly by, apparently content to wait for one of them to emerge the leader.

Jim seemed introspective, observing the smugness of Graley and Hill without appearing to. After a long, reflective pause, he glanced around at the three of them and then said, "The one thing that I've heard the most throughout this whole thing—in fact, I've heard it so much I'm getting sick of it—is 'We've got to get organized.'"

The three men looked at him expectantly, half nodding in agreement yet waiting for the point.

"I hate to say it all over again but that's exactly what we've go to do. We've got to get organized." He looked around at them, letting this sink in. They mulled this over, each of them obviously trying to fit his own meaning to the remark.

It was Marvin who finally broke the silence. "Well, I guess we all agree, Jim, but what are you getting at?" he asked innocently.

Jim took a deep breath and said softly, "Each of you has your followers who will listen to what you tell them. Ezra, most of the people there last night flocked around you." Graley tried to look humble, but his triumphant countenance wouldn't be squelched.

"Avis, the people loyal to you won't listen to anybody else." Hill nodded his firm acknowledgement of this. Jim had looked into their eyes as he spoke to each. He knew that neither of them was aware that he had intentionally left Marvin for last. In their minds, the spotlight was on them, and they liked it that way.

"Marvin here also has his followers," he said almost as an afterthought. "Our big problem, and I think all of you will agree, is that as long as we have three leaders, we're going to continue to have the confusion that we've had in the past. It's taking all our time and energy just trying to keep it all together."

"We know all about this," said Graley, "but what do you propose to do about it?" The eagerness in his question and tone of voice made it clear that Graley was certain that he was the considered leader.

Jim knew the bait had worked. Graley and Hill were eagerly waiting now to hear what his plan was, each appearing confident that the outcome would be in his favor.

He looked at them as though in deep thought. At last, he said, "I believe that we should give the people themselves the opportunity to choose the one they want as the supreme leader. Once that's decided, the other two would take secondary positions in charge of their own groups."

He paused, looking around at them, waiting for an answer. When none came, he asked, "Well, what do you think?'

"I'm for it, myself," Graley answered. "It's up to you and Marvin, Avis."

"I don't see anything wrong with it," Hill added.

They all turned to look at Marvin, who seemed to be reluctant to agree. He stared at the table and then said, "Yeah, okay, I'll agree to it."

"All right. That's settled, then. If it's agreeable to all of you, I suggest we call a mass rally for this Sunday afternoon at Watt Powell Ballpark. Each man will have equal time to deliver his proposal—his platform, if you will—just as they do in a political campaign. Then we can judge by the response from the crowd just who they want as their leader. Is that agreeable to all of you?"

Each of them said that it was.

"Fine," said Jim. "Marvin, since you've dealt with the newspapers before, would you mind making the arrangements?" Marvin said he would be glad to.

The meeting was starting to break up when Hill spoke up. "Boys, we forgot something."

Jim asked apprehensively, "What have we overlooked?"

Hill looked at him with his one good eye and said, "What about Charley Quigley? He's got a stake in this too."

Jim looked quickly at Marvin for the expected reaction. Catching his meaning, Marvin allayed his fears with a wave of his hand. "No, I think he's right, Jim. Charley has tried as hard as the rest of us. Maybe in the wrong way at times, but which one of us hasn't made mistakes? No, I think Charley should have his say along with the rest of us."

Jim sat back with a sigh of relief. "Okay, then, we include Charley."

Jim regretted to admit that as a novice at the beginning, he'd thought of the same solution. Hold an election. But he was not a reporter, informed with the facts.

The elections have been held in our legislature, our school board, by our governor, and so on. It is up to them to enforce the laws they have passed within the guidelines set by the constitution—if they will first take the time to understand those laws and become aware of when they are being violated.

An editorial in the *Charleston Daily Mail* on Wednesday, October 9, 1974, was an example of the simplistic, shallow thinking of the media concerning the textbooks, the controversy, and the solutions: "Half of the fury aroused by the textbook disturbance stems from a simple question of who is the majority, and what are its rights."

This quoting from the first paragraph of the news article illustrates the first misconception that confronted Alice early in the struggle and hounded her through to the end. Jim remembered her patient tone as she systematically explained to him that this was neither the point nor the issue. It was not at all a matter of who was the majority. (There are eleven instances in the Constitution where the majority does not rule.) To say the majority should decide in an election, as the editorial suggests, would be to qualify the objection to the books as a matter of opinion, which would be erroneous.

The objections were based on individual human rights: invasion of privacy and teaching what was, in effect, religion in the public schools, contrary to the Constitution. It is undermining parents' authority over their children and exposing them to obscenities that not even one child should be submitted to.

In other words, the matters objected to by most of the protestors gave each individual parent the legal right, following guidelines already established in the Constitution, to demand that his child not be compelled to be submitted to these books.

The editorial makes the absurd inference that 80 percent of the parents must be in favor of the books, since this morning, 80 percent of the pupils are in school, which must mean that the parents want them there. Jim wondered why they didn't grade it that way three weeks earlier, when the attendance was down to 20 percent, with the 80 percent majority was on the streets."

To so rate the figures either time would have been misleading. Parents kept their children out of school for various reasons, many having nothing to do with their objections to the books—but because of fear, anger, confusion, apprehension. The list could go on and on.

Parents put their children back in school for just as many reasons: fear of retribution from authorities, respect for the law, weariness of the hassles, so Jimmy wouldn't miss football practice and Susie wouldn't miss band (Jim personally witnessed an example of this in Marvin Horan's headquarters), and many more.

PROTEST LEADER PRAYS FOR GOD TO STRIKE BOARD MEMBERS DEAD.

Under normal circumstances, Jim would have thought it a hoax, but in the last several months, the unreal was the norm. He read on. "The Reverend Charles Quigley, one of the fundamentalist leaders of the forces objecting to the controversial textbooks, made a statement to this reporter this morning that he had spent a large portion of the night before praying that God would strike the members of the school board dead if that was the only solution to the problem.

He cited biblical precedent, but frankly, this reporter failed to take note of what the precedent was."

Charley, Charley, he thought. I sympathize with your desperation, but you have given the opposition ammunition to blow us out of the water. Jim laid the paper aside, shaking his head. He cringed when he thought of what the media was going to do with this.

He couldn't believe that Charley of all people would do something so stupid. Okay, if your belief in God to solve problems is all that great, pray for whatever you like; but for Pete's sake, did you have to tell the whole world so as to make us the laughingstock of the nation?

The article went on to quote Charley as saying that he was seriously considering dropping out of the protest due to the lack of cooperation between the Christian leaders: "They're just not doing what they should be doing."

He parked his car in the lot of Charley's church and went inside. Charley was on the phone, so he waited. As soon as he was off, Jim came straight to the point, "Charley, I'm withdrawing my offer of the ten thousand. I'm sorry."

Charley only nodded without speaking. Jim took that to mean that he understood. In any event, he just turned and left.

CHAPTER 11

Anson's Pastor

ANSON'S MINISTER APPROVES HIS ACTION.

The headline caught Jim's eye, and he felt a groundswell of rage mounting in him as he began reading the accompanying article. "Dr. Conley, the pastor of the prestigious First Presbyterian Church of St. Albans, where school board member Albert Anson Sr. is a member, told his congregation yesterday in his Sunday service that he fully endorsed Mr. Anson's position on the controversial textbooks. Conley made it clear he felt that Anson, the board member strongly in support of the books, was doing his Christian duty and a service to Kanawha County."

Jim was trembling with fury when, even though it was almost midnight, he reached for the phone. He got the number from information and dialed. The pastor's voice answered. "Do you have any idea what you have done?" Jim's rage superseded all protocol.

There was a long pause at the other end ... Jim heard a heavy intake of breath. Finally, the voice asked, "Who is this, please?"

"My name is James Farley, and I've just finished reading your statement concerning Mr. Anson's role in the textbook selection. I repeat the question, Doctor: Do you have any idea what you have done?"

There was another long pause, and then the pastor asked, "Could I have your phone number and call you back, Mr. Farley?"

Jim had grown accustomed to being checked out these days, but it still angered him.

"I assure you, Doctor, I am not a nut or a radical. I'm just a father who loves his daughter, and also a member of a community and country that I'm very concerned about."

"I didn't say you were a nut, Mr. Farley. It's just that there are some things I have to do. It will only take a few minutes, and then I will be happy to talk as long as you like."

Jim didn't like it but he agreed. "All right, Doctor. I'll be waiting." He hung up the phone, satisfied the pastor would call him back just as soon as he looked his phone number up to make certain that he was who he said, and that he was home, not around the corner.

It seemed like a long time, but he knew it was only a few minutes when the telephone rang. "Hello."

"Mr. Farley?" said the voice of the man he had been talking to.

"Doctor, now that you've satisfied yourself that I'm who I say I am, and I'm where I said I was, could we begin discussing this rationally?"

"Mr. Farley, I wasn't trying to ...," the man began.

"Doctor, I know you were checking me out, and that's all right. I can't say that I blame you after what's been going on in the valley these days. I understand that for all you knew, I was one of these radicals and was in a phone booth across the street from you with a bomb in my hand. But now that you know that's not the case, I'll repeat my original question: Do you have any idea what you have done by taking your stand behind Mr. Anson on the issue of these textbooks?"

There was a long pause, then Conley said, "Mr. Farley, what I have done is give my approval of an act of a very good man, an act that I happen to agree with, and to lend my moral support to that man in his greatest hour of trial and anguish."

"What you have done, Doctor, is put the stamp of respected Christianity on books that are specifically designed to destroy Christianity."

There was another pause, much longer this time, and then the Doctor said, "I can't believe that, Mr. Farley. I'm sorry."

Jim started to explain it but realized it was hopeless to try to convince him over the telephone. "Doctor, could we meet in person? You name the place; have whomever there that you feel safe with ... and under any circumstances you deem necessary to protect yourself." He could tell that his offer had allayed most of the good doctor's fears of violence, but it was still taking him a long time to decide about the meeting.

"Doctor, if you will give me thirty minutes of your time, that's all I'll ask. If I haven't convinced you that what I say is true, then I promise you that you'll never hear from me again. I'll bother you no more."

That did it. "All right, Mr. Farley, that sounds fair enough. Do you know where my church is?"

"No, but I can find it."

"Fine, my office is in the main building of the church. Can you come there tomorrow afternoon at three o'clock?"

"I'll be there, alone. And thank you, Doctor."

The next day, Jim left early for his appointment with Anson's pastor. St. Albans was in the lower end of the valley with Nitro, down from Charleston, parallel to Nitro but across Kanawha River. A bridge connected the two. He'd taken care of some business with J. D., finished some things at Elmer's office, and was now driving across the bridge toward St. Albans. He could see almost the whole town from the high point of the arch at the center of the bridge. As his vision swept from one end to the other, taking in the neat, attractive, though not extravagantly expensive, homes making up the little town, the words of a reporter doing an article on Avis Hill, who lived here, came to him. They were an example of the distortion of facts (almost all of them) in the media coverage of the controversy. "Avis Hill's base of operation lies in the brawling mining town of St. Albans, downriver from Charleston ..." (There wasn't a mine anywhere around and very few miners. Avis was a plumber.) "... with its dreary tar-paper shacks being a natural breeding place for discontent and potential violence." (When the local paper did an editorial on the article, they began by saying the people of St. Albans were going to be surprised by the description of their town. They were. And they were infuriated.)

Jim knew firsthand that the people of St. Albans had more

civic pride and went to greater lengths to keep their community clean and attractive than any town or city in the state—and probably ranked as favorably in this as any in the country. He had made the remark one time that you could get away with shooting the mayor more quickly than you could get away with building anything without a permit there. To describe St. Albans as a "brawling mining town with tar-paper shacks," automatically stereotyping its inhabitants as whiskey-drinking, moonshine-making, brawling rednecks, was more than a distortion of news. It was a blatant perversion of truth. He doubted the reporter had ever seen St. Albans.

As he pulled up in front of the impressive building that housed the First Presbyterian Church of St. Albans, he couldn't help but wonder what the common denominator was that polarized the prestigious churches from those that were working-class oriented. He was certain that it was not the degree of education of members, as the media and the educrats were claiming. He had not found a person with any measure of intelligence or common sense, regardless of the level of formal education (just as long as he had enough schooling to be able to read), who could not recognize the plan once it was pointed out to him. As he stood by his parked car looking up at the hand-cut stone and the ornate trimmings adorning the front of the church, he felt he had the answer.

Everything about this church fairly screamed expensive and status. Thinking about the "ignorant rabble" image of the typical protestor projected so vigorously by the media, he could understand why people of this class would automatically take the opposite stand, and he really couldn't blame them. He felt certain that few of them, if any, had taken the time to examine the books for themselves, taking the media's explanation of them instead.

The caliber of people attending this kind of church would obviously favor progress and improvement, and that alone would cause them to favor the media's version of the books. They would be against violence, so the exaggerated, distorted reports of all the havoc caused by the protestors would strengthen their position, and the fact that the protest began as a movement of "fundamentalists" would solidify their stand in their enclave of ignorance. Not ignorance from an educational standpoint, but ignorance of the true facts of the contents of the books and what the protest was truly about.

He thought of an article published in the October 7, 1974, issue of the *Wall Street Journal* with the bold headline KANAWHA PROTEST WORKING-CLASS WARNING. When he read it, he wanted to scream at the top of his lungs, "It's not a working class issue; people of all levels are upset about these books!" He wanted to scream it loudly enough that it would carry to the editor in New York and his counterparts across the nation.

That was the idea behind, and the purpose for, the building of the Alliance: to acquaint the country and the world with the fact that the business community and the professional people were equally concerned about what these books were teaching and what the end result would be. (He didn't know it at the time, but a copy of the national *Presbyterian Journal* would come across the desk of the pastor of this very church and would make it clear that this purpose had been accomplished. It would read, referring to the business and professional people of the Alliance, "When people like this start to speak, you'd better listen."

The article in the *Wall Street Journal* continued relating the usual misunderstandings of what the protest was all about, zeroing in, as always, on the four-letter words in the high school books; and one of the most common misunderstanding, and I quote, "The Kanawha County movement naturally makes all the obvious mistakes of such protests: stifling ideas, restricting education," and the last and largest misunderstanding of all, "banning major authors on trivial points."

We are not guilty of this—it's only that we want to provide good ideas and restrict only morbid, negative education. We do not want to ban good authors, he thought in frustration. We object to the selection of the very worst of their work compiled in these books.

The article stereotyped the protest and the protestors once again by stating, "The deeper motive of the protestors seems to be resentment—against the schools, the bureaucrats, and the upper classes in general. 'Even hillbillies have civil rights' read one sign."

Strange, he just couldn't imagine a statement like this (the one on the sign) being made by Mick Staton or Bill Hamb or Roger Banks or Elmer Fike or Dr. Cracraft or Betty Rogers or, and especially, Alice Moore; and they were all avid protestors. Alice even had the distinction of being the original protestor. It reminded him of the seemingly intentional promotion of misconception by the national news reporters at the Gabler rally at Wall Powell Ballpark, when they passed right over well-dressed, intelligent-looking people by the dozens, seeking out the seediest-looking, tobacco-chewing character there.

The *Wall Street Journal* article seemed to be attempting, however, to be fair this time. It suggested that although they (the *Journal*) agreed that in our pluralistic society, different points of view and different lifestyles should be aired, they said, "Yet too often a hidden assumption operates behind the attempt to show 'life as it is.' The way to broaden the sheltered white middle-class 1950s outlook is to confront it with the amoral, if not criminal, outlook fostered by our most pathological social conditions ..." (Amen.) As he read, he thought, so you introduce students to Eldridge Cleaver and the world of convicts and prostitutes.

"We don't object to these books, but we feel this viewpoint distorts life even more than the other. The average experience in the 'ghetto' would probably be that of a hardworking, churchgoing family trying to raise children in spite of surrounding vices. Religion would play a major role in their lives, and we think people in Kanawha County would understand them well." This was the most accurate statement ever made by the media in the entire controversy. The reporter knew what he was talking about; we found the Kanawha County counterparts of the 'ghetto' blacks that he described incredibly similar.

But then the article switched back to the more typical nebulous and erroneous suggestions, such as "Book burning must be deplored." Jim remembered only one time, by one person, out of the thousands of protestors, that the suggestion was ever made to burn books; and that one time was a case of a small mind groping for a grand statement (sensational, in reality) in front of the television camera, flattered and awed by this first experience.

Jim was pulled out of his reverie by the opening of the front door of the church and of a matronly woman walking out. He headed for the door, wondering what kind of man he was about to confront. Would he be reasonable enough to admit seeing what Jim was about to show him? (Jim knew that he would recognize it; admitting it was something else.)

His footsteps resounded off the marbled walls as he walked down the elegant corridor toward the door at the end, marked OFFICE. He knocked and a woman's voice told him to come in. He opened the door, walked in, and said, "I'm James Farley. Dr. Conley is expecting me."

The middle-aged woman looked at him searchingly for a moment and then said, "Have a seat, Mr. Farley. I'll tell him you're here."

She disappeared into the inner office for a few minutes. He heard the murmur of subdued voices. She came out with a good-looking man in his mid-thirties. Jim's sixth sense about people told him the man was, by nature, pleasant and mild-mannered. But just then, he was obviously tense. He gave Jim an appraising look as he extended his hand.

"Mr. Farley, I'm Dr. Conley."

Jim accepted the handshake, finding it surprisingly firm, and said, "Thank you, Doctor, for seeing me."

Conley motioned him toward the inner office; Jim started for the door. Out of the corner of his eye, he caught the stern nod of the good doctor toward the outer door, indicating with a meaningful look for the receptionist to leave. Jim did not turn to look, but he could feel the woman's grateful eagerness to depart. He thought he had grown accustomed to the aura of intrigue permeating the battle they were in, but this unnerved and irritated him. He kept the feeling subdued, walked in behind the pastor, and sat down across the desk from him.

"Now, Mr. Farley, you told me on the telephone that you could show me in a few minutes what was upsetting you so much in these textbooks."

"Yes, I can, Doctor, and I have all the proof I need right here." Jim started rummaging through his briefcase to get the third- and fourth-level readers of the D. C. Heath Communicating series.

"Before you go into that, Mr. Farley, I want to make it perfectly clear that I haven't changed my attitude toward Mr. Anson in the slightest, and I still maintain the position that I took in relation to his stand on the textbook issue."

Jim glanced at him but did not answer. He was leafing through the Communicating reader, level three. Finally, he found the place he was look for. He leaned across the desk. "Doctor, if you will, read this story, noting, please, that it's emphasized strongly as a myth. It states over and over that it is a myth."

The pastor looked at him curiously, took the book, and began reading. While the pastor was absorbed in the passages in the books, Jim waited patiently. His gaze wondered around the plush mahogany-paneled office. A card on a bulletin board caught his eye. It was the size of a business card and read "God can work wonders through the man who doesn't care who gets the credit." It reminded him of the statement he had made to his daughter-in-law when she bemoaned the fact that Jim was doing so much good and working so hard with no recognition. "I don't care who gets the credit, Brenda. I just want to get the job done." He thought of Avis, Ezra, and some of the other protesters basking in the limelight.

> Telling Your Own Myth (suggested lesson plan from the teacher's manual)
>
> Objectives:
>
> 1. To make children more aware of the nature of myths
>
> 2. Children make up myths. Read and discuss the page with the pupils. At some appropriate time, explain that the purpose of a fable is to teach a lesson, and that the purpose of a myth is to explain why something is the way it is or how it came to be that way. Composition: You may wish to work out a sample myth on the chalkboard. The pupils can have the choice of working out their own on the chalkboard. You may

wish to use the following:

Purpose:

1. Why Roses Have Thorns. Characters: The God of work and a village of people.

> Action: The people of a village always work very hard. The God of work wishes to reward the villagers for their hard work by making beautiful roses. The thorns act as a reminder there is still work to be done. Some pupils may find it stimulating to discuss their ideas in groups before actually writing. Other pupils may prefer telling to writing their own myths. These pupils can meet in a corner of the room and, of course, have the option of writing their myths at some other time.

2. (Written in the margin, apparently connected with the myth section, is the following.)

> You could ask if anyone knows and wants to tell the story of 'Daniel in the Lions' Den.' If it is told in any detail, you could then discuss any similarities between that story and 'Androcles and the Lion.'

Jim noticed a pause in the doctor's reading and figured that he had finished reading. Conley looked reflective.

"Did you read the part where they draw the students' attention to a direct parallel between 'Androcles and the Lion' and 'Daniel in the Lions' Den'?"

"Yes," answered Conley, without further comment.

"Doctor, can you explain to me why they would do that?"

Conley turned this over in his mind for a time; twice he started to speak, as though he had the explanation, but he stopped each time, as though still searching for the answer.

"Let me give you some of the reasons that I tried to convince myself of why they did it," said Jim. "At first, I thought, 'Why not the Bible?' They have to draw their material for the lesson plans from somewhere. But then I wondered why profane educators, whether they writers, editors, or teachers, who are struggling so hard to keep prayer, the Bible, or any form of Christian religion out of the schools, would go to such great lengths to draw attention to the Bible. If this were the only instance of it, I could overlook it as a coincidence, a lazy writer finding it easy research, or any number of reasons. But this is typical of the theme for the entire selection for the elementary levels. It prevails throughout, from cover to cover, from first to sixth grade, and then the thread of the theme can be followed through middle school, high school and college.

"I asked you for only thirty minutes of your time, Doctor, so I can't possibly cover all of it, and that's what makes these books so infuriating. The plan is scattered through so many pages and so many books that it's difficult, most of the time impossible, to keep people's attention long enough to show it to them; I think this also was deliberate, and it's very effective. If a challenger of the books attempts to abbreviate the meat of the plan by quoting certain passages, he is automatically accused of taking things out of context. But as Elmer Fike said, it's only when the entire story is told *in* context that the full implications come across. But who will take that much time reading the whole thing? Or even listen while someone else tells about it? It's exasperating, Doctor.

"I came across a book, *Have the Public Schools Had It?* by Elmer Towns that does an excellent job of explaining the conditions in the educational system. It told of a time when the slums of London were infested with rats. An extremely strong poison was used in an effort to eradicate them. Corn kernels were dipped in the poison and set out for the rats. Upon their first taste, the rats promptly dropped over dead, yet the poison was ineffective. After the first rat went into convulsions, the others avoided the poison; they connected death with its source. The experimenters diluted the poison so that its killing effect took several days, and large swarms of rats were killed. The rats couldn't connect death with its source.

"If Americans could identify the problem of the schools, they would make the necessary changes. That is why the plan is so effective; it is very much diluted.

"My thirty minutes are up, Doctor, and I will abide by that. But I would like to give you this list to take with you, if you will, and study it when you have more time. You will see that the plan you have already recognized in the third and fourth grades is carried on through middle school, high school and college."

Doctor Conley took the list and skimmed it briefly. Jim knew this is what he was reading:

Man in the Expository Mood, page 99: "How the boy trembles and delights at the white excrement of the bird."

Compas, page 112: "One Saturday Afternoon." It's the story of how a ten-year-old boy helps a man hang himself.

"Man in the Poetic Mood, page 48: picture of Marilyn Monroe's face "pondering her perfect breasts."

Jim had made notes here. "These books are designed to make protestors look foolish—designed to confuse and frustrate searches for evidence.

There is the high school history book *Search for Freedom* (note the title), published by Macmillan. It devotes seven pages of rhetoric to Marilyn Monroe, while giving George Washington one—yes, one—paragraph.

In that same book, Martin Luther King and Cesar Chavez are likened to Jesus Christ, but the text omits Benjamin Franklin's call to prayer at the Constitutional Convention because of the words of the publisher's representative: "That would be teaching religion." (The blatantly obvious asininity of their method overwhelmed Jim—whatever happened to presenting opposite points of view?)

As evidence that it is carried on through college, we find the following in *Mythology and Psychology*, page 191 (italicizing is mine): "A great many *myths* deal with the idea of rebirth. Jesus, Dionysus, Odin and many other *traditional* (underlining is ours) figures are <u>represented</u> as having died, after which they were reborn or arose from the dead ..." This was in a course called "Psychology for You" at Oxford.

"Let me ask you another question, Doctor."

Conley, looked up from the list he had been reading, looking a bit startled. His expression had softened from its original stern defensiveness to one of intense interest, almost sympathetic. He gave Jim his undivided attention, hanging on to every word.

"You don't have to answer this one for me; just think about it and come to a conclusion for yourself. What will happen to a generation of children with basic Bible teaching lax in the home—the home being preoccupied with television—becoming exposed to books that constantly and consistently teach stories directly parallel to the Bible, almost verbatim, under the label of *myth*, being reminded again and again that a myth or fable is untrue, and that it is only a trumped-up way of trying to explain something?"

Jim was looking straight into Conley's eyes when he asked this. He saw a flicker of fear there. Conley didn't answer.

"If you're not convinced, read on. But before you do, I think you've seen enough to give credence to this; if you want to take the time, you'll find many stories in there, such as "The Cow-Tail Switch" in the third-grade reader, again under the bold heading of fable, making it clear that it is not true. The story tells of a village—the setting is not established but is typically biblical—where the natives go through the process of weaving meat around the dry bones of a dead cow, thereby proving that they, being mortal, are capable of resurrecting the dead.

"Laughable, isn't it, Doctor? Laughable to you and me, but what about an impressionable nine-year old?

"I'm not that much of a student of the Bible, but I was informed, by an old man who is, that this story is a direct analogy to the story of "The Valley of Dry Bones" found in Ezekiel.

"I could go on and on about these stories, which cover almost the entire scope of the Bible, from creation to damnation, and they are all told as myths and fables, always making certain that the student is fully aware that both are untrue.

"The method here, Doctor, is like that in the children's games that are so popular these days. One, for example, has two pencils connected by a rod. When the child draws a picture with one pencil, a 'ghost,' or 'clone,' shows up on the other page, an exact duplicate, yet on different paper. Now, suppose that the paper the child is working on directly has, at the top, the heading TRUTH, and at the top of the other page the heading FABLE—or, in other words, false or untruth or more strongly put, lies.

"After six consistent years of this, will a student be able to tell which page is which; and even if he can, will he be able to distinguish the difference? Will he even want to? And if all that fails, what happens if the headings on both pages are removed and the papers shuffled?

"Confused, Doctor? Superimpose this over the effect these books will have on this generation of children's belief in the Bible. And, of course, since the Bible is the cornerstone of Christianity, if you can erode that foundation, the citadel of Christianity itself will crumble."

"But even if all this—mind you, I said if—is true," said Dr. Conley, "that still doesn't give people, 'protestors,' if you will, the right to start a conflagration the likes of which is raging through this valley, burning everything in its path, including private citizens' cars, shooting people and terrorizing the community in general."

"I agree with what you say about that not giving them the right, Doctor. Where you are wrong, however, is that the protestors, per se, are no more guilty of starting this war than the man who stops a bullet with his heart is guilty of murder. The person who fired that bullet is the culprit. By the same token, the people who initiated this play are the ones who started all this. The protestors are in the unenviable position of the man stopping the bullet—with their hearts, if necessary.

"Secondly, the man who shot Philip Cochran through the heart is a man named William Noel, the avowed leader of a group calling themselves Concerned Citizens, a pro-book organization that is fighting to keep these books in the classrooms. He is far from being a protestor. Doctor, at this moment, Cochran is lying in the intensive care unit of Memorial Hospital, struggling to live.

"Furthermore, to my knowledge, none of the violence has been proven to be the work of any protestor at this point."

"But what do you attribute all the violence to? The other side?

Come now, there has been bombing, shooting ..." (Like the two state police officers' cruisers that had holes put through them by snipers' bullets). "Why would a pro-book force member do a thing like that?"

"Well, I could give you a lot of possible reasons, Doctor, but let me give you the one that, in my opinion, is the most plausible. We both know there is an element out there that is always present in our society, containing everything from the lunatic fringe to the disgruntled misfit carrying a grudge. It also contains the hotshot braggarts just looking for a reason and a target to get their frustrations out. This presents a witch's brew of potential people. With the format of violence presented by this controversy, every nut in the valley will vent his feelings in any way he is capable of, with any means available to him. This element couldn't care less about the books, one way or the other."

He could tell the good doctor was relenting from his hard stand of before, but he was still skeptical.

"But the way these people are going about this thing is all wrong, Mr. Farley. I don't mean the snipers and the bombers; I'm talking about the protestors as a whole, including the ones the media refers to as 'fundamentalist leaders.'"

"That's all too true, I'm afraid," said Jim, and then he leaned over the desk in an impassioned attempt to lend emphasis. "That's the sad thing about this textbook situation, Doctor. The people who would do something about it can't. And the people who can ... won't.

"You're under the impression that I agree with all the people in the protest, everything they do and say. Let me set you straight. I disagree with eighty-five percent of their points of view, ninety percent of their methods, doubt the sincerity of fifteen percent, and know for a fact that at least eight percent are thrill seekers and troublemakers. But I agree one hundred percent with the goal of all of them, which is to remove these books, or rather the plan in them, from the educational system. I'll work with any and all of them to accomplish that end, no matter what their reasons are for being in the fight, and no matter who they are."

"But why work so hard when the fundamentalist preachers are saying that God is on their side—and 'If God be with us, who can be against us?' asked Conley.

Jim knew he was speaking in generalities, but he thought of Avis Hill at the St. Albans roadside park that night several weeks ago, when he had said that very thing: "If God be with us, who can be against us?"

"In the first place, how do we know that God is with that particular person saying that?" Jim said. "How do we know what's truly inside that person? As the Bible says, 'Outside they are as white as snow, but inside they are like a sepulcher, filled with rotting flesh and dead men's bones.' That's loosely translated, of course. But really, how do we know what their real thoughts and motives are, to say nothing of their lusts? So maybe we can't depend too much on God helping that particular person get the job done. Besides, God also tells us that he will help those who help themselves. Frankly, I'm willing to do my part, and I want his help."

"But you're not even a Christian."

"True, but I've got sense enough to know what kind of life we'll have if the plan in these books accomplishes its purpose."

The doctor was visibly aghast. He looked as though he were pouring over the formula for the alchemy of the devil. But he was a cautious man. Reserving any comment, he simply asked, "Mr. Farley, would you mind if I take these books home and show them to my wife? She is a schoolteacher, currently active in the educational system of public schools. I would like to get her opinion."

Jim was pleased. "I'd be happy if you would, Doctor." This was more than he had dared hope for. Not only was the good doctor an extremely well-educated man, a Doctor of Divinity, and thus as far removed from Marvin, Ezra, Avis, and the fundamentalist image as the North Pole from the South Pole, but he was also from New York, which removed him from the hillbilly image as well. Now it was turning out even better—his wife was currently a schoolteacher. Add to that the fact that he leaned basically toward Liberalism, was the pastor of the most prestigious church in St. Albans, with many influential people in his congregation, most of them liberals; add the fact that he was not only interrelated with but was the leader of these liberals, and it was perfect.

He couldn't think of a more formidable way to test his convictions about the plan. If it passed this obstacle, any remaining doubt would be dissolved.

"Mr. Farley, could you come back tomorrow afternoon? Say, about the same time."

As Jim came down the marbled corridor for the second and what he hoped was the last time, his feelings were mixed. He had had no communications with the good doctor since their original conference, so he had no inkling of what the outcome was or what to expect when he confronted the man this time. He caught himself analyzing the sound of his own footsteps for a clue—a portent or omen, a particular sound or rhythm to enhance or give a gut feeling ... anything—but he heard nothing indicative either way, only the hollow sounds of footsteps resounding off impersonal, uninterested marble walls.

The doctor was expecting him this time too, but unlike the first time, the door was open and the receptionist was absent. He walked in, straight past the receptionist desk and into the doctor's office. Dr. Conley was on the phone. He looked up, saw Jim, and brought the conversation to its quickest conclusion.

His face was drawn, as though he had just had a draining experience, with very little sleep to relieve him. But there was also the hint of another emotion there: one of a man who has had a great burden lifted from him.

He put the telephone back on its cradle with his left hand, extending his right for a handshake, and Jim took heart, noticing the greeting was much warmer this time. He got right to it.

"Mr. Farley, it's good to see you again. I have just spent a prayerful afternoon with Mr. Anson. He has done a lot of soul-searching along with the praying. After this and a long discussion of the matter between Mr. Anson, Mrs. Anson, my wife, and myself, Mr. Anson has decided to resign from his position on the school board. He just told me on the telephone that he will make the official announcement to the public in a press conference he has called for five this afternoon. That was Mr. Anson I was talking to when you came in."

Jim was speechless; this trait was foreign to his personality, almost unheard of, but he was stunned. He had not expected such reverberating results as this. He hadn't dreamed of something like this happening. The most he had hoped for was to rattle some more chains. Not really trying to tabulate the anticipated results; pressuring Anson, maybe causing him to reflect to the extent of having possible second thoughts. But get him to resign! That had never crossed his mind. The card the good doctor had given him earlier felt heavy in his wallet as he walked out the marble corridor for the last time, its words burning in his mind: "God can work wonders through the man who doesn't care who gets the credit."

Amen, brother.

The footsteps sounded like the muffled drums of history being made as they resounded off the marbled walls.

Anson resigned October 11.

The day of the rally came before Jim was ready. So many things had to be done; so many things were left undone. But ready or not, the day was here, bright and sunny. He filed into the park with the rest of the crowd, a face among many. In looking around him, he was pleased with the size of the crowd. It looked like a packed house would be the result of the full-page ad that Marvin had placed in the paper, announcing the day's event. At the end of it, he hoped to see Marvin in undisputed control of future happenings in the protest.

He walked, or was rather carried, along with the throng, until he became disentangled enough to find a seat in the bleachers overlooking the speaker's podium.

He impatiently waited for the rally to begin. After what seemed like a long time to him, Ezra appeared from the dugout, heading for the podium. It was fitting, he supposed, that since Ezra was the current hero, he should be the first speaker. Graley was dressed in his best finery, the light tan sport coat with the lighter shirt and blazing red tie. He had been wearing the same outfit when all the pictures were taken for the newspaper.

"Ladies and gentlemen," Graley began, "it does my heart good to see as many people as there are here today who are interested in their children's future and eternal souls."

Graley, as usual, went into a long, repetitious, and boring explanation of what the fight was all about, and how he knew that all the parents there were concerned. Jim squirmed in his seat, figuring everybody else in the packed park was doing likewise. C'mon, Ezra, get to the point, he thought.

As though he had heard Jim's thought, Ezra finally began his pitch. "Ladies and gentlemen, the people pushing these filthy books ain't gonna listen to reason. I talked to Underwood and the rest of them at the school board that day until I was blue in the face. They had me arrested. The only thing that them people is goin' to listen to is pressure. Now, I don't mean goin' out and blowin' up schoolhouses and shootin' at the school buses and state police cars. That ain't gonna git us nowhere but in jail. What I mean is to put pressure where it hurts. With people like this, that's the ole pocketbook."

Jim though of Graley's anger and tone of voice that time in the Alliance office when he, Graley, said to Jim, "You don't care; you got all the money you need."

Graley continued. "We shut most of this valley down once, and it was hurtin' 'em. That's why they was eager for that thirty-day double cross. We'd have 'em on their knees."

Jim winced at this blatant slap at Marvin.

"But it ain't too late. We kin still do it. It's gonna be harder now, but we kin do it. This time we'll close down the whole valley ... not just a part of it. All of it."

The crowd's response was difficult to evaluate. The applause was heavy, but was it in support of Graley or just vented feelings against the books?

It was Avis Hill's turn. "Ladies and gentlemen, hittin' these people in their pocketbooks is fine, but what about our pocketbooks in the meantime? I ain't worked a day since all this started, and I don't mind tellin' you, it's startin' to hurt. My kids ain't had no new clothes since the first day of school; the bank is threatenin' to take my house, and to tell you the truth, we ain't even eatin' too good. If we go gittin' into a war of dollars, who do you think is goin' to win, people like us or them people on South Hills with their fat savings accounts and all that money rollin' in from stocks and bonds and other investments? I don't think that's a hard question to answer, do you?

"No, a war of dollars is not the answer. They got us outgunned there. The way to do it is to close down their schools. All of them. And keep 'em closed until they holler uncle and git rid of the trash in 'em. They can't teach kids if they don't have any kids to teach and no schools to teach 'em in."

As Avis left the podium, the applause was sparse and sporadic. Looking around him, Jim could see people giving each other nervous, appraising glances.

Marvin stepped to the microphone, wearing a look of concern that even Jim could see clearly from his position high in the bleachers. What bothered Jim was the knowledge that the crowd didn't understand, as he did, the reason for that look. A rousing cheer went up for Marvin from his supporters. He broke into his gleaming smile.

"Ladies and gentlemen, I know some of you don't agree with what I did in signing the agreement for the thirty-day period, whatever you want to call it—cooling-off period, moratorium, or whatever. I'm not sure it was the right thing to do myself. But I'm not sure it was the wrong thing to do either.

"What I do know is that although each of the plans offered by Avis and Ezra might work, our final solution to this problem is going to have to be negotiating. That's what these people understand: negotiations. Eventually, that's what it's gonna have to come down to. Somebody is going to have to sit down at the table and talk this thing out. It's going to take representatives from each side presenting their case—compromises from both sides, like Elmer Fike keeps telling us. Carry out all the violence you want and they're just gonna get meaner and harder. Put economic pressure on them and they'll just wait us out. Close their schools down and they'll just bring in the federal marshals and open 'em up again. Folks, we might as well face it, and the sooner the better: the only final solution to this is to negotiate! "

The crowd seemed thoroughly confused. The people made a feeble attempt at showing their appreciation of Marvin with scattered, unenthusiastic applause; but everybody in the park was turning to look at his neighbor with an expression that clearly asked, "What in the world is going on?"

Charley Quigley's delivery was totally anticlimactic. The crowd only half heard his offered solution. "Ladies and gentlemen, we can't hope to beat the establishment at its own game, especially when they're fighting us with our own money. I have had extensive experience with the educational system"—pointing out that he was college educated, setting him apart from the three leaders—"and I know what I'm talking about. We can't beat 'em, so let's leave 'em." Charley paused, a smile spreading slowly across his face. "You thought I was going to say, 'If we can't beat 'em, join 'em'... didn't you? No, I will never suggest that. The only solution to this problem, ladies and gentlemen, is alternate education. Establish Christian schools. Establish enough Christian schools and you'll put the public schools out of business. Accomplish this and not only do we win this battle, but we will have won the war that has been going on ever since certain factions in this country have been leading us astray from what the Founding Fathers originally intended for us. They intended for public schools to teach Christianity. In fact, the sole reason, originally, that the public schools came into being was to teach children to read so they would be able to study the Bible. The only reason.

"So, in conclusion, ladies and gentlemen, violence is not the answer, economic pressure is not the answer, nor is boycotting the schools per se, as according to Avis; you can negotiate all you want and 'they' are going to have the final say. Why? Because their very label—'The Establishment'—dictates it. They are already established. So let's not expend our time and energy fighting them; let's get established ourselves." Charley beamed at his finish, exuding confidence. No one noticed except Jim. The rest of the crowd at the ballpark, more than ever, seemed to be in a state of total bewilderment, confused by not three, as before, but now four completely different approaches to the problem, with four totally different offered solutions. The murmuring of the park suddenly became vocal, voices shouting angrily, "What are we supposed to do? Tell us what to do."

The cold reality of what had gone wrong settled in on Jim like fog from a grave.

His idea was good; his plan was good; the execution was good; only one small thing had gone wrong. Nobody had bothered to tell the crowd that the whole purpose was to select a leader from these four, selecting him as they would a political candidate, according to his platform. The crowd didn't know!

When the basket for donations was passed, Jim did not put anything in. A friend sitting with him dropped a twenty-dollar bill into it and, giving him a searching glance, asked, "Don't you believe it's a worthwhile cause?"

"I've got a better place to put my money," he answered. He was thinking of the Alliance. It was time to put the pressure on forming the Alliance.

As he left the park, he was already making plans. Finding the first phone booth he could, he called Elmer. "Elmer, can we get the guidelines and bylaws of the Alliance together in time to have our first meeting Thursday night?"

"Ah, I don't know, Jim. That's awful short notice."

"The opposition isn't giving us much time, Elmer."

"Well, I suppose we can. Where are we going to have it?"

"I'll leave that up to you."

"Well, all right, but I'll let you figure out where the steering committee is going to meet. We should call it together Tuesday night to lay the groundwork."

CHAPTER 12

The Alliance is Born!

Tuesday evening at seven o'clock, he was headed for the Heart o' Town, a local hotel in Charleston where they had booked the conference room. Jack Douglas had suggested it for the meeting because all they had to do to use it was buy dinner, and they got the conference room free. He figured you had to eat anyway, so it seemed like a good idea.

He found the conference room just as Roger was going in. "Hello, Jim, you the only one here?" asked Roger.

"I guess so; how are you?"

"Oh, all right."

They went in, found their table, and put their briefcases on it. They had just started for the salad bar when Elmer came in. "Isn't Betty here yet?" He'd no sooner gotten the words out than the door behind him opened. Elmer turned his head toward it, his brow knitted in that part frown, part-curious, part-accusing look that was peculiar to him, watching Betty Rogers as she came toward them.

"I'm sorry I'm late," she said. "I had to fix Frank and the children's dinner before I left."

"That's all right. We understand," said Elmer. You never knew what Elmer's reaction to a given situation was going to be—sometimes anger, sometimes impatient irritability, and sometimes a compassionate understanding, like now.

They served themselves salads and sat down.

Jim saw it as accidental that he and Elmer wound up at opposite ends of the oblong table, either end of which could be considered the "head of the table," and he wondered if it was intentional. He thought of the six weeks it took head negotiators in the Vietnam peace talks to agree on the shape of a table to avoid a "place of importance." Whatever the case, sitting at one end of the table made him feel better.

His mother had died when he was six. An assertive, authoritative older brother, and a grief-stricken father who was too burdened by the awesome task of raising two small boys alone to recognize the sensitive nature of the young boys, had inculcated him with the world's worst inferiority complex. It had withered his soul as a boy, followed him through adolescence, and occasionally come back to haunt him as an adult if circumstances warranted. He had to be on guard always or it would color his decisions and sometimes even control him. Sometimes he wondered if it was a complex or if he really was inferior.

In any event, it always surprised him when people in authority, important people, listened to what he was saying with attentive respect.

Sitting there dressed in a suit that he was unaccustomed to, in plush surroundings that were above his norm, he felt almost as if somebody else had occupied his body. He couldn't believe the voice that spoke now with such authority and commanded the attention of everyone there was his own. And yet, in one sense, the role fit like a glove.

He decided that the desperation of circumstances must be forcing confidence and courage into his inadequate being. He had read a true story of a man who'd lifted a car off his family, single-handedly, when it overturned in an accident and pinned them beneath it. When it was over and his family was safe, the man realized what he had done. He went back to prove it to himself. Try as he might, he could not budge the car. The same thing must be happening to him now.

"Elmer, the first thing we need is an office, preferably downtown."

"What for, Jim?"

"For the Alliance."

"You think so?" Elmer asked, giving him that searching,

uncommitted gaze.

"Oh, it's absolutely vital."

"We could hold the meetings in my office." Elmer was still missing the point. He was groping for Jim's reasoning. All eyes were on Jim.

"Image, Elmer. That's what the Alliance is all about. We have to set ourselves apart from the other protestors, especially the street protestors and the fundamentalists. We have to project an image of organization, stability and rationality, and of course, as being representative of the business and professional communities. That dictates an office."

The others half nodded. Elmer clearly still wasn't convinced, for the searching look remained on his face; it was obvious that he was analyzing his own thoughts as well as Jim's.

"All right. If you think it's that important," Elmer acquiesced, but Jim knew he still wasn't convinced. After they agreed on that, the meeting was adjourned.

Six o'clock these days always found Jim glued to the TV set, and this evening was no exception. He lay on his unmade bed amid the rumpled blankets, watching the day's events unfold on the tube. It had become almost a status of involvement of a protestor to have an unkempt house. The more cluttered the house, the more dedicated a protestor seemed to be—the less time for housekeeping. The extent of clutter indicated the extent of involvement.

The lead-in to today's report concerned the review committee. The camera panned the room, where the group was trying to come to a consensus. There was much disagreement and some bickering.

Then the camera switched to a lone figure for a personal interview. The announcer introduced him as Mick Staton, the chairman of Alice Moore's group.

Jim was close to the set, and he could see the man clearly. He was impressive on camera: handsome, with black hair and a mustache, and he spoke like a professional. Now there's the kind of people we need, thought Jim. A few like that would counterbalance the ignoramus image the media was pressing so hard upon the protestors as a whole.

Staton gave an intelligent résumé of the proceedings, presenting his own views of what should be done to resolve the problem. Jim was greatly impressed. He picked up the phone to call Elmer.

"Elmer, did you see the news just now?" he asked.

"No, I've been too busy this evening to watch anything. What was it about?"

Jim was starting to tell him about the man he had just seen, when he heard Elmer's door open and close and heard Elmer say to someone who had just come into the room, "Just put them over there, Mick." He got to his feet.

"What did you say, Elmer?"

"I was talking to Mick about some of the books he was bringing in."

"Mick who?'

"Mick Staton," Elmer said in his usual flat tone. "He's on Alice's review committee, and he brought some of the books here for me to look at."

Jim wanted to blurt out, "You know Mick Staton?" and explain that this was what had excited him about the news this evening. But he decided to play it close to the vest until he learned a little more about the man and his relationship with Elmer. He said instead, "Is he there now?"

"Yes, he's right here," answered Elmer.

"May I talk with him a minute?" Jim asked, trying to hide the excitement he felt.

"Mick, Jim wants to talk to you," said Elmer.

"Hello, Jim. This is Mick Staton," said the cultured voice with quiet dignity.

Jim had the dizzying feeling of having just watched *Gone with the Wind*, then getting a phone call from Clark Gable.

As he was watching the news on television, it was a little hard to separate Walter Cronkite, a national news correspondent, interviewing John Kennedy from Jim Reader, a local news anchor, interviewing Mick Staton. All of them were figures in the news. They all had that same aura of mystique about them, as if they were figments of another world. And now here he was, actually conversing with Mick Staton.

His voice didn't betray him as he calmly said, "I'm Jim Farley, Mick. I understand that you're chairman of your segment of the screening committee, and I was wondering if it would be possible for us to get access to some of the books."

"Sure," answered Mick matter-of-factly. "Any of them you want."

Jim was ecstatic; his mind reeled. After the difficult and tedious struggle he had gone through these past several weeks in search of a book here and a pamphlet there, here was the top man of the screening group himself telling him he could have all the books at once, which boggled his mind. These particular books would even have the offensive passages marked for him. He couldn't believe his good fortune.

He and Mick talked a little more about different things and then hung up after they arranged for Mick to leave at Elmer's house the books Jim currently wanted.

When he got off the phone, his mind began racing as he made plans. He could see all kinds of possibilities with Mick in the picture. He had to get him as a member of the Alliance. He just had to.

His impulse was to jump in the car and head immediately to Elmer's house and make a desperate attempt to recruit Mick. With great effort he persuaded himself it would be much more effective to wait and talk to Elmer alone about it. It was obvious the two of them were close, and he was counting on Elmer's influence to help get Mick as a member of the Alliance.

Early the next morning, he was on his way to Nitro where Elmer lived.

Jim was not the type to be impressed with status, power, or money. But he had to admit that something about Mick Staton had intrigued him during their first meeting. Perhaps it was the incredibly coincidental way they talked the first time.

No, it was more than that. The man's handsome good looks were enhanced by the black mustache that matched the color of his hair, which was groomed in the semi-long fashion that was just reaching popularity among the professional people. The emerald eyes were constantly curious, always studying the person he was talking to. The mark of intelligence was clear. Jim was to learn that he was well educated and extremely well read as well.

Mick was the vice president of one of the larger banks in Charleston and was very good at his job, but he was considerably overqualified.

His principles were cast in concrete, and he made it clear to his bank at one point in the textbook fight that he would sacrifice his position with them before he would compromise. The bank, like a lot of other companies and organizations depending on the public for survival, was concerned about their image and what the stigma of the involvement of one of their executives would do to them.

The loss of the job would not have been a small matter; it would have been catastrophic. Like most people, Mick was just starting a young family and, in spite of his position at the bank, was heavily in debt. He had bought a new home, which along with all the other expenses involved in raising a family, was strapping him.

Although he was painfully aware of this, Mick held his ground with the bank, and they finally relented because of his qualifications and his value to the bank. They would not help him in the fight, but neither would they stand in his way.

Most of this, Jim learned later from Elmer. The three of them were in Elmer's office now, discussing the bylaws that were to govern the Alliance and set its policy, which Jim and Elmer had worked up the previous Sunday.

"Well, what do you think, Mick?" asked Elmer after he had introduced him to Jim.

"Sounds good to me," answered Mick.

Elmer was agitated when he called him Tuesday afternoon. "Jim, we've got a problem. The Elks Club got cold feet about letting us have our meeting there and canceled on us. Now we don't have any place to hold it unless you agree with the only alternative available that I can find."

"Where's that, Elmer?"

"The Ambassador Room at the Daniel Boone Hotel. It's expensive, but it is available."

"I think you'd better grab it." He was in no mood to discuss economics or frugality. He wanted to get on with it. The Daniel Boone was the oldest and most respected hotel in Charleston and in the valley. It would do their image a lot of good. Whether the rest of them were aware of it or not, that was what the Alliance was all about: image.

He was excited as he walked through the side door of the Daniel Boone, dressed in his best suit and carrying his briefcase full of textbook material. He glanced casually around the lobby as he headed for the stairs leading to the Ambassador Room. When he walked in, he saw that the room was already packed with people. He saw J. D. Landers sitting near a vacant seat. Jim walked over and took the seat. J. D. smiled at him.

He looked around at the crowd, pleased at the better quality of attire and behavior. He cringed a little when his examining gaze swept along the left wall; there were the street protestors, Frances McCune and all, about twenty in number. He had hoped to avoid this. He wanted it to be a meeting with dignity and reason.

Hope for this began to dim further when he saw Ed Miller come in the door, armed to the teeth with protest material. Miller was a faction all by himself, waging a one-man crusade against the books. For whatever motives, only he knew.

A squat, powerfully built man in his late forties, Miller had admitted to serving eight years in prison. He never did specify what the charge had been; only that he "had made a mistake and had paid his debt." (He was the man responsible for the future introduction of the Ku Klux Klan into the fight.) He remained a man of mystery throughout the struggle. The only thing clear about him was his open vow to stop these books with any means necessary. When making this statement, most groups and individuals added "within the law." Miller added nothing but a period.

Jim saw Elmer seated at a long table at the front of the room. There were two other men seated with him. At seven thirty sharp (Jim liked that), Elmer called the meeting to order, as brusquely and efficiently as if at a business luncheon.

"Ladies and gentlemen, I am Elmer Fike, the acting president of The Business and Professional People's Alliance for Better Textbooks. I would like to make you welcome and thank you for coming. We hope this is the beginning of a forum for moderate thinkers here tonight."

"Hah!"

Elmer, scowling, glanced at Frances McCune, who had made the remark, then ignored her and went on. "We are of the opinion that violence never settles anything, but rather, reason is the tool that will get the job done. I have with me this evening Gene Hoyer, my attorney, to explain the legal possibilities."

Hoyer took the speaker's stand and went into a dreary harangue of dead and legal avenues, finishing with, "I regret to sound so dismal, but I'm afraid your legal recourse is nil."

Jim felt the frustration surge once more. "I thought we were coming here for something constructive tonight," he said angrily, with only J. D. to hear.

J. D. leaned over and whispered anxiously, "Now, take it easy, Jim. Let's lay back and see what's gonna happen."

This only angered him more. "Hang it, J. D. We can't wait for it to happen; we're the ones who have to make it happen." He was furious as Elmer droned on.

According to Elmer, Alice Moore was supposed to be here to speak if she could make it. It seemed fitting, and if she did make it, maybe the evening wouldn't be a total loss.

"Mr. Fike, are we gonna be allowed to join your group?" The sarcastic questions, sprinkled with derision, came from the predicted source of Frances McCune.

Elmer looked her over appraisingly and said, "Anyone subscribing to our principles, who will stay within our guidelines and observe our bylaws, will be admitted to the Alliance. Provided they pay the initiation fee, of course, which is fifty dollars per member." (Jim had wanted the fee to be a hundred dollars, to keep out the riffraff, but he settled for fifty at Elmer's insistence.)

Jim winced at this. He had hoped to keep the Alliance pure in its membership, embracing only the people the name implied: "business and professional. But the street protestors were a necessary part of the struggle, with a vital role to play. So be it if some of them wound up in the Alliance.

Suddenly, Jim's hair bristled on the back of his neck. He had just remembered there was no one posted at the Elks Club to direct to the Daniel Boone anyone who showed up. He seethed, wondering how many people they'd lost.

A stir at the back of the room caused heads to turn, and then the ripple of whispers began: "Alice Moore is coming."

Jim looked around in time to see the striking figure of "Joan of Arc" striding daintily, but with a purpose, down the aisle. Dressed dramatically and in good taste in red on white, she was a vision of elegant beauty as she took the speaker's stand amidst a standing ovation.

When the applause finally stopped, she said, "You are very kind. I came here tonight to lend my total support to this newest organization formed to combat the threat in our schools. I have known Elmer Fike for many years, and I know him to be a man of integrity and dedicated to the same principles I hold dear. In this man, you will find a determined fighter, intelligent, always using reason as the most effective weapon. It is because of these traits—and others that I am so familiar with—that I endorse this new group without reservation."

That was enough for the crowd to come to its feet to express its praise of Alice Moore and to embrace the Alliance. After all the labor pains, Jim had the gratification of hearing the first cry of his newborn brainchild come to life, spanked into being by the garrulous Elmer Fike and nurtured by the lovely Alice Moore. The Alliance had been born!

CHAPTER 13

The Alliance Office Opens

Jim was excited as he drove along the quiet street, looking for Country Club Boulevard. Betty Rogers had given him that address last night at the meeting of the Alliance. He was going to pick her up at her home and the three of them (June was to meet them uptown) were going to look for an office for the Alliance. The feeling of frustration of last night returned when he remembered Elmer saying at the steering committee meeting, "Jim, do you think it's really that important to have an office?"

He had exercised patience, holding a tight rein on his temper when he answered, emphatically, "Yes, I do, Elmer. It's vital." The look of unconvinced bewilderment on Elmer's face added to his frustration, but since Elmer acquiesced, he didn't pursue it. He didn't know which was more frustrating, trying to explain the plan in the books to unbelievers or trying to make his fellow protestors understand that "image" was all-important to the Alliance. But the frustration of last night was replaced this morning by the excitement of knowing they were finally moving forward in establishing a new face in the protest.

Seeing a sign reading KANAWHA COUNTY CLUB, he slowed the car. It was spelled out in individual wrought iron letters spanning the entire street and supported by two large brick piers. He drove past it, figuring this would have to be the private entrance to the club. Country Club Boulevard must run parallel to it. He drove several hundred yards with no luck. Then he passed a street sign for Spring Hill Avenue, then another street with another sign, but no Country Club Boulevard. He was confused. He pulled up across the street for a few minutes, pondering the matter. Deciding he had better backtrack, he turned around.

He drove back to the brick piers with the sign. He sat reading the sign and looking up the opulent drive beyond, noting the well-groomed berm and the attractive shrubs lining either side. He glanced at his watch. He was already late due to the time lost looking for the street. He decided he had no choice; bracing himself for the possibility of being thrown off a private drive, he pressed the gas pedal, sending the car up the hill.

As the street leveled out, he saw a pickup truck parked in the grass, maintenance men working nearby. He tensed, expecting one of them to step in front of him and throw his hands up to stop him. He hoped he could make it to a stop and ask them for directions before that happened. A rolling golf course lay beyond.

Just then, he saw a driveway to his right, leading to a residence. He quickly turned into it and parked. He was relieved, feeling that he was on neutral ground; at least, he hoped he was. He got out and looked around. The grounds around the house were almost as spacious and beautiful as the country club itself, with shrubs and flowers placed just right, in a manner that connoted professionalism and good taste. He saw no signs of life anywhere, so he started up the wide flagstone walk toward the house, noting the slate roof and copper gutters. It must have been built some time ago, he thought. Not many people could afford to build a house of such quality at today's prices. The brick structure, a Williamsburg-style home, seemed spacious as it rambled over the brow of the hill, molded expertly into the landscape.

Majestic chimes responded to his finger on the doorbell. A moment later, the door opened, and to his surprise, Betty herself stood there. She smiled when she saw him. "Hello, Jim, come in."

He followed her into a spacious living room, elegantly furnished. She motioned him to a luxurious sofa. "I'll be right back; there's some material I want to show you." He looked appreciatively around the room as he waited. After a short time, Betty came back into the room.

"This is some of the stuff we came across in the sex education fight that resulted in Alice getting elected to the board," she said, handing him some papers. He leafed through them, and Betty sat down at the other end of the sofa, watching him. He understood her intense interest in his reaction when he came across certain subject matter in the papers. He could feel the crimson spread across his cheeks. He was too embarrassed for a moment to look up.

"Do you mean this was actually shown in the classroom?" he asked, shuffling the papers.

"Not only shown, but taught," answered Betty softly.

"It boggles the mind, doesn't it?"

"Yes, it does."

He put the papers aside. "Betty, could you give me some idea of what I can count on from you?"

She sat looking at him, not answering, analyzing the question. He couldn't help but think that Betty belonged here in this house. Her classic beauty, the soft, cultured voice, and the elegance of carriage and dress reflected the decor of the dwelling.

When he saw that she wasn't quite sure of what he meant by the question, he said, "I mean, how much time can you devote to the office, what are your capabilities, can you type, and so on? I'm sorry to be so blunt, but I'm totally ignorant about everybody in the protest—who they are, what their credentials and potential are, and so on—and time is short."

A look of understanding crossed her face. "Oh, I see what you mean. Well, yes, I can type. I do some shorthand but not much. I'm good at answering the telephone, and I've had a lot of experience in dealing with people. As far as the time is concerned, I'll spend whatever is necessary, as long as it doesn't interfere with my responsibilities to Frank and the children." Frank was her husband.

A frown knitted Betty's brow; her soft brown eyes became thoughtful. "Frank just took over a mining company, and the strike is over. These books are causing a lot of problems," she said.

"How bad is it?" asked Jim.

She thought a long time and then said, "We may have to sell

the house."

Jim looked at her appraisingly, slightly shaking his head in sympathy. "It would be a shame for you to sell this house."

She looked around as if she were seeing it for the first time ... or the last. "Yes, it would be a shame. Oh well, that's another problem." She pulled herself back to the issue at hand. "Just call on me anytime I'm needed, and if I can't make it, I'll tell you in time for you to find someone else. But the serious nature of these books dictates they take first priority. Maybe even over the children's immediate needs. After all, what kind of people will they grow into and what kind of world will they be forced to live in if the plan in these books is not stopped?"

He felt a compassionate admiration for this woman.

Jim and Betty had driven from her home in their separate cars to the parking lot uptown to meet June, who was already there when they arrived.

Betty had told him that she had joined Alice in the sex education fight that got Alice elected to the school board, and she had taken care of the job of renting an office for that purpose.

"Where was the office, Betty?"

She lowered her eyes a moment, then answered, "Well, it was in the Holley Hotel building."

Jim cringed a little, thinking of the winos that used the Holley Hotel for home base.

Betty saw his reaction and said, "I know ... I felt the same way, but we were operating on a shoestring budget, and this man I knew let us have it free." After a pause, she said, "To tell you the truth, I always wondered how true the rumors were about his being connected with the Mafia. He did have some mysterious habits.

Jim looked at her searchingly. He overcame the curiosity about the man, deciding it had nothing to do with them and the present problem and didn't warrant the time it would take to explore. That was the second hardest thing he was discovering about this situation, needing to sort out priorities and stick with the issue. The first obstacle was getting organized. That brought his mind back to the entire purpose of the Alliance: image. It had to be impressive ... if not impeccable.

"I've known Guy Erwin, who runs Erwin Realty, for years," he said. "Let's give him a call and see if he has anything. We've got to get something respectable and reasonably nice."

"That's going to be expensive," Betty said.

"I know, Betty, but we either do it right with the Alliance or we serve no purpose." June gave him a concerned look but said nothing.

Erwin happened to be in his office when Jim called. "Guy, I need an office—today. What do you have available for immediate occupancy?"

"Are you expanding your business, Jim?"

Jim hesitated, took a deep breath, and thought, Oh well, he'll find out sooner or later; might as well tell him now. You never knew where anybody stood on the textbook issue. Some people, especially executives, shunned it like the plague, keeping their true feelings to themselves, fearful of the effect it could have on their businesses.

"No, I need it for a new organization that we're putting together to fight these textbooks."

"Oh." There was a long pause ... "I see." Another long pause. Jim waited, wondering if the pause meant that Guy was running through a mental list of possibilities ... or whether he was trying to find a tactful way to tell him to get lost.

Finally, there was a deep intake of breath at Erwin's end, and he said, "I've got three empty offices I could show you in the Union Building."

Jim was relieved that Guy didn't turn them down cold as the Elks Club had. He thought of the Union Building; it sat all by itself on the riverbank of Kanawha, across the boulevard of the same name, right at the head of Capitol Street, which was the center of Charleston. In fact, if you were driving a car up Capitol at high speed and didn't swerve, you would hit the Union Building dead center. Perfect, he thought. He liked the independence of the lone building, and being at the head of Capitol Street made it like a hub in the center of town. Even the name—Union—connoted organization.

He knew immediately that they were going to take it, but always the businessperson, he didn't tell Erwin this. He wanted to negotiate the best deal possible.

He covered the eagerness in his voice and said matter-of-factly, "Okay. Could you meet us there now?"

Erwin said he could, and it took only a few minutes for all of them to get there. Erwin's office was just across the street, and the three of them were already on Capitol Street.

Guy fumbled with a key in the door to the first office. When they walked in, Jim noticed a second door leading off to the right. Erwin, noticing the curious look, opened the door, showing a second connecting office. "I told you on the phone that I had three offices; these are two of them, and the third is on the next floor up by itself."

"I didn't notice as we came up. What floor is this?" asked Jim.

"Third," answered Guy.

Jim thought that was perfect. Just far up enough to discourage people from dropping in—and not too far to be inconvenient enough to discourage true protestors. Hiding the excitement he felt, Jim asked casually, "How much are they?"

Erwin thought for a moment and then said, "Well, Jim, they're supposed to rent for two seventy-five a piece, but since it's for you, and if you want them both, I'll let you have the two of them for four hundred a month."

Jim hesitated, trying to negotiate the best deal he could get. It was going to be his money financing it initially, and later, if he did get his money back, it would be the nickels and dimes of people all over the country who could not afford extravagance.

"Is that the best you can do?"

He doubted that Erwin was truly giving him a special rate because of their friendship, but was instead trying to make it sound like a good bargain.

"I'm afraid so, Jim. I have some other people who have asked about them. I don't figure you're going to need them for too long a time for your purpose, and that could be just long enough to cause me to miss out on a long-term lease with the other people."

He noticed that Erwin hadn't commented on the issue of the textbooks or the fight, and there was an air of distaste about his manner, as if he were forcing himself to handle a tainted object and he would just as soon get it over with.

"Okay, we'll take these two. Do we pay in advance?"

"It's customary for one month's rent in advance," answered Erwin in a flat tone.

Jim wrote him a check from the several he had purposefully brought, and Erwin quickly handed him the keys and left, obviously relieved.

He turned to Betty. "Do you have any ideas on how to furnish this place—what we will need, where to get it, and so on?"

She thought for a moment and said, "Well, we could ask people like Elmer to chip in whatever they can spare. A piece here and a piece there, and we could eventually put it together."

"That would take too long. Is there any place in town that could rent what we need?"

Betty was taking this quite seriously. She frowned in thought and then said, "Rose City Press rents office equipment."

He dealt with Rose City occasionally and knew it was only two blocks away. "Sounds like what we need. Come on. We'll walk over."

Going through the storeroom of furniture made his head spin. Shopping, especially for furniture, always did this to him. That's why he usually left this sort of thing to June.

But this time June was hanging in the background, watching him and Betty go through the desks, typewriters, tables and chairs, and so on. Finally, she got him gently by the arm and led him off to the other side of the room, pretending that she had seen something she thought they needed. When they were out of earshot of Betty, she said in a low voice filled with concern, "Jim, don't you think you're going overboard? This is going to cost a lot of money. And then there is the telephone that I heard you order to be installed in the office. Where is it going to stop ... and where is all the money going to come from to pay for all this?"

Jim, who was usually mild-mannered, was short-tempered these days. "I've never made you go hungry yet, have I?"

A hurt look crossed her face; she stared at him for a moment and then shrugged. "I just hope you know what you're doing."

"I always do, don't I?"

She walked away as if thinking this was not the Jim she knew.

What June didn't know was he had been putting a little money away secretly for a long time, saving for a rainy day. The rainy day was here. He had decided that when he had committed the ten thousand dollars to Charley Quigley a couple of weeks ago. In his own mind, if necessary, he had already committed every nickel he owned to stop these books. He would then liquidate everything he had and use that money too, if he had to. He had never had such strong feelings about anything in his life as he did about these books. Right now, the only thing he could think about was that they had to be stopped, at any cost.

June gave in and helped Betty finish picking out the furnishings. Before leaving, they arranged to have everything delivered.

Jim opened the door to the office, walked in, and looked around. He was pleased with the way June and Betty had furnished it. It looked impressive, businesslike, with the big desk against the side wall, complete with swivel chair; the second chair and couch on the opposite wall for visitors; and the table at the far end to display the books. He walked into the second office and looked around. Satisfied, he came back to the front office and sat down behind the desk. Sitting there in his best suit, he looked like an important executive waiting for a busy day of business to begin. Looking out the window at Kanawha Boulevard, he felt good. At last, they were organized. Swiveling around in the chair, he looked expectantly at the door, waiting for the shadow of their first "client" to darken the glass of the top half of the door. No one came. Nothing happened.

Oh well, he told himself, it will take time for word to get around. The ad he had placed in the paper announcing the opening of the office wouldn't even come out until today's paper. While he looked at the glass half of the door, he felt something was missing. He tensed in concentration, trying to put his finger on it. Then it hit him. No business office had a blank door. He grabbed the phone. Dialing a familiar number, he got Jack Walker, a friend of his who ran Walker Sign Company.

"Jack, I need a favor."

"Okay, what do you need?"

Jim explained, and Jack said, "I'll have a man over there the day after tomorrow."

"You don't understand, Jack. I need it now."

Jack took a deep breath, started to explain his busy schedule in an exasperated voice, and then stopped. He'd likely remembered the favor that Jim had done for him just a few weeks ago. "Oh, all right. I'll do it myself. Where is the office?"

Jim told him the location, excitedly thanked him, and hung up to wait. Jack was there in twenty minutes and they began.

When the job was finished and Jack had gone, he stood back and admired the neatly lettered sign that announced with class that this was THE BUSINESS AND PROFESSIONAL PEOPLE'S ALLIANCE FOR BETTER TEXTBOOKS.

Now he was satisfied.

CHAPTER 14
The Allies

Donna McCallister's thoughts were of a brooding nature as she rode along beside her husband. They had taken turns driving their little VW station wagon on the long trip, and now it was his turn during the last twenty miles or so they had to go before they reached Charleston, West Virginia.

Charleston, West Virginia. My God, she thought, six months ago, I thought the only Charleston was in South Carolina. West Virginia was the outback section of Virginia, somewhere west of Norfolk.

After leaving Chicago, they had first gone to Norfolk. Her husband, Neil, had been sent there by his company to inspect a plant similar to the one they hoped to build in Charleston—or rather in South Charleston, the industrial suburb of Charleston.

Even that sounded strange to Donna. She, like most people across the country, had the stereotypical image of West Virginia, picturing hills and hillbillies furtively flitting through the woods to their moonshine stills in their bib overalls, carrying their mountain rifles and swinging earthen jugs with corncob stoppers.

The only industry she knew of up to now was the coal industry. The inhabitants of the hills called it King Coal, in triumph by the rich; in bitterness by the poor. This brought visions to Donna of overworked wage slaves, their faces blackened by the choking dust of the mines, almost to the color of their early African American brothers in slavery.

Before Lincoln, the methods were more direct. Now they were deceptively subtle, in Donna's opinion, in grudging obedience to the law.

Before Lincoln, you bought a healthy young black on the block at auction, and he was yours—body and soul—bought and paid for. Feed him just enough grit and gruel to keep his strength up and it was your right to work him until you had wrung every drop of production from the machine that was his body. Then send him, each night when he was exhausted, to his dirt floor shack to collapse on the bare cot. Repeat this day after day, until his lungs were filled with black dust and he died from black lung. Since Lincoln, you bought a young white trash slave out of the bar on Skid Row (Lee Street). You bought him with glowing promises of good wages, big bonuses, and top living conditions in company houses and fine bargains in the company store.

Once you had him securely imprisoned in the stockade of the mining village of company shacks, surrounded by the invisible walls of fear and poverty, solidly held by the chains of his debt to the company store, he was yours—body and soul—to be paid for in installments of small amounts each month. Feed him just enough grit and gruel to keep his strength up, and it was your right to work him until you had wrung every drop from the machine that was his body.

Send him each night, exhausted, to the rough board-floored shack to collapse in the swing on the front porch of rough board, listlessly swinging to and fro, watching, helpless, as his offspring grow up, their only recreation kicking a can up and down the dirt street that ran in front of the shacks.

Through the numbness of his fatigue came a muted awareness that they, his offspring, would take his place in the endless cycle of debt and work—when he had spit the last of the black dust out of his lungs into the black dust of the street.

The horrid picture painted by these thoughts depressed Donna. She shuddered slightly and shook her head as though to erase it and bring her mind back to the present.

She looked out the window at the bright sunlight bathing the rugged mountains, interspersed with rolling meadows, picturesque farmhouses, and the ever-present red barn out back. She had to admit it was beautiful country, and seeing it for the first time on such a glorious day lifted her spirits a little.

But the beauty was not enough to make her glad to be here. She still regretted having to leave their home, the lovely house they had built just outside Chicago. Also, she was apprehensive about the unknown that was facing them in the hills of West Virginia.

The image she carried of the place caused her to have the feeling of being on a wagon train with Dan Boone, heading into the wilds of Kentucky in the frontier days. She could almost see herself going to the creek to wash clothes or to the outhouse instead of the indoor bathroom.

Her map told her that the West Virginia Turnpike they were currently traveling was beginning to run parallel to Cabin Creek now. The creek was in the heartland of the mining industry, running its weaving path some sixty-seven miles from its source to where it dumped into Kanawha River. Jerry West, the all-star basketball player, had spent his youth here, dribbling and shooting baskets on his school court, determined to overcome his ineptness at the game of basketball. He went on to become one of the top NBA players in professional basketball, leading the Los Angeles Lakers to many victories in the years of their heyday. (West Virginia University, where Jerry West began his career, now has one of the largest and most modern basketball facilities in the nation.)

The hollow and the creek ran along the base of one of the richest seams of coal ever discovered in the state.

Donna had a clear view of the miners' homes, situated on every spot of ground wide enough to accommodate a structure of any kind. Most were of the type she expected, shabby, run-down frame houses built of rough oak. Some really did have tar paper on them, as she had heard.

This brought back her previous thoughts of the wage slaves. She could hardly wait to get to Charleston to see the other side of the mining industry, the recipients of the fruit of all the labor here in Cabin Creek.

She fully expected to find elegant mansions, their huge white columns rising high in their splendor, reminiscent of the *Gone with the Wind* era, paid for with the sweat and blood, the very lives, of the wretched souls that lived in these shacks. She burned at the thought.

But then a house or two caught her attention. They were different, better. She even saw a brick house, then another. She leaned forward in interest, waiting to see what was around the next bend in the road.

Then, suddenly, Cabin Creek and its inhabitants disappeared from sight as the turnpike circled the last mountain and the Kanawha Valley came into view. Donna was in wonder of the vista that spread before her. The turnpike cut into the mountain on her left. Running parallel to the mountain range across the valley, it gave a bird's-eye view of the valley and the city (suburban) in between. Then the houses were replaced with smokestacks of factories, stores, and modern shopping centers.

Donna sat enthralled as the stereotypical image of primitive West Virginia crumbled in her mind and was replaced with the reality of a city so modern, so middle class that it could be any thriving city in the country. The commanding mountains that bordered the valley tucked the city in securely at their base.

They got off the turnpike and directly onto a modern interstate, which took them past the most beautiful capitol building her eyes had ever beheld, its gold-covered dome rising in glorious splendor over the ultramodern administration buildings of state government.

She had been to the national capitol many times, and it could not compare with the magnificent beauty of this one here "in the hills."

Donna found out later that the gold on the dome was genuine. This was the poverty-stricken, backward Appalachia she had heard so much about?

The interstate crossed the river and continued past the business district of Charleston, and since it was elevated, sometimes on solid mountainside, sometimes on concrete pillars, it was like watching a parade from a reviewing stand. The only difference was that the stand was moving instead of the parade.

She was spellbound as she watched, from her moving vantage

point of five stories high, the diverse and interesting buildings of the city glide by. Some were new, some not so new, some ultramodern, but all were a part of an attractive city. The cars bustling in the crowded streets were almost all late model, not the Ma and Pa Kettle pickup trucks she had expected. And there were more big cars than compact economy cars.

They crossed the Kanawha River, a Mississippi in miniature. She looked upstream when they were at the middle of the bridge and drew her breath in sharply. The scene from there looked like a panoramic postcard. Looking straight up the middle of the river, it appeared wider than the Mississippi, disappearing finally around a bend just above the capitol, whose stately dome of gold rose with authority above the total domain, like a king guarding its own.

The city itself lay on the left side of the river; a brand-new Holiday Inn drew her attention. The modern building rising just beyond, the latest design in expensive high-rises, with its sign Charleston National Bank suggested money ... lots of it.

She saw the stately mansion she had expected high on the hill to her right, complete with white pillars.

Her attention was drawn away from the mansion by the movement of an enormous body of people going up the four-lane expressway to the left side of the river. She wondered what the big occasion was. Political, she thought, since they were evidently heading for the gold-domed capitol. This was October 17; Election Day was less than a month away.

Kanawha Boulevard, a grand four-lane expressway, separated the city from the river. She noticed one single building on the riverside, standing tall in its loneliness. She had no way of knowing about the group of desperate people gathered there in the office behind a door marked THE BUSINESS AND PROFESSIONAL PEOPLE'S ALLIANCE FOR BETTER TEXTBOOKS.

Sharon Mason stood on her terrace, looking down at the city. It was normally a magnificent scene. Right now, she could not see the panoramic grandeur that lay at her feet. It had always been enthralling, making her feel a little like a goddess on her heavenly throne as she surveyed her domain.

The hill broke away from the edge of the terrace so steeply that it really wasn't there, visually. It created the illusion of standing on a stationary cloud above the valley, watching the river find its winding way down through the mountains, taking Kanawha Boulevard with it as its modern border. The boulevard, with its riprap running down the bank to the water's edge, separated the city from the river like a castle wall from the moat.

The elegant woman who lived in the stately manor on the hill epitomized the elite of "Snob Hill" to the protestors.

As they trampled along in their hopeless marches and stood at their futile posts of vigil in front of the school board building or the capitol, they could always see the majestic sentinel of the other side, its four white pillars rising to support the Roman-type roof fifty feet above, giving it such a stately splendor that it gave one the feeling that nature's architect had built the mountain just to support the house atop it. It could be seen from any part of the city.

Unknown to the protestors who occasionally raised a clenched fist toward it, the house had a heritage. The man who built the house was on an excursion with his wife on the Hudson River in 1915. He saw a magnificent house high above the river on a cliff. They were so impressed by the house that they asked the owner permission to look through it. He came home to Charleston and requested a local architect to duplicate it for him on the hill above the bend in Kanawha River. He later sold it to Admiral Jones, now retired from the navy, who apparently enjoyed watching river traffic, gleaming of days gone by.

But Sharon's mind was on none of these things now; her thoughts were focused entirely on the massive throng of people marching their defiant way up the boulevard, toward the state capitol. The writhing mass of bodies seemed endless in its length and covered the boulevard from curb to curb.

She couldn't believe there were people like this. She had heard of them, but she never thought she would actually see them carrying out their crusade of rebellious ignorance.

Before moving to West Virginia, she held the same

stereotypical image of the natives that most of the country shared. It was that of a backward people—clannish, narrow-minded, and resistant to change. But she never dreamed it would go this far. This was a revolt, almost treason. They were natives all right. More like the natives of Africa—or rather the savages of Africa that the word native brought to mind.

She remembered Hitler's takeover power of Germany and had horrible visions of huge bonfires with these people dancing around them, gleefully flinging book after book atop the crackling flames, howling in raucous laughter. She shuddered involuntarily.

She thought of the story she had read about Spain in the olden days. There had been a castle there that had been a center of learning, with such excellence in teaching that it was considered the standard of education. Then the people became concerned with the material being taught and decided to take a hand in the selection of such teaching matter. The more they became involved and the more books they censored, the more the quality of the education deteriorated. Finally, it dropped to such a low that all the people stopped sending their children to school. No one came anymore. (This can go both ways; censor value and you have deterioration.)

Why couldn't these people down there on the boulevard below her understand that?

To get her mind off the problem, she turned her gaze down the boulevard until it came to the bridges crossing the Elk and Kanawha rivers where the two met. The one across Elk River was a secondary bridge carrying traffic from one section of the city to the other. The one across the Kanawha River was the hub of the largest interchanges in the interstate system east of the Mississippi. She watched with distraction the heavy flow of traffic, wondering superficially where all the people in the cars were going and where they were from. What were they like? Why were they hurrying so?

With neither of them being aware of the other, Donna McCallister was in the center of the bridge at that very moment, looking up at the huge white columns of Sharon's house, wondering about the people who lived there. What were they like? What were their drives and ambitions? Neither of them knew that also at this very moment, there was a group of dedicated people huddled together in the tall building they both could see, feverishly and desperately formulating plans for the next battle of the war they were waging, the war that Sharon was observing and Donna was as yet oblivious to. But aware or not, it was raging all about them.

Although both their lives would be affected tremendously by the textbook controversy, it would remain the only common denominator in their lives. This moment now would be as close as they would ever come to meeting physically. Their lives followed different paths.

Jim's car seemed to weave its own way down Louden Heights Road, the steep, twisting main artery into Charleston, out of South Hills, like a faithful horse picking its way down a familiar trail. All his thoughts were directed toward the coming day, the second day in the Alliance office. The road he was traveling had been blasted by dynamite and hacked by hand out of the solid rock of the sheer face of the mountain, the cliff dropping straight down below it and only slightly less steep above. His father had been in charge of the blasting; and the Works Progress Administration or WPA, formed by the Roosevelt administration to give the people something to do in the throes of the Great Depression of 1929, did the work. Jim had acquired his proficiency in blasting with dynamite from his father and had developed it into a lucrative part of his business. Presently, he was the only licensed demolitions expert in Kanawha County. He, solely, was allowed to use the nitroglycerin in clay form, anywhere in the valley, including within the city of Charleston itself. This made his service much sought after ... and expensive.

When he rounded the bend that brought the city into view, his eagerness was that of a newly graduated law student who had just been awarded his degree to practice and was on his way to his spanking-new office to begin. As he looked down on the city from his vantage point halfway up the mountain, he saw it as his college of learning, with "the plan" in the textbooks as his thesis and Marvin's first rally at Campbell's Creek as the day of enrollment. Today was graduation.

Normally, this spot in the road gave him the feeling of driving through the rugged wilderness of Wyoming and abruptly, as if by magic, dropping in on New York City, but today the feeling was buried beneath his eagerness to begin the fight.

He was totally unaware of Sharon Mason standing on her terrace immediately above him.

His excitement grew when he saw the long, ragged line of street protestors stomping angrily up Kanawha Boulevard, carrying their signs. He watched them during the remainder of his trip down the mountain and across the bridge. Then his interest shifted to the lone building on the riverbank: the Union Building. It had a good sound to it, a sound of solidarity, and he was warmed by the thought as he eagerly searched for the three windows on the third floor that marked the offices of THE BUSINESS AND PROFESSIONAL PEOPLE'S ALLIANCE FOR BETTER TEXTBOOKS. He left his car in the adjacent parking lot and hurried upstairs to begin the busy day.

CHAPTER 15
Is Victory Worth It?

The first couple through the Alliance door that morning wasn't exactly Russ and Martha Werhle, but at least it was a start. They came meekly, the little old man timidly leading the way, followed by his grandmotherly wife, looking as though she would rather be home with her darning needles. They both inspected the office apprehensively, glancing at Jim behind his desk with the look of two frightened children on their first day of school. His worn suit and felt hat and her outdated dress spoke of intermittent usage in Sunday school and funerals over the years.

"Can I help you with anything?" Jim asked, trying to put them at ease.

The man cast him a nervous look, vainly attempting to assume the assertive role of head of the family.

Thinking of his own father and the mother he never knew, Jim's heart went out to them. But even though he felt sorry for these people, he also had a contradictory feeling of satisfaction; the Alliance image was working. It was confirmed in the awe shown by these good people. Rough on them, but necessary, he thought grimly.

"We saw your ad in the paper," said the man in his aged schoolboy voice, "and figured you all would be the folks with the answers."

Jim smiled warmly and said, "The books you're looking for are on that table over there. You can look through them all you like, and if you need help, just holler."

His friendly voice and soft tone, speaking in their vernacular, set them at ease. They relaxed a little; the man nodded his head gratefully and led his woman firmly by the elbow to the table.

Jim was basking in the warmth of the moment when the door

burst open, shattering the mood. His jaw dropped along with his hopes when the blustery figure of Frances McCune came crashing in, looking arrogantly around as if to say, what can I do to upset things here?

He had never acknowledged to Frances that he even knew who she was, and he wasn't going to now. He chose to ignore her and let nature take its course, dealing with the problems if and when they came.

"Where's all them dirty books, and where's all them fancy people that's gonna git rid of 'em?" she asked in her derisive, raucous tone.

The elderly couple at the table glanced at her nervously and then looked at Jim to see how he was going to handle it. He cringed inwardly but said nothing. He calmly began shuffling some papers in front of him. The couple at the table took their cue from this—deciding everything was under control—and went back to their examination of the books.

Frances looked as though she had just slammed a door only to find out it had a hydraulic brake on it. Jim looked up from his papers and casually said, "The textbooks are on that table over there. Anyone who wants to may examine them."

"I don't need to look at the filthy things. I've already found out what's in 'em," said Frances. Jim didn't bother to ask why she was here if she had no interest in the books, because he knew. He went back to his papers, hoping she would just go away. Some of the people who were supposed to be on the protestors' side of the fight did the protest movement more harm than did the "enemy." Some allies, like Frances, were just out to get their kicks; some were out of well-intended ignorance; some out of grinding their own axes, religious or political. Many of them would try to ride the wave of publicity and pseudo popularity into public office, everything from justice of the peace to governor and the Congress of the United States.

Frances was about to launch into a tirade of disruption from a different approach when she was distracted by the door to the office opening. All eyes in the room turned in that direction to see the frail figure of Avis Hill make his entrance, stomping in with an unsuccessful attempt at appearing authoritative, as though he were here to take over. The only semblance of real authority was the impressive mustache above his otherwise weak lip. Even his bodyguard, following close behind, seemed odd. The bodyguard had been his constant companion due partly to the threats made to Alice and to Underwood and the actual acts of violence. Anyone coming closer than four feet to Avis got a fierce, warning look from the bodyguard for his pains.

Avis ignored Jim, as though acknowledging him would be recognizing him as master of ceremonies, which Avis wasn't about to do. Jim was not bothered by this but was rather amused. After glancing at the newcomers, he went back to his papers. June, sitting in a chair at the side of his desk, was passive.

"Folks, if any of you need help, that's what I'm here for," said Avis. "Hello, Frances."

"Avis, we ain't gonna git nothin' done like this. Let's go back to the street and raise some hell. That's the only thing that's gonna git the school board's attention."

Avis looked at her for a moment, obviously trying to decide which way to go, always on the lookout for support for himself—from any quarter. But even Avis couldn't stand Frances.

"Frances, let's give these people a chance before we judge 'em," he said in a grand display of tolerance. (Toward the Alliance, not Frances.)

Avis and Frances's discussion was suddenly buried under the wave of people beginning to pour into the office. The telephone on Jim's desk began ringing. People of all walks of life were calling to get information on everything that the Alliance was about: who was in it, what they planned to do about the books, and why hadn't it been done already. Betty was busy answering the phone in the other office. Jim looked across the room at Betty and could tell by the look on her face that the call was disturbing to her. Jim hung up, went in, and took the phone from her hand. "Hello."

"What are you perverts up to now?" The voice was clearly that of a teenager, possibly high school age. Jim was at a loss for a moment, but then he recovered. This was a new twist for him, but he would soon become accustomed to it.

"I don't have the time for you, friend." He hung up.

June came to the door. "There's somebody who wants you on the other phone." Jim would learn that this was going to be a pattern.

"Hello, this is Jim Farley."

"Mr. Farley, this is Reverend Fred Bailey of Mt. Calvary Baptist Church, and I want to make it clear that our church is against these books one hundred percent. We are praying for you and your success in stopping them. If there's anything we can do, just let me know."

Jim made a mental note of it, thanked him, and hung up. There was someone waiting for him on the other phone. "Mr. Farley, this is Jack Dunlap of Hillside Christian Temple, and I would like to state our position on these books. There is no way our convictions will allow us to accept them." The man went on and on, finally ending in the same way: "We're praying for you."

Jim began to see possibilities in all the churches banding together for strength. If this could be accomplished, they would make a powerful force. He thought of all the causes that different churches supported financially. If each church would lend its financial support as well as its voice, they could whip this thing. He had read the declarations of positions by the many churches in the newspapers, all adamantly against the books. Some differed in their reasons, most objecting to the vulgarity, but a few noticed the true threat of the plan.

Jim spent a good portion of his time explaining to these ministers and Christians that he was not a minister himself; in fact, he was not even a Christian, always adding, "I don't say that proudly. I should be because it's the only thing that makes any sense, but I don't want to give any false impressions or travel under false colors." He still got calls asking for "Reverend" Farley.

To himself and to the people that new him well, he admitted that he was far from being a saint. In fact, he and L. T. Anderson even had some things had in common. One thing he and L. T. did not share, however, was the consensus on these books, the plan, and what they would eventually do to the county, as well as the whole country ... or did they? Maybe they did agree on the result; maybe each desired a different result.

Jim was beginning to understand Dr. Underwood's statement made some time back, when he said to the newspaper reporter, "I feel like I have telephones growing out of my ears." He was beginning to get the same feeling.

On top of the phones, the outer office was wall-to-wall people, all of them talking at the same time—some to each other, some grabbing his ear between trips from one office to the other and one phone and the other.

His head was spinning like a top, all rational, lucid thoughts hopelessly fading. The only bright spot was the fact that Avis and Frances had disappeared. Thank God for small favors.

The day eventually, mercifully, ended. He had made it clear to June and Betty in the beginning that to enhance the image of professionalism and business, the office would hold strict hours just like any business office: open at exactly nine in the morning and closed at exactly six at night. At six, he announced it was closing time and gently but firmly ushered the reluctant visitors out the door. He sat down with a weary sigh. He felt as though they had accomplished exactly nothing.

The next morning, before he was fully awake, there was a dread coming over him. Why get up? To face another futile day at that miserable office that he had had so much hope for? His ears started ringing already at the thought of it. None of the people that he had hoped for—the influential people of the valley—had shown up.

But then he remembered something. Through all the fog of faces and the haze of voices, he remembered the idea that had come to him about the consolidation of the churches. Maybe a side benefit would come out of it.

As he opened the door to the office to begin the second day, his mind was torn between the regret of the previous day and groping for ideas for a more productive use of his time for today. He stopped midway while unlocking the door. Why not call all the businesses and professional people that he knew while he had to be in the office anyway? It may not prove as fruitful as going to see them in person, but he could sure cover a lot more people.

He hurried to his desk and got out his little book with the telephone numbers of people he dealt with on a regular basis. He dialed the first one, Jim White, a general contractor and a good friend. He was out. This may not have been such a good idea after all. Everybody seemed to be out. He wondered who was running the world. He decided to try one more. He dialed Al Marino, who ran the largest plumbing business in the state. He had known Al practically all his life.

The phone rang only twice before he heard a voice saying, "Al Marino's, may I help you?"

"Is Al there, please?"

"Yes, he is. May I say who's calling?"

"Jim Farley."

After a slight pause, Al's voice said, "Jim, how are you?"

"Fine, Al. How about yourself?"

"Oh, just fine. What can I do for you?"

Jim hesitated. Although he had known Al for a long time, he didn't know where Al stood on the issue of these books. This time he decided to be blunt. "Where do you stand on the textbook issue, Al?"

"Oh, I'm against them," Al answered immediately.

"Good," said Jim. "You wanna help get rid of them?"

"Just tell me what I can do, Jim. I've got a fleet of trucks that we can put signs on. I'll contribute whatever money is needed. Just tell me which way to go. You know us Davis Creek boys have always been fighters, and that hasn't changed."

Al's enthusiasm overwhelmed him. "Well, to tell you the truth, Al, I didn't expect this kind of response from you. I don't know at this point what to tell you, except to hang in there. I'm in the process of putting together an organization of business and professional people to fight the books. You wanna join?"

"Name it, you've got it. What do I do?"

"Well, for the time being, Al, just hang loose. I'll get back to you, okay?"

"Sure, Jim. Anytime you're ready, just say the word."

Jim hung up the phone, feeling a little like the times he had gone to J. D.'s and then to Elmer's—from a lull to a hurricane.

CHAPTER 16

The Alliance Grows

Ginny Cracraft was the wife of a surgeon. A former practicing RN herself, Ginny had already been immortalized in the book *The Child Stealers*, about the sex education fight that put Alice Moore on the school board.

She had commented about her husband that she had fallen in love with him as a surgeon before she fell in love with him as a man. She had been his nurse, assisting him on many operations long before they were married.

Good-natured but cryptic, Ginny was a repetitive and dedicated crusader.

Jim had just hesitantly asked her if she would be interested in becoming a member of the Alliance. He had noticed a lack of mention of joining from Ginny, although she had been one of the hardest workers in the office. He attributed it to the fact that she was afraid her name being officially linked with any group involved in the protest would affect her husband's practice because of the stigma poured on by the media.

Ginny looked at the floor, obviously reluctant to answer. He regretted bringing the question up, as he hadn't meant to embarrass her.

He was about to apologize and ask her to forget the whole thing when she spoke.

"I'm not sure you would want me."

Perplexity clouded Jim's countenance. He just stared at her in silence, wondering if she was going to explain—not feeling entitled to ask.

Finally, after an embarrassed silence, she began to speak. "There are some things you should know about me before you consider taking me in as a member."

Jim's curiosity was piqued, to say the least. In the ensuing silence, his mind sifted through far out possibilities. Had she become hooked on drugs in her professional career? He new that people who suffered from chronic pain or had experienced a horrible tragedy in their personal lives had been known to have started out with a mild tranquilizer and gradually progressed to stronger and stronger drugs that were so readily available to them, until they were hooked.

Was that it, or had she, in her foolish youth, become a member of the Communist Party ... premaritally pregnant ... what?

Finally, Ginny began to explain. "A few years back, I was a member of The John Birch Society."

She paused to let this sink in, watching him carefully for reaction. She seemed puzzled when she saw none. She went on. "Bill let us use his office for some of the meetings, and we stored some of the records there. One night, someone broke into the office and ransacked the place, taking most of the records as evidence. The press had a field day, playing it up big."

She paused again, looking even more bewildered by his total lack of reaction.

Finally, when she realized that none was forthcoming, she said, "Now that you know that, you wouldn't want me to add that blemish to the Alliance, would you?"

Jim was incredulous. For a moment, he was even speechless, which was a rare thing for him.

"Ginny, to stop the plan in these books, I would welcome Khrushchev himself, as long as he was on our side." Ginny smiled gratefully, relief spreading across her face.

Jim said excitedly, "I'd be very honored and glad to have you as a member. If that's all there is to it, do you think Bill would want to come in as well?"

"Bill's not a joiner." She smiled. "He'll back me in any cause that I deem worthwhile, but he stays on the sidelines."

Jim was ecstatic over having her as a member. The Alliance could use all the members and their money that it could get, and a prominent surgeon's name couldn't do any thing but good for the image. He was almost laughing about the misunderstanding between the two of them about the reluctance to join. Besides, he thought, The John Birch Society is a bunch of bird-watchers.

Jim's big fear throughout the entire battle, progressively so, as the issue became more and more important to him and his involvement deepened, was that the key people, especially the influential ones, would discover his naivety. On many occasions, ignorance forced him to improvise. The time Elmer brought up the political slate was such a time.

Having been active in political affairs for a number of years, usually on the fringes, Elmer had decided to run for the legislature. He had his hands full, trying to run his campaign for that office, manage the affairs of the Alliance, and oversee his chemical plant—although the statement he made at the meeting in the West Virginia Room, when he introduced Jim as "the man who does all the work that I get the credit for," wasn't too far from the truth.

He'd interrupted his busy schedule to call the Alliance office to ask, "Jim, I've been wondering—do you think we ought to put out a slate for the election?"

"I sure do," answered Jim without hesitation, not having the vaguest notion of what a slate was. It sounded to him like the little thing his teacher used to give him in the first grade to make figures and draw pictures on.

Elmer replaced the previous apprehension in his voice with cautious enthusiasm, explaining how he tentatively thought the slate (whatever that was) should be handled.

Jim had just hung up the phone when Ginny walked into the office. Jim had no qualms about being candid with Ginny. She was the only one with whom he could let his hair down. She accepted and respected him for his qualities, not his credentials.

"Ginny, what's a slate?"

Anybody else would have laughed, assumed a superior air,

and started explaining as though to a child—but not Ginny. She was much too understanding and knew quite well the man who was asking the question out of blameless ignorance.

She looked at him levelly, clearly trying to decide how to explain it to him.

"Well, it's a list of candidates for public office, put out by different groups and organizations. Each slate has the names of the candidates who are preferred by the group for their respective offices. In other words, the candidate listed is endorsed for a particular office by the group putting out the slate."

Now he understood. He thought again of Elmer's question in the light of what Ginny had just told him, and he saw where it could have a tremendous impact on the election.

He didn't suffer the delusion that every man, woman, and child in Kanawha County, or the state, was against these books, but he certainly hadn't met many who weren't.

He had discussed it with so many people in all walks of life, and almost all of them were appalled; they would do almost anything to be rid of them. He knew the county like the back of his hand from traveling all its roads, hollows, and ridges for his business. This would come in handy in the distribution of the slate, as well as cutting up the county into battle zones (or precincts.)

The vision of all the crowded rallies and the much-participated-in parades flashed through his mind. He could see the same crowds going to the poles and the effect they would have on the outcome of the election if they knew which candidate was against the books.

He had no doubt the protestors, known and private, were a powerful voting bloc. Perhaps this was the vehicle they needed for a voice. The message would be clear if all the candidates on the Alliance slate were elected. Especially the ones considered at the bottom of the poles. He liked it very much.

Moreover, this would give the silent majority an opportunity to speak loudly without the fear of betraying their identities or jeopardizing their jobs, businesses, or their positions in the community.

The ringing of the telephone interrupted his thoughts.

"Hello," said Jim as he answered.

"Reverend Farley?" Here it was again.

"No, this is Jim Farley, but I'm not a minister. I'm not even a Christian, I'm afraid. May I help you?" There was a long pause on the other end of the phone, and Jim almost knew what was going through the mind of the person who had called him under the misconception that he was a practicing minister.

"I do have the right Jim Farley, don't I, the one who put together the business people's group?"

"Yes, you do have that Jim Farley."

"Well, Jim ... Do you mind if I call you Jim?"

"I prefer it."

"Well, Jim, this is Henry Thaxton, and I am a minister of God, pastor of the Wolf Pen Baptist Church, but that's not why I'm calling. Whether you're a minister or not, it's obvious that you're on our side in this fight, so that makes you one of us, an unsaved Christian, I suppose you might say. I called you to invite you to a minister's meeting to be held at the Cathedral of Prayer in the Elk Valley. Are you familiar with it?"

"Yes, that's Charley Quigley's Church, correct?"

The surprise in Thaxton's voice was evident. "Why, yes, that's right. The meeting will be held on Wednesday at seven thirty. We'd like you to come if you can."

"I'll be there," said Jim. You bet I'll be there, he thought to himself. This was an excellent opportunity to initiate his plan stemming from his idea about consolidating the churches. Maybe it had begun already.

Jim thought about the Christian schools that were springing up due to the textbook controversy, especially the one at Pocatalico. (The name Pocatalico stems from the Native Americans who once settled there, meaning "plenty of fat doe."

At one time, there was an abundance of deer and elk in both valleys, hence some of the names, such as Elk Valley, Pocatalico, etc. Even the name of Kanawha itself was derived from a Native American chief.)

Six forty-five Wednesday evening found him heading up Elk River in his car. Elk Valley ran at a right angle from the Kanawha Valley, with its river splitting its bottomland like the Kanawha. In fact, it was a Kanawha in miniature, topographically, but it was less populated and had no industry at all, save a few gas wells and a booster station farther upstream. Some stretches of the river were almost a wilderness. Jim glanced at the waters, thinking of the many canoe rides he and his son had taken up and down the Elk in more tranquil times.

Quigley's church was halfway to Mink Shoals. He pulled into the now-familiar parking lot, noting that it was already crowded with cars.

He sat near the back of the church to observe as many people there as possible. He would get a glimpse of a face now and then when new arrivals entered and when someone turned to talk to a neighbor behind him.

So far, he hadn't seen anyone he knew. This didn't surprise him, not being a churchgoer himself, for most of these men were ministers. J. D. wasn't even there.

He was gratified, though, by the apparent quality of the crowd. It was more than the fact that they were all dressed in suits. The mark of intelligence, what little dialogue he could overhear, and the decorum in general gave an atmosphere of a business luncheon on a high level. He glanced at his watch: 7:25. The church was almost full. If his guess was right, in exactly five minutes, the meeting would come to order.

Sure enough, at precisely seven thirty, a slender man wearing glasses walked to the pulpit and introduced himself as Henry Thaxton. "Some of you know me; some of you do not. The introduction is for those who do not."

Jim studied Thaxton closely. He looked and talked like Ichabod Crane from *The Legend of Sleepy Hollow*, or more understandably put, like an old-fashioned English schoolmaster. He formed his words carefully, spoke clearly with impeccable grammar, and kept a stern though pleasant look on his thin face. The long, thin nose completed the illusion.

"I won't take up a lot of our time here tonight explaining to you about the problem we are facing. I think all of us are all too familiar with that. The time will be better spent, I believe, in exploring our options to a solution and making decisions as to paths to follow."

After all the rallies with the three leaders and the street protestors thrashing around blindly, crashing into one another, this approach was as refreshing as a breath of spring to Jim. He sensed this was going to be a very productive evening, at least a beginning.

"Most of you here are pastors of churches. I recognize some of you. I don't know how many of you are convinced of the reality of the threat we are facing and the extent of it. Some of you may have come here tonight to be convinced. In either case, those of you who are convinced at the close of this meeting, I would like to set up schedules for speakers at each of your respective churches. There are people familiar with the contents of these books who will be happy to come to your church and enlighten your congregation. I think this is vital to gain the support that we need.

"I would also like to meet with you individually or collectively to discuss other plans with you, such as announcing our resistance to the books publicly. We can do that with paid ads in the newspapers, listing our specific objections and the position we intend to take. There are many things we, as Christian leaders, can and must do to bring this lunacy of Lucifer to an end. And without violence.

"There are many things that I would like to say to you tonight; there is much ground to cover. But we locals can get together at another time for that. Time is short for us all, but especially so for our guest speaker tonight from California. He is only here for a few days, and in view of that, I would like to introduce him at this time and give you the benefit of his views and comments. Ladies and gentlemen, please welcome Mr. Bob Dornan." The introduction was without fanfare, delivered unemotionally in Thaxton's moderate voice.

Dornan walked to the podium—or in this case, to the pulpit. He turned to face the congregation, palms down on the pulpit. He was a good-looking man in his mid-thirties, with sandy-colored wavy hair combed straight back. The only negative feature about his face, in Jim's opinion, was that his eyes were just slightly closer together than they should have been. He was dressed in a suit this time.

"Ladies and gentlemen, for those of you who were not at the Watt Powell Ballpark for the rally this past Sunday, I would like to give you a brief profile of myself. I won't be quite as generous to myself as Marvin was," he said, "but I will l try to be accurate. I was an actor in television for a period of time, although I never quite gained the stature of John Wayne." He smiled and said, "Actually, I was the copilot on the series *Twelve O'Clock High*, a story about bombers in the Second World War." His smile widened ruefully. "I was the one who always said, 'Bandits at two o'clock, Skipper.' That was about all the lines they allowed me." The audience chuckled.

Dornan became serious. "I saw the moral decline in our city, which mirrored the situation nationally, and ran for the office of mayor of Los Angeles. Although I never seriously expected to win—I only had a budget of two thousand dollars—I was running to make a point. I came in second in a field of thirteen candidates. You get a lot of free media coverage when you're running for that office, and since I was running on a reform ticket, I was satisfied that I got my point across and accomplished my purpose.

"I am now working for an organization called Citizens for Decency through Law. We try to get laws passed that will improve and maintain the moral fiber of our nation. A resident of your fair city is a member of CDL and a good friend of mine, J. D. Landers. He sent a request asking for our help on this situation, so they flew me in.

"I had never been to West Virginia, before and I shared the hillbilly image the rest of the country did. So before I left Los

Angeles, I went out and bought some clothes that I thought would be appropriate. I felt I would have to 'dress down' to the natives here in order to fit in and be accepted."

He paused, looking around at the crowd. "I apologize for that. I was wrong. When I showed up at Watt Powell Ballpark Sunday, dressed like a modern-day Daniel Boone, and saw all the well-dressed people there, I felt like an idiot. Hollywood had better come take a look at modern West Virginia. They might find a few things that would help them improve their own communities.

"But enough of that; when I came in here, I expected to find some bad things in these books. There had to be some fire to cause all this smoke. I expected to find a few four-letter words and some 'new grammar.' But I never expected to find what I did." Dornan paused, taking a deep breath while looking the crowd over.

"Ladies and gentlemen," he began in a moderate but serious voice, "looking beyond the gutter language and four-letter words, I discovered in these books an insidious"—hissing the word insidious—"plan that boggles the mind." His voice began to rise. "If this "Plan" is allowed to be taught to our children, it will undermine everything we, as Americans and of the Judeo-Christian ethic, believe in. This country is on a collision course with disaster."

Jim was impressed with Dornan's impassioned climax to the speech. After the meeting was concluded, he waited for the people who crowded around Dornan to satisfy themselves. When Dornan finally broke free and walked to a water fountain, Jim walked up behind him and waited for Dornan to finish drinking. When he did, he said, "Bob, I'm Jim Farley. We've known each other all our lives; we've just never met before."

Bob turned, took Jim's extended hand, and answered, looking him over curiously, "I know what you mean."

Jim let it drop at that and left.

The more he thought of the slate and its ramifications, the more it appealed to him. He was eager to get started on it, but he didn't have the slightest notion of where to begin. This was one that he was going to have to leave up to Elmer entirely. He waited impatiently each day, or more like each hour, for some word of progress from Elmer. Occasionally, the latter would call him to get his feeling on a particular candidate. Jim would blunder through the best he could, trying not to sound too ignorant, lest Elmer lose confidence in him. He couldn't afford that. If Elmer discovered how much he had kept his head in the sand for so long, and how little he knew about politics, he would likely be looking for a new associate. Fast.

The truth of the matter was that he didn't know one candidate from another. Had it been left up to him, he probably would have just found a list of protestors—genuine protestors, that is (some running for office were trying to use the issue for a bandwagon)—and make the slate up.

The list was almost complete and just about ready for the printer when Elmer called him one day. "Jim, are you busy there at the office?"

"Well, pretty much so, Elmer. What's up?" There was a pause, which, for Elmer, was typical.

"Well, I'd rather not discuss it over the phone. Is there any way you can get free and take a run down here?"

Jim ran over the list of people that he was expecting today, on top of the unexpected ones. Elmer sounded urgent. The people would have to wait.

"Okay, Elmer, I'll be right down."

It was a relief to get out of the office and away from all the people. In the act of unwinding, he tried to make the most of the drive to Nitro. But the urgency in Elmer's voice kept haunting him. He wondered what the problem was.

When he got to Fike Chemical, he didn't bother with the receptionist; he just went on past and up the stairs. She merely glanced up, saw who it was, and went back to her work. She was used to this by now.

He barged into Elmer's office, only taking slight note of another man being there. "What's the problem, Elmer?" he blurted. Elmer broke his conversation off with the man, excused himself, and walked out of the office, motioning Jim to follow. They walked around the corner and down the corridor to the conference room in the back.

When Elmer had gone as far away from his own office and the man as he could go, he stopped and turned. "Jim, we've got a problem."

"What's the matter?"

Elmer hesitated, and then said, "Well, some of the people in my party are objecting to the slate."

"What's their objection?"

"I tried to think like a protestor instead of a politician and honestly seek out only the candidates that were genuinely opposed to these textbooks."

"So?"

"More of them were Democrats than I expected. It surprised me."

Jim, in his naivety, still didn't see the problem. "So?"

"Consternation clouded Elmer's features. "Jim," he said in exasperation, "my people didn't like that. Putting out a slate loaded with Democrats, I can understand their point." Elmer was Republican. "What are we going to do?"

Anger began to mount in Jim. "Elmer, I don't care what their politics are; we're looking for protestors. If we don't put out an honest, accurate slate with people that are really against these books, then we've served no purpose, except to waste a lot of time and money"—so far, it was Jim's money—"and do the voters a great injustice, to say nothing of the people who could have gone on the slate in legitimate protest."

"Well ... I know," said Elmer patronizingly, "but still, I've got to live with these people in my party for a lot of years after this book thing is history."

Jim shook his head perplexedly. "Elmer, it's your baby. You thought of it—I never would have—and you've put it together. I never could have, so it's your decision. I'll leave it up to you. If it were left up to me, it would go as is."

Elmer stared at the floor, frowning. "Ah, I don't know, Jim. Let me think about it."

Jim left and Elmer turned into his office to resume his conversation with the man.

As soon as he walked through the door at the Alliance office, June picked up a newspaper off her desk. She waited until he had shouldered his way through the crowd and made it to her desk, and then she handed it to him. He gave her a curious look before reading the headline: TEACHERS' MARCH TO TAKE PLACE SATURDAY. NEA WILL ATTEND.

He didn't know whether to be shocked, amused, or just disgusted. He handed the paper back to June with a shrug. He decided to reserve feelings and comments until after the protest march.

Saturdays were usually slow anyway, so they didn't open the office that morning. They had decided that both of them would go watch the parade, to make an evaluation of sorts of the enemy's strength. The day was bright and sunny, not a cloud in the sky. Just our lousy luck, thought Jim. They get a day like this; if we were having a march today, we'd have a downpour.

Strange, he thought, when he realized what he was thinking. He was feeling bitterness and hostility toward these people whom he had always had the greatest respect and admiration for ... up until just a few short weeks ago. He wondered how things could change so much so fast. Of course, nothing had changed in that short period except feelings and opinions caused by awareness replacing ignorance. The condition in the educational system had existed for years, getting worse each year.

The air was still crisp and chilly at noon in spite of the sunshine. Maybe it'll snow, he thought, hopefully looking up at the sky. Not a cloud anywhere.

The march was scheduled to begin at one o'clock. They'll probably be right on time, he thought bitterly, thinking of the protestors straggling up to all their rallies and marches somewhere between thirty minutes to an hour late as a rule.

They stood on the corner of the sidewalk in front of the Civic Center, watching the marchers gather. He saw Dr. Underwood a few feet away, standing with three women, apparently teachers. He felt near hatred for the man, as though this whole mess was his fault.

Sure enough, at five minutes to one, a crowd began to form an orderly line in front of the Civic Center, the starting point of the march. Jim noticed a curious thing, remembering his brother-in-law's remark at the school board rally: there was a profuse amount of black faces sprinkled through the crowd.

At precisely one o'clock, to Jim's disgust, the march began, led by Dr. Underwood and the three women he had been standing with. Jim had learned from Karl Priest that the women were NEA representatives.

He and June followed along on the sidewalk, along with some other protestors. The march was orderly and brisk. Naturally, Frances McCune was there to heckle; and heckle she did, along with a few others. Jim wished they wouldn't do that. Couldn't they realize they were only making fools of themselves and adding to the already bad image of the protest?

The march was scheduled to go up Virginia Street, out Capitol Street, and back down Washington Street—and then stop for a question-and-answer session. Dr. Underwood carried a sign, hardly in keeping with his dignified posture, that read EDUCATION IS A JOURNEY, NOT A DESTINATION. Ed Rable, a hometown boy, now in the big time, was the reporter covering the event for CBS.

The billboard made a perfect stage for the NEA representatives. The wooden catwalk built along the bottom of the sign, used by the workers to change the advertisements, was about three feet off the ground, putting the speakers above the crowd and in plain view.

It was interesting that a African American female was the first to speak. She was deft, Jim had to give her that, cleverly weaving the moonshine drinker and the tobacco chewer into the rhetoric without using either phrase. He wondered if she had any other function or if this was her full-time profession, giving talks of this nature around the country when their cause was threatened. Lots of training in her background was in evidence. She also had a figure like Lena Horne and a voice like Pearl Bailey. Perfect casting, thought Jim.

"There is a saying: 'To be successful, you have to look successful,' she said. "I've often wondered if they didn't have that backward. Wouldn't it be more reasonable to say, 'When you're successful, you will show it?' If you have watched the filmed footage of the protestors in their marches as I have, or seen those marches in person as some of you have, and then observed the people in this march today, it should tell you something." She was referring to the shabbily dressed tobacco chewers segment of the protestors always picked up on by the media and holding that up in comparison to the well-groomed participants of today's teachers' parade. Jim thought of all the well-groomed people at the Gabler rally, conveniently passed over by the cameramen, and seethed. He kept his silence.

"The people objecting to these books do not want change. They want to remain primitive and backward. They are afraid of new philosophies. They claim they are 'Christians.' These pathetic pawns have groped blindly for a culprit to blame their malaise on. They have come up with the bogeymen, ranging from the devil to the NEA."

"Mainly, they point their finger at Communism." She looked the crowd over, a sarcastic smile flickering at the corner of her mouth, then finished in a vehement shout, "But if you'll pull back the sheets, you'll see who they're in bed with!"

The best defense is a good offense, thought Jim. She's good, very good. There was loud applause from the teacher-packed crowd. The protestors in the crowd weren't hard to spot. They were the ones not applauding.

"We teachers and educators have to stick together to preserve academic freedom for the good of the students."

Jim doubted she had ever actually taught in a classroom.

There was more applause. Encouraged by the response, her voice rose further in its lusty delivery. "These people don't know what's good for them. We have to tell them what's good for them! After all, we are the professionals." Loud cheering went up, along with clenched fists.

When the cheering had subsided, Bob Dornan got the woman's attention.

"Yes, you have a question?" she asked.

"Yes, I do," answered Bob. "My question is this: Does the 'academic freedom' you're talking about include a teacher using the phrase 'f– you' in front of children in her classroom?"

She fairly shrieked her answer, her face contorted. "That is her right." There was no applause this time. The crowd was noticeably stunned, even the teachers. Bob smiled; he had made his point.

Jim began thinking of the recent report in the newspaper about a young teacher in New York. She had decided to lend realism and emphasis to her sex education course by bringing her boyfriend in and proceeding to perform the sex act, complete with running narration, right in front of the class. This actually happened and can be documented.

CHAPTER 17
Horan's Headquarters

The homemade sign hanging across the front of the dismal, abandoned storehouse read PROTEST HEADQUARTERS FOR UPPER KANAWHA VALLEY. The sign did little to discourage the image of the protest projected so lavishly by the media.

It was Marvin Horan's base of operations, and Jim had business with him that day. He walked through the rickety front door into a small, crowded room. It had a dank odor, smelling of dampness and sweaty bodies. There were wall-to-wall people, and all of them seemed to be talking at once. Jim was trying to get his bearings when Marvin appeared in another doorway, leading to a back room.

"C'mon back, Jim," he said.

Jim had been elbowing his way through the crowd and now made his way easily along the passageway that suddenly opened up between him and Marvin.

They stepped into the back room, where there was an assortment of photocopiers, books, handbills, and other now-familiar paraphernalia of the protestors.

"Jim, you've got to give me something." Marvin looked terribly serious. "I'm running out of ideas. You're going to have to help me ... anything. I'm desperate."

It suddenly registered with Jim what all the voices in the other room had been saying. They had all been trying to tell Marvin of their difficulty persuading their children to stay out of school any longer. Johnny was tired of missing football, Mary was going to lose her position as cheerleader if she didn't go back soon, and Jane was falling behind in band practice.

Jim looked through the small doorway at the people of the same caliber he had seen at the first rally with Marvin:

hardworking and coarse but honest and dedicated. They were scared and battle-weary. If the school boycott crumbled, Marvin was finished, and he knew it. His haggard face showed the toll the battle had exacted from him. The brown eyes, normally piercing, were now desperate, urgently searching Jim's eyes for an answer.

Jim studied him carefully. Marvin was losing control. He was losing control of the protest, but worse, he was losing control of himself. The confidence, the ring of authority, was gone.

"You told me when we started working together on that day at Shoney's that you could pick up the phone and have a whole chemical plant closed down instantly. Let's do it."

Jim chided himself for his over exuberance at Shoney's that day. He had been feeling the desperation that Marvin was showing now, and it had pushed him to exaggeration almost beyond truth. He thought of what Elmer's reaction would be if he blandly called and said, "Elmer, shut her down." Inwardly he cringed, but outwardly he remained calm and confident. This was going to be a real test of diplomacy.

"Marvin, it's not that simple." Marvin's face started to show an "I knew it" expression.

"Now wait a minute," said Jim. "Let me finish. I understand your urgency, but you've got to understand that things like this have to be organized and coordinated. You can't do it like calling a rally together or putting up a picket line on a grocery warehouse. What good would it do for Elmer to close down his plant when Carbide, Westvaco, Libbey Owens, and all the rest are still going full blast? It wouldn't mean a thing to anybody except to Elmer, losing a lot of money." He countered Marvin's look of disdain with, "Now don't sell Elmer short. I have no doubt he would do it and will do it if and when it will be worth it. I know Elmer well enough to know that money is not that important to him. In fact, money is low on his list of priorities. Right now, stopping these books heads that list."

Marvin's expression softened. Encouraged by this, Jim went on. "I'll start working on it, I promise, but it's gonna take time." He felt he could figure something out during that time, some way to get out of actually asking Elmer to do the ridiculous.

"All right. I can accept that," said Marvin. "But how do I keep this thing together in the meantime? What do I do?"

Jim looked at Marvin levelly before answering. "Marvin, I've had more confidence in you than any of the others since this thing started," he said honestly. "You've done a tremendous job. You've overcome the insurmountable and accomplished the impossible many times over. Your problem right now is battle fatigue. You're tired. And no wonder. You've put a lot into this. A flicker of hope showed in Marvin's eyes, but it didn't erase the desperation.

They lapsed into silence, each in his own thoughts. What to do? Where to go from here? Jim's eyes wandered about the room, only half seeing. Through the clouds of his thoughts, a glimmer of something familiar kept trying to penetrate to his conscious awareness. Suddenly, it hit him. A five-gallon gas can was sitting in one corner, partially covered by a rag. He stared at it, reminded of the rally just up the road that night before the first day of school—the first time he had ever seen Marvin. God, it seemed so long ago. So much had happened; so much had changed. He felt a strong yearning for the impossible: if only he could turn the clock back to before that night. Or if he could wake up and find out this was only a run-of-the-mill nightmare. The kind you have at three in the morning after too much lasagna, not the nightmare of reality that he knew it to be.

The can looked exactly like the one that Bob Burdette had loaned him gas in that night.

"I don't care what Marvin says." The shrieking female voice brought both of them out of their reveries, Marvin first, who snapped his eyes toward Jim for response, then followed his gaze across the room to discover that it was the gas can holding his interest. He looked back at Jim and then abruptly came to his feet.

"We'd better find out what's goin' on," he said, starting around the table that separated them.

Jim got up and headed for the other room. Being the closest to the door put him in front of Marvin. He glanced over his shoulder just in time to see Marvin furtively make a quick swoop and cover the can completely with the rag. Jim jerked his attention back toward the crowd in the other room; Marvin hurriedly followed.

"What's the matter here?" Marvin asked in a scolding tone. A hush fell upon the room. Every face turned toward him, and though reactions seemed mixed, the mood was that of children being caught in a rebellious act by a stern father.

The woman who'd made the remark tried to maintain her defiance, but an apologetic tone crept into her voice. "Marvin, you don't know what we're up against. I'm running out of answers to my daughter's questions when she wants to know what we're accomplishing by all this. She wants to go back to school; she's the head majorette, and she worked hard to get there. It was her dream all her childhood, and now she sees it goin' down the drain if she doesn't get back in school."

Jim studied the woman. The wrath of a protective mother knew no master, save her love. It would brave any danger, jump any boundary, and defy any authority if the mother considered her child in grave peril. Fear was forgotten in the lioness rushing to protect her cub.

In this case, physical harm to her daughter was not the woman's concern, but rather she saw it as physiologically damaging, possibly terminal, if current conditions worsened. The death of a promising personality can be a greater loss than a body ceasing to breathe. If the tenant of the soul departs, why maintain the structure that housed it?

In truth, perhaps this was magnified, but in the woman's mind, it was reality. The murmurs in the room rising to a roar made it obvious that the others shared her concern, even though they were less vocal. Fierce loyalty to their own and timidity in themselves forced them into line behind the outspoken woman, now their leader. But they all had reached a common crossroads; the future of their offspring, their growth in a normal lifestyle, was at stake, and the issue of the textbooks was withering in comparison.

Jim marveled at Marvin anew as he watched him study the woman with that lazy gaze of his, which gave the impression that he hadn't even listened. His noncommittal expression gave no clue whatsoever to his thoughts. And yet the brown eyes penetrated like a soft cannon shot. His outward appearance of being completely relaxed made it hard for Jim to convince himself of what he knew was true—that inwardly, Marvin was in turmoil of doubt himself. The man truly was a wonder.

Finally, Marvin spoke, first sweeping the room, then fixing his attention on the woman who had spoken. "I know you've got problems, all of you. And I know it hurts. I know well the anguish you all are suffering. I share it with you, and I carry it in myself because of my own children. But does that excuse any of us from our responsibilities? Does that relieve us from our obligations?" He slowly looked around the room again. "Does our suffering and our love for our children justify us giving in to their immediate needs and desires," he said, coming back to the outspoken woman, "or does it compel us, as loving parents, to apply restraint and discipline, on ourselves and our children, in order to offer guidance? Does the relief from the short-range suffering justify the long-range consequences? We all know they're there." He looked around the room; some of the women looked away, some looked at the floor.

Marvin's timing was always impeccable. "Give me two more weeks. That's all I ask—for two more weeks. We've got some things in the works"—that's the closest Jim had ever heard Marvin come to skirting the untruth—"that will turn this thing around. I promise you."

Marvin paused, looking slowly around the room again. The silence was pregnant.

"One more week," he said, his tone making it sound as if he had decided it wouldn't really require two weeks. Jim hoped the crowd was convinced of the reason for cutting the time, but he knew better. Marvin had sensed the reluctance in the crowd concerning the two weeks and had quickly averted head-on rebellion with the cut. It was the first time Jim had ever seen Marvin give ground on a decision once it was made. It bothered him. He hoped the crowd hadn't noticed.

"All right, Marvin. You're the boss," said the woman who had silently been put in the position of leader. "One more week." She looked at the other women. "If Marvin says to keep my girl out for one more week, she's gonna stay out for one more week." It gave an air of finality when she turned and walked out of the building.

The balance of the crowd milled around a bit and then followed. Marvin looked at Jim in the empty room, his relief evident. Then the fear returned to his eyes.

Jim came bursting through the Alliance door, bracing himself for the onslaught of people who were always in the outer office. The quietness stunned him like an explosion of silence. He looked around disbelievingly at the empty office. The lone figure of June staring at him from behind her desk was the only human form to soften the hardness of the inanimate surroundings.

His mind teeming with a kaleidoscope of thoughts, as usual, he only glanced at her and started for his office.

"Jim."

Something in her voice stopped him cold. There was more wrong here than the fact that the office was mysteriously empty.

"I just had a phone call."

"So?" The phone rang constantly. What was the big deal?

He looked at June more closely. Her face was ashen. She sat silently for a moment.

"The call was from a man."

"June, what in the world is wrong with you? Get it out."

"Jim," she said, her voice unsteady, "the man said that if you don't get out of the protest, he's going to blow up my car."

He stared at her, trying to make sense of it. Finally, he said, "June, you know there's all kinds of nuts out there making crank calls. Look at how many times different schools have been emptied by bomb threats that never materialized."

"Yes, but also look at how many schools have been bombed. Midway Elementary was firebombed this morning."

The gas can in Marvin's headquarters flashed through his

mind, but he pushed it out.

Trying to ease her mind by appearing nonchalant, he shrugged and casually walked into his office. But the haunted look on June's face followed him. Why did they threaten to blow up her car? Why not his? He mulled it over for a moment and then pushed it out of his mind, convincing himself it was only a prank.

He sat down and began shuffling through the papers on his desk: suggestions from well-meaning people and excerpts from books, meetings, and news items. Jim read with interest the editorial in the *Charleston Daily Mail*, which began:

"Levittown, N.Y., isn't like wild, backward uncouth West Virginia. It is much more sophisticated. Nonetheless, Levittown, just like Kanawha County, is up to its knees in controversy over books and their place in the public school curriculum."

Sounds familiar, Jim thought, and he continued reading.

"It began abruptly when the Board of Education ordered the removal of 11 titles from the junior and senior high school libraries as unfit. Among the teachers, there were two responses — first the plaintive cry at the violation of 'academic freedom'; second, the cautious silence at the fear of reprisals."

Jim saw the teachers' reaction as typical, especially the silence for fear of reprisal. This was a culprit that ran a close second to ignorance (both on the part of the general public and the teachers) in effectiveness in squelching the uncovering of the philosophy and plan in these books.

> "And sure enough, there was the president of the teachers' association, draped in red, white and blue, declaring: "Here we are, celebrating the bicentennial of the greatest nation of the history of the world, and they (the board) act as King George III reacted to our Declaration of Independence."
>
> The public school is an institution its students are required to attend. No freedom here. It is also the place they are required to study some subjects and are denied others ... English, say, instead of comic books. No freedom here either. The public schools are a gentle exercise in thought control because the American people want them that way.

"Since the school system itself can develop into a closed system with only those teachers paid by the state, the students become a captive audience to particular points of view approved by the public school. In this context, the Supreme Court has stated: "In our system, state-operated schools may not be enclaves of totalitarianism. School officials do not possess absolute authority over their students. Students in school as well as out of school are persons under our Constitution. They are possessed of fundamental rights, which the state must respect ... In our system, students may not be regarded as closed-circuit recipients of only what the state chooses to communicate."

So much for infinite "academic freedom," thought Jim. Also, the First Amendment of our Bill of Rights begins: "Congress shall make no law respecting an establishment of religion, or prohibiting the free exercise there ..." It's great that the highest court in the land ruled this way. But as Earl Rogers, one of the greatest trial lawyers who ever lived, once said, "Even if the judge says 'strike that remark from the record,' how can you erase it from the jury's mind?"

Could we not, using the liberals' rationale, call this a denial of our constitutional rights, even censorship, when the Bible and even prayer are not allowed in the public schools?

Jim sat back in his chair to reflect on the article. His first reaction was being glad that people in other parts of the country were beginning to be alerted to the danger, even if they didn't realize the depth of it. We protestors all have one thing in common, he thought. We're not advocating censorship, in any way. We are advocating selectivity. Not what can be read or said, but by whom, to whom and where.

Jim's phone rang, and he picked it up. The one in the outer office was the only one listed, and it rang constantly with calls from the public. This one ringing usually meant a call from the "inner circle." This time it was a stranger. "Mr. Farley?"

"Yes," answered Jim.

"My name is Patsy McGraw. Has Ginny ever mentioned me to you?"

"Yes, many times." Ginny had told him all about Patsy. She was the female counterpart of the old-time precinct bosses, which due to their clout, consequently, the outcome of an election.

"I heard through the grapevine that your organization is putting out a slate for the upcoming election."

"Yes, we are."

"I'd like to distribute it for you in Cabin Creek."

He mulled this over for a minute. Cabin Creek was the largest precinct in Kanawha County. There was a saying that "as Cabin Creek goes, so goes the county," and Patsy McGraw controlled Cabin Creek, which was like saying Patsy McGraw controlled the county. But politicians were politicians, and Patsy was a politician. Could she be trusted?

"Patsy, I've heard you're a staunch protestor, but you're also a politician. Before I give you the go-ahead, I'd like one straight answer. Which are you first, a politician or a protestor?"

There was a slight pause, and then Patsy answered, "I'm a protestor first."

The emphasis in her voice removed some of the doubt in his mind, but not all. He was thinking of the pressure exerted on Elmer by his party concerning the slate. But then, what choice did he have?

"All right, Patsy. I'd welcome all the help you can give me."

"When will the slate be ready?"

"In a couple of days."

"I'll keep in touch, and when it's ready, we'll arrange to meet." The line went dead.

Abrupt woman, Patsy McGraw. This was one of the things that made this fight so hairy: dealing with people you didn't know; having to put your trust in them for important things when, for all you knew, they might be the biggest crooks in the world. Or even worse, the enemy. It was a "plainclothes" war; there were no uniforms to designate who was who.

When a situation like this came up, you crossed your fingers, made a decision, and prayed that you were right. For him, however, praying was a figure of speech. He never prayed. It wasn't that he didn't believe in God; he did, very strongly. It was just that he had never made a commitment; therefore, he didn't feel he had the right to ask God for anything.

Jim knew that the battle they were waging here in Kanawha County was not in vain, even if they never got the books out of the schools here. More and more frequently, articles from all over the country appeared in the daily newspapers, magazines, and other publications, attesting to this.

One was about a Baptist minister urging his Brooklyn congregation to "follow the example of the school book protestors in West Virginia." The Reverend Roy Thompson had been the pastor of the Cleveland Baptist Church, 4431 Tiedeman, for sixteen years. He was quoted as saying, "I believe God has chosen a group of people in West Virginia who have lit a flame that's going to burn across the nation."

At the same time, reports came in about headlines screaming, TEXTBOOK CONTROVERSY THREATENS TO BECOME NATIONAL PROTEST, from such places as Keysport, New Jersey; St. Paul, Minnesota; New Hanover, North Carolina; Houston, Texas; and Prince George and Montgomery counties, Maryland.

An article appearing in the *Charleston Gazette* newspaper, dated Tuesday, November 19, 1974, from the *Washington Star-News* reads:

IS NATIONWIDE OUTBURST AHEAD?

> WASHINGTON – From Kanawha County, W. Va.., to Keyport, N.J., St. Paul, Minn., New Hanover, N.C., Houston, Texas, and Prince Georges and Montgomery counties, Md., battles over books in the classroom are surfacing daily in what threatens to become a nationwide outburst.
>
> Parents are protesting what they consider dirty, disruptive, subversive, irreligious, immoral, or racist and sexist books and materials. And frequently school boards are responding by banning the objectionable books, films, slides, charts or other

materials.

"It's extremely serious, and it's spreading across the country. I can only equate it with the McCarthy era," says Judith F. Krug, director of the Intellectual Freedom Office of the American Library Assn., which for the last 23 years has issued a newsletter monitoring censorship in the nation's schools and libraries.

To the protesting parents; however, it is not an irrational, know-nothing wave of book burning but a movement, bordering on a crusade.

"It's not a few dirty books we're objecting to. It's the secular humanist philosophy that pervades the curricula; the concentration on what you think and what you feel, rather than academic skills and the basics," said Mrs. Mary Bowen, information director of Citizens United for Responsible Education in Montgomery County.

Teacher organizations, such as the National Education Assn., which is carrying on its own investigation of the violence-wracked Kanawha County situation, fear that the academic freedom of teachers may be threatened.

The flames were spreading across the country like a prairie fire. One report in particular brought Jim great personal satisfaction. He had come across a national Presbyterian publication, *Presbyterian Survey*, published in Atlanta, Georgia, several weeks ago. It held in derision the "protest of the ignoramus hillbillies against change." In the latest issue of the same publication, put out monthly, they specifically mentioned the Alliance by name, saying, "When people like this start to speak, you'd better listen."

Another article on the same day quoted Mrs. Mary Bowen, information director of Citizens United for Responsible Education in Montgomery County, Maryland, as saying, "It's not a few dirty books we're objecting to. It's the secular humanist philosophy that pervades the curricula."

Well, finally, thought Jim. Finally, somebody is beginning to understand what the real threat is all about. He knew now how frustrated Alice Moore must have felt at the beginning when she was trying to point this out to people and they persisted in focusing on the four-letter words and poor grammar.

The protest was getting recognition and support from many different parts of the country. Following is a five-page pamphlet that Bob Jones University circulated in their January/February 1975 newsletter. It's an investigative report and analysis by Elmer L. Rumminger, the director of Bob Jones University Press.

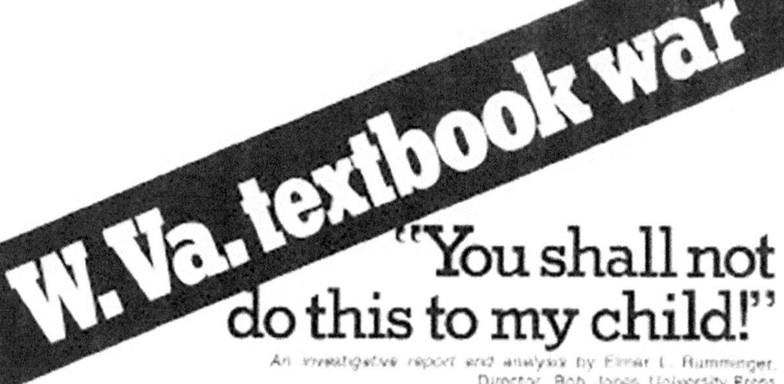
W. Va. textbook war
"You shall not do this to my child!"

An investigative report and analysis by Elmer L. Rumminger, Director, Bob Jones University Press

Demonstrations in the streets. Schools shut down. A massive general strike in the heart of coal country. Gunshots in the night. A dynamite blast. What's it all about?

Textbooks. Bad textbooks in the public schools of Kanawha County, West Virginia.

Robert Dornan

"West Virginians: Stand tall. Be proud. You are fighting a battle for the whole country."

1. Is the child the parents' responsibility, or is he a ward of the state?

2. Do parents have the right to determine what their children shall be taught, or does an elite group of professionals have the power to impose an alien philosophy upon public education?

3. Should an elected school board be responsive to the will of the people, or should it merely "rubber stamp" recommendations of a hired superintendent, his staff, and selected teachers—even when those recommendations are clearly contrary to the best interests of the students and the expressed wishes of the parents?

Alice Moore

Textbook War

they show pictures of a mother scolding her child—in some cases scolding the child unfairly, because she's misunderstood—and the pupil is to look at these pictures and tell his own story about something that happened in his life that relates to those pictures. Not once do these books show a picture of a child who is being hugged or treated affectionately by his mother. Not once do they show a child anything that would reflect a pleasant home life—it's always something unpleasant."

Matthew Kinsolving

"We've had a good school system here in the county and I certainly don't want to destroy it."

"In the junior high book called *Right On* by Harcourt Brace Jovanovich, they have the children keep a record of things that cause trouble in their home—things that cause problems between them and their parents—and they bring these to school for classroom discussion. They also tell them to make a list of things that parents do to interfere in the personal lives of sons and daughters and cause trouble in the home. Can you imagine suggesting to a child that parents interfere in his personal life, and that in fact this is not their role or their responsibility? These books put the child in the position of thinking critically about his home and family."

Mrs. Moore attaches some danger to the way in which the modern educational technique of "role-playing" is employed. "They even have the children in the classroom act out having a disagreement with their parents and arguing with their parents in order to change the parents' mind about something like dress length or hair style. Rather than teaching the children any respect for parents, it's always conflict.

"Generation gaps are created artificially—and obviously they are being deliberately created by many public schools and by the publishers of some of these textbooks. I think it's to bring the child's loyalty to the school community and away from the home. Some people think that the nation is in a bad way because parents are training their children improperly and if they could get these children into the school atmosphere and could bring them up according to some bureaucrat's idea of what is the right way to rear up a child, they could create some kind of a Utopian society."

Elmer Fike

"As long as we've got schools in this country, we're going to have to realize that there are people who are trying to destroy our basic concepts. We've got to be on guard from now on."

The anti-Christian philosophy of most of the texts is of grave concern. "The books project the philosophy that Christianity is a mental illness and if we could remove guilt from the world, we would remove all mental illness. They claim to present reality to these children, but what they call reality is nothing but ugly and depressing hopelessness. I don't think most teachers want to do that, and I cannot understand why some teachers would recommend adopting books that portray life in this manner."

Mrs. Moore told me that she couldn't believe the kind of material she saw in the textbooks. "I brought it to the attention of the other board members, and the amazing thing is that every other board member (except lame-duck president Albert Anson, who later resigned) reacted with shock and with such remarks as 'profane' and 'That's terrible. I agree with you, Alice.' But about two weeks later, their attitudes began to change."

Mrs. Moore did not want to make a public issue of the textbook matter "because I knew that any time one objects to textbooks, there is always the cry of book burning, and someone tries to make a lot of trouble out of it. I really thought there had been some kind of mistake, and I had hoped we could quietly correct the error without making a big scene. But when I saw that they were going to go ahead and purchase the books, then that's when I took the books to the public. I spoke at about five or six public meetings to groups of parents. I said, 'Here are the textbooks your children are going to be reading.' I read sections from the books, and from there it grew on its own—the people just took over."

Mrs. Moore cannot understand the change in the position of Matthew Kinsolving, long-time board member who was named president following the Anson resignation. "The things that seemed to upset him most were references to disrespectful treatment of the flag, some of the references which were obviously teaching racial hatred, and a story on draft-card burning."

BJU Faculty Supports Protestors

More than 500 members of the faculty and staff at Bob Jones University unanimously passed the following resolution on Wednesday, November 20: "Because Bob Jones University is loyal to the freedoms guaranteed by our American Constitution and believes in the right of parents to protect the minds, emotions, and moral values of their children, we strongly support those parents of Charleston, W. Va., who, because of their godly convictions, are striving to maintain public schools which respect and teach morality and patriotism.

"We deplore the action of school officials in forcing upon the people material which is, without question, anti-American, anti-God, immoral, detrimental to the home, and in many cases devoid of any educational value.

"Our prayers are with these dedicated Americans in their opposition to those required texts which undermine the moral and patriotic values being taught in their homes."

Matthew Kinsolving is, in the classic tradition, the tragic character of our drama. A tortured man, apparently befuddled on moral issues, he is being destroyed by his weakness. A Boy Scout leader, churchman (United Methodist), civil servant (postmaster at Belle), he has tried to play the role of peacemaker, but has failed pitifully—because he is willing to sacrifice principle (and the children of Kanawha County?) on the altar of expediency in a vain quest for peace at any price.

He says with quavering voice, "I feel that the text material we are now getting is not the best, much because of pressure from the National Council of Teachers of English who have, we'll say, an extra liberal view. This has been transmitted to the publishers, and in their rush to be in accord with the National Council of Teachers of English, they haven't got the best. There is much to be desired in the material they're producing in their hasty approach to be multi-ethnic."

In a pathetic way, Kinsolving bemoans the permissiveness of the age and of the textbooks. He says he wanted to hold off purchasing the books for a year, but now supports their use. "There are," he says, "issues of academic freedom." Kinsolving speaks vaguely of maintaining "school authority" (parental authority, anyone?) and a fear of overthrowing the school system. Although apprehensive of "mob violence," he quails before pressure from "professional educators."

The sad fact is that this one man might have turned the textbook battle, had he been able to muster the courage to embarrass the teachers on the textbook selection committee by voting against their recommendations. He yearns for respect, but has earned contempt.

Mrs. Moore's analysis of the Kinsolving "cop-out" is refreshing in its directness. "Kinsolving sees that

Ezra Graley

James Lewis

faith

teachers with pro-textbook leanings. They were supposedly there to provide information of a technical nature as needed, and were, in their own words 'to speak only when spoken to.' As it turned out, they consistently engaged in gallery tactics, ridiculing and embarrassing the anti-textbook members of the committee. They injected themselves into the proceedings and the chairman (board-member-elect F. Douglas Sharp) would not restrain them. Yet, when one of our people became somewhat outspoken, he was immediately restrained by the chairman."

Freeman says that at the first two meetings "the committee was given 4½ hours of indoctrination in progressive education. This is a humanistic philosophy that advocates the supremacy and professional infallibility of the professional educator. It provides for no input by the parents or the community. The only thing the parents are supposed to furnish is the children."

Early in the proceedings, Freeman called for balance. "In all fairness, I felt that there should at least be six anti-textbook teachers on the 12-member advisory panel. This was hooted down. They were so frightened of some of our proposals that they wouldn't even discuss them. We suggested that we learn the community feeling by polling the parents. That was hooted down—no discussion."

By the fourth meeting the pressure on the six conservative members of the review committee had become so intense that some became physically ill. On October 8, the six—along with one alternate member—announced to a press conference that they would withdraw from the committee in order to write a minority report and thus fulfill the original charge of the school board "to review the books and make a report on them." They examined 254 books. An additional 71 books were not given to the committee for consideration.

The "minority report" was detailed and specific about the objectionable matter, but Freeman says the basic conflict goes even deeper. "The textbook problem is a surface issue emanating from the basic ideological differences between some professional educators and The People. It's a battle between their humanistic philosophy and the historic American approach to education.

"This is a matter that the people in our community feel so strongly about that we feel we have been given a choice between our God and our Board of Education. We must oppose this material in every way that we can. We have come to the place where we must say: Whatever decision you have made as a board of education—you shall not do this to my child."

Larry Freeman

"We must guarantee a legislative climate where private education can survive and flourish. This is essential to the survival of our society as a free society."

Reprints of this article are available at the following rates:

1 to 99 copies — 10 cents each
100 or more — 7 cents each

Order from: **Bob Jones University Press** Greenville, South Carolina 29614

Please add 10 percent for postage and handling; minimum charge, 30 cents. South Carolina residents add 4 percent sales tax. Dealer discounts available.

Alice Moore notes that the pro-textbook forces were loudly in favor of majority rule, "until it became apparent that the overwhelming majority of the common people opposed the textbooks." Now Mrs. Moore feels the only thing that can reach the liberal establishment is economic pressure. She sees the formation of strong, new private schools as part of this pressure.

Robert Dornan, national spokesman for Citizens for Decency through Law, spent the better part of six weeks in West Virginia. Dornan brings it to a personal level for parents nationwide: "Don't look at PTA night as just a time to go pick up a report card. Make the PTA evening a meaningful experience (to use a current, in-vogue word). Lean on the teachers, and let them know that you are not just furnishing children for their schools. 'Trust us,' they say. 'Trust us (s-s-s),' (like a snake). 'We are the professionals.' Well, parents are professionals, too. Parents love their children, and they must be involved with what textbooks, approaches, and goals are adopted for their children's education. The educators have failed in lots of areas—like phonics and the new math—and here in West Virginia they are wrong on English, too."

Larry Freeman agrees that "public educators must realize they are public servants and must be responsible to the taxpayers." He is also deeply concerned about the future of private schools: "Private education is being 'hunted' like a hunted animal. Too many of those modern-day educators are dedicated to a humanistic philosophy and a 'professional elite' approach, and they are determined to stifle or destroy private education—especially Christian education. They don't want private education as an alternative to their Pavlovian conditioning and programming of children. They recognize that private education thwarts their objectives."

The first hint of real progress came at the Kanawha County School Board meeting of November 21, 1974, when at the insistence of Mrs. Moore the board voted to adopt the following guidelines in future selection of textbooks:

1. Textbooks must respect the privacy of students' homes and may not ask personal questions about inner feelings or behavior of students or of their parents.

2. Textbooks must not contain profanity.

3. Textbooks must not ridicule the values and practices of any ethnic, religious, or racial group.

4. Textbooks must not encourage or teach racial hatred.

5. Textbooks must not encourage sedition or revolution against the United States Government or teach that an alien form of government is superior.

6. Textbooks used in the study of the English language must teach that traditional rules of grammar are a worthwhile subject for academic pursuit and are essential for effective communication.

7. Textbooks must not defame the nation's historical personalities or misrepresent the ideals and causes for which they struggled and sacrificed.

Lest the reader think the end of the battle is at hand, let me sound a word of warning. There may be a few token concessions in attempts to cool the protests. The liberal forces may even concede the West Virginia skirmish. If they do, watch for redoubled efforts to smear the good people of the Mountain State as "ignorant" and to discredit their leaders as "extremists." The whole idea is to discourage concerned Americans in other states from taking action for fear of ridicule and slander. This is not a time for fear.

It is the time for courage. American parents are engaged in an historic struggle. Robert Dornan likes to quote Herman Kahn: "A religious war is going on in the country, a war of values. The middle class is having its values taken from it by a thin slice of the upper-middle class [upper-middle class by intellectual pride, rather than by income]. That thin slice has an overriding influence in the media, in the schools, and in our court system."

Textbooks are just one part of the battle. This is a war that America cannot afford to lose. □

An unusual sound penetrated Jim's thought. He stopped reading to pinpoint what it was. He listened and heard it again: the sound of children playing. Odd, he'd never realized until now that even though children were what this whole thing was about, none of them ever came to the office. This was the first time he had heard children's voices bouncing off the walls. It was as refreshing as a breath of spring.

Bob Dornan came bouncing through the door, followed by Ginny's twins, who were pretending to try to catch him. Bob ran around the desk and stood behind Jim, grabbing him by the shoulders. "Jim will protect me," he said to the twins. Jim smiled, and the twins pretended to look serious, as if they were trying to decide how to handle this development. They studied the situation for a moment, huddled together to whisper back and forth into each other's ear, then smiled and broke into a run, one around each end of the desk, pinning Bob between them.

Bob threw his hands up and said, "You caught me. I give up. Jim, you weren't much help." Jim laughed.

It was a welcome relief from the seriousness of their situation and the usual somber atmosphere that constantly hung over the office. He was tempted to join in and keep it going awhile to get himself out of the state of depression he had been in ever since he had left Marvin's headquarters. But he had to get something worked out to get Marvin moving again or the man was going to topple from leadership, whether from lack of direction, disgust, or just plain exhaustion. And all three were understandable.

"Bob, I need to talk to you," Jim said.

Bob was wrestling with the twins, pretending to be attempting an escape. With his arms still locked around them, he looked at Jim with seriousness. "Okay, kids, you win. Game's over."

"Aw," the twins complained.

"Game's over, kids," Bob said sternly. "Go out in the other office with your mother." Bob had moved out of J. D.'s motel and was now a guest of Dr. and Ginny Cracraft. It was much more convenient to the office and downtown, and as Bob put it, "more like home." J. D.'s motel in Hurricane was twenty-five miles downriver.

When the twins were gone, Bob looked at Jim with a serious expression. "What's up, Jim?"

Jim took a deep breath and told him about his visit to Marvin's headquarters. "If we don't help Marvin come up with something, he's gonna fall, or worse, just plain quit. And if either happens, the protest is going to collapse. Marvin is the heart of the street protestors, and they in turn are the heart of the protest itself."

Bob nodded. "You're right about that." He became thoughtful. He looked out the window at the heavy traffic on the four-lane Kanawha Boulevard. He thought of the image of West Virginia he'd carried with him on the plane ride here from his home in California. What he expected to find were log cabins, homemade rafts floating supplies down the Kanawha River, and practically all the natives wearing overalls. He was struck by the similarity between the boulevard he was looking at now and Hollywood Boulevard in his hometown of Los Angeles. In fact, he was amazed at the similarity of the two cities themselves, except for the size. Charleston was nothing at all like what he had expected it to be.

He looked at Jim, who was also in deep thought. "Got anything yet?" he asked.

"No," answered Jim. "Have you?"

"No." They both went back to their thinking.

"You say the people are getting tired of the school boycott?"

"I'm afraid so, Bob. It's obvious not only from what I heard at Marvin's headquarters but also from the school attendance, which is going up every day."

They lapsed back into silence.

"How about your plan to close down the whole valley? The chemical plants you said you had control over, plus putting picket lines on other things, like you told me about the Kroger warehouse incident. Plus, we could close the mines down again, the construction jobs as before. Everything, like you said."

Jim winced slightly, and his face reddened. "Well, Bob, I might as well confess. I was a little guilty of Avis's tactics on that one. I delivered more enthusiasm than I felt. Oh, don't get me wrong. It could work ... and might yet. But it's gonna take time and an awful lot of planning and support. Especially support. We need assistance from inside the plants, like Elmer, plus we'll need an awful lot of manpower for the synchronized picket lines. To get all that support, we need something to fire people up to fever pitch again. Like Marvin, they're getting tired, and some of them are giving up."

Bob looked around the room, thinking. His eyes fell on a calendar hanging on the wall. He looked out the window at the boulevard, noting the stars and stripes flapping in the breeze atop one of the buildings. His eyes snapped back to the calendar. "What's today?" he asked abruptly.

The question startled Jim; he thought a minute and then said, "Thursday. Why?"

"No, I mean the day of the month." They both looked at the calendar. It was the twenty-fifth day of October.

"I've got it!" Bob shouted.

Jim looked at him puzzled, waiting. Bob glanced at the metal bracelet on his left wrist. It was known as a POW bracelet. It symbolized the fact that people in America had not forgotten the prisoners of war still locked in concentration camps in Vietnam. Bob had started the movement in sympathy with the prisoners and their families. It had grown into a national-scale activity, with people all over the country wearing the bracelets.

The one on Bob's wrist was the original. The very first one made.

Jim was still looking at him expectantly. "Veteran's Day," Bob said simply.

"What?" asked Jim.

"Veteran's Day. Don't you get it?" Jim shrugged without speaking. Bob got enthused. "One of the big issues of this controversy is patriotism, right?"

"Right."

"Every city has a Veteran's Day parade; I assume Charleston is no different."

"We have a parade. So? What does this have to do with our problems?"

"Everything. We'll have a parade on Veteran's Day," said Bob, extending his arms in a gesture of grandness, smiling broadly.

"The people will see through it," Jim said skeptically.

"What's to see through? I'm a veteran, you're a veteran, and how many of the others are? Probably most of them. We do only one small thing that might be construed as underhanded."

"What's that?"

"How far in advance do they usually make the announcement of the parade?"

"I don't know. I never was that interested in it to notice."

"Okay, we'll find out. That shouldn't be too hard. Then the one sneaky thing we'll do is to preempt them with our own announcement of 'our' parade. Then we'll become a part of their parade, or vice versa. With you, me, and Marvin at the head of all those people, complete with uniformed veterans, some of them carrying guns for effect, it will have a tremendous impact."

Bob was getting excited. "Jim, I think we've got it. How do you feel about Marvin, Avis, and Graley?"

"What do you mean?"

"I mean, how do you rate their qualifications ... and how do you compare one to the other?"

He thought this over and then said, "Marvin's the most intelligent of the three and has the most charisma. He's definitely the leader. Ezra is the kind-hearted one of the bunch. He has a heart as big as all outdoors. He's sincere and dedicated, and he has a likable personality, but he's short on logistics. Avis, in person, up close, is very disappointing. Maybe it's the same handicap that Sammy Davis Jr. has, his small size. But you put Avis up on a stage or platform with a microphone in his hand and he's impressive. He becomes a tiger."

"Avis strikes me as the one with the most street savvy."

Jim said, "Yeah, I guess you could say that."

"Do you think Avis and Graley should help lead the parade?"

He smiled and said, "Why don't we label this a rehearsal for the big parade? We'll bill it as representing the upper half of the valley only. That way, Marvin can head it up alone—along with you, of course."

"What about you?"

"No, thanks," Jim smiled. "I'm not a public figure. You two are the ones who like the limelight. I'll stay and take care of the office. I can watch it from here."

"Let's go tell Marvin." Bob was visibly wound up about this. On the way to Campbell's Creek and Marvin's headquarters, Bob noticed a pack of gum on the dash of Jim's car. Reaching up and helping himself, he said, "I see you like to chew gum too."

"Yeah, it helps to relieve tension."

"It does, doesn't it?" answered Bob, stuffing a stick in his mouth.

"You'll have to overlook the mess in this car, Bob. It's my rolling office. I spend more time in it, in my business, than I do at home."

Bob glanced around and smiled. "Don't worry about it. You ought to see mine." With that, they lapsed into silence, and Jim knew that Bob, too, was preparing himself for the meeting with Marvin.

Out of the corner of his eye, Jim studied Bob Dornan, the man whose measure of perceptivity was exemplified in the khaki bush hunter's outfit he was wearing once more. Remembering Bob's apologetic explanation at the ministers' meeting of "dressing down" to the people to conform to the nationally accepted image of hillbillies, Jim knew he now understood the analogous nature of West Virginia and her people.

Bob's movie actor instincts had directed him to adjust to a

role befitting the level of the people he was dealing with, so he had arrived at the Gabler rally dressed in his khaki bush hunter's outfit in the certainty he would blend right in with the bib overalls and gingham dresses. In his mind, there was no doubt about the dress code.

Try to imagine his shock and embarrassment when he stepped to the speaker's podium dressed in this fashion—only to face a multitude of people wearing Saks Fifth Avenue business suits and button-down collars.

Donna McCallister had undergone a similar experience, unknown to Bob or Jim. When she first moved into the tiny community of Pinch (next door to Quick, believe it or not), the clannish natives did not accept her as one of them for more than a year. Although the neighborhood was definitely middle class, with modern brick one-story homes, this one hillbilly characteristic persisted.

She became acquainted with all her neighbors easily enough, even becoming friends with one of them, Jane Carson. On the afternoon of the first New Year's Eve they lived in Pinch, Jane came to Donna's house to invite her over that evening for a "small" celebration for the occasion.

Donna was overjoyed. She had been lonely since she had moved here, feeling like an outsider. She hungered for close female companionship. She felt this invitation was an act of acceptance.

Trying to hide her excitement, she asked, "What should I wear?"

Jane looked the sophisticated girl from Chicago over, dressed in her jeans and shirt, complete with sandals. "Oh, what you're wearing will do just fine," she said casually.

After Jane had gone, Donna could hardly contain herself. She had been accepted!

How strange, she thought, looking out her window at the peaceful alcove of her backyard, with the hills going up from it so steeply that you could not see the sky. None of the elaborate balls and black-tie affairs she had attended in Chicago had ever excited her nearly as much as the thought of this small, informal gathering here in the hills. The afternoon dragged. In her eagerness, she felt evening would never come.

When it finally did, she showered and put on a pantsuit—but not her best one. Although she hadn't taken Jane literally about coming as she was dressed, she didn't want to overdress either. Neil slipped into slacks and a sweater and got out the red and black plaid woodsman jacket he had bought when they first moved here. It would keep out the bite of the December wind while they made the short walk to Jane's house.

They were lighthearted and happy as they made their way down the snow-covered street, heading to the friendly warmth of the lights at their destination.

Donna gaily rang the doorbell. Jane, dressed in an elegant black full-length evening gown, opened the door wide. She stood there, silhouetted against a backdrop of a roomful of tuxedos and evening gowns, smiling coolly at the shocked expression of "the sophisticated girl from Chicago."

Hillbillies have a cryptic way of putting one in one's place.

At the other end of the valley, Jim returned to the present when they arrived at Marvin's headquarters. The dreariness of the moment was made complete by the bleakness of the fading light of evening, the steady drizzle of cold rain that had begun, and the barren storefront, with a once-used sign banging against it in the wind. It was depressing. Not a good backdrop for cheering a man up and firing his ambition.

They watched curiously as a shabbily dressed woman got out of a rattletrap car, opened the trunk, and got out an assortment of ragged bags and cardboard boxes. She began carrying them into the dismal building. Bob looked at Jim questioningly.

"Groceries for the miners that are staying off their jobs protesting these books," Jim said simply. "Different people are going around collecting them, and then they bring them here for Marvin to hand out."

Bob gave him an incredulous look of disdain, grimaced, and shook his head. They got out and went inside.

The front room was even more crowded this time. It was so noisy that their entrance wasn't noticed for a moment. Then a sudden hush fell over the room when the people realized the celebrity from California was in their midst. Bob smiled. Marvin came out of the back room to see why the roar of the voices had suddenly stopped. The grimness of his face was softened just slightly by a weak smile when he saw Bob, followed by Jim. However, the usual sparkle was missing from his haunted eyes.

Clearly recognizing this in an instant appraisal, Bob made a fast decision and moved on it. "Ladies and gentlemen," he said, extending his arm outward toward Marvin, like an emcee announcing the star of a show, "there is a natural leader if I ever saw one."

The crowd was pleased. Marvin just appeared noncommittal.

Bob went on. "As all of you probably know by now, I've spent many years fighting, in my own way, a similar fight to what you people are waging here. I've met many people in doing that. I've observed senators and congressmen battling out an issue on the House floor ..."

Jim never suspected at that point that Bob himself would become a congressman in a few years.

"I've watched lobbyists working their charms, top-flight lawyers eloquently weaving their spells, and many others that I could tell you about." He paused.

You're doing a little spellbinding of your own, Bob, thought Jim.

"But this man," he continued, indicating Marvin, "commands my respect as a leader more than any I have ever met." Marvin's expression did not change.

The crowd was impressed; Jim was puzzled. In view of Bob's remark on the way up here, cautioning him about inflating Marvin's ego, he was stunned at what he was hearing now. Apparently, he had convinced Bob of Marvin's regal humility and his awareness of his own capabilities.

"Jim brought me up here today at Marvin's request. He said

that he had some plans for some big doings that he wanted to discuss. So if you folks will excuse us, I'm sure Marvin will be ready to make the announcement to all of you shortly."

Marvin took his cue and led the way to the back room, Bob deliberately following. Jim brought up the rear.

When they were behind closed doors, Marvin turned and said, "Bob, I sure appreciate that buildup. But I hope you knew what you were doing announcing my 'big plan.' I think you'd better tell me about that part because I don't know of any such plan."

Bob smiled to set Marvin at ease. "It's an idea that came to me this afternoon when Jim and I were talking, Marvin. We kind of worked out the preliminaries between us. See what you think and we can take it from there." He brought Marvin up to date on what he and Jim had discussed and then asked, "Well, what do you think?"

Life was beginning to stir in Marvin's eyes. He said, "To tell you the truth, Bob, I had already thought of doing that, but I was afraid to bring it up for fear of Avis and Graley thinking I was trying to take over or steal the show. I love it." Marvin was out of his chair now, excitedly pacing, his eyes beginning to sparkle. "When can we get started on it?"

Bob smiled. "Thought we already had, Marvin. Why don't you give the folks in the next room a few more minutes to make it look like we're really deliberating this thing and then go out and make the announcement?" Marvin's pacing quickened.

When the three of them came out, Marvin led the way. The crowd turned to face them in a hushed expectancy. Marvin had his old air of exuberance back, smiling broadly once more. He waited for the right moment and then said, "Folks, I told you a few days ago that we had some plans in the works, ones that would turn this thing around. Well, I think it's time for all of you to know what I was talking about." He paused to let their curiosity build before continuing. "We have just decided that on Veteran's Day, which is not too far off ..." He paused again, looking the crowd over, smiling, letting the tension build. They were starting to fidget nervously. "On Veteran's Day, we are going to show this valley just how many people are against these textbooks."

"How are we gonna do that, Marvin?" asked the outspoken woman who had become the unofficial leader of the mothers here.

"By having a march from the civic center to the capitol ... with more people than you can imagine." Marvin's confidence and excitement were becoming contagious; the crowd was stirring.

"How do you know you can get that many people, Marvin?" asked a skeptic weakly.

Before Marvin could answer, the leader spoke up. "If Marvin says he can do it, he can do it. He ain't failed us yet." Marvin smiled appreciatively at the woman, and she continued. "I don't know about the rest of you, but I'm with him all the way." She turned and said, "Marvin, just tell us what you want us to do." The rest of the people joined in, loudly displaying their support.

Bob Dornan, who towered over the crowd, his head almost touching the low ceiling, said. "I'm gratified to see the dedication you have to your leader and the cause." Bob had an unwitting knack for upstaging people, but Marvin wasn't a man easily upstaged. It wasn't that he fought it. Actually, he did nothing to combat it. It was just that his regal humility and relaxed yet poised stance made it impossible. He retained the usual noncommittal gaze.

Jim knew Bob was trying to make certain that Marvin was implanted firmly as the leader and make sure that everyone there was aware of it. It was clear that it soon became obvious to him, as it had to Jim, that he was wasting his time. The crowd made it clear they would follow Marvin to the limit. He changed tack, directing his attention toward the crowd.

"This has been a whole new experience for me, and I thank God for directing me to come to West Virginia. You people of this state..." He paused, smiled, and said good-naturedly, "You 'hillbillies' are the most marvelous people I have ever met—the salt of the earth. I believe God knew what he was doing when he chose you to lead this fight. As President Kennedy said on his visit here, the year of your centennial, 'The sun may not always shine in West Virginia, but her people always do.'"

The crowd chuckled gratefully, some glancing through the dirty windows at the steady downpour.

"Make no mistake, people. You're not just fighting a battle for your community or Kanawha County, or even the state of West Virginia. You're fighting a war for the whole country. What you're doing here ..." Bob paused as two men, roughly dressed and one with a beard, came blustering through the door. Rainwater spilled from the brims of their hats. They stopped, blinking as though startled to see all the people; or was it because of seeing Bob? They glanced at Marvin, who furtively jerked his head toward the back room. They went back, closed the door, and didn't reappear.

Bob watched as the two men disappeared, glanced at Marvin, and then picked up where he had left off. "What you're doing here," he said, pulling his eyes from the closing door back to the crowd, "will alert this great nation to what the root of the problem is in our country. If you can keep the lid on the kettle long enough, and keep the fires burning, this whole thing is going to explode from coast to coast. You are a chosen people. It's up to you what you do with it."

The electricity in the room was tremendous. Marvin's body seemed like the receptacle and his eyes the outlet for that current. His eyes sparkled with it. Jim knew at that moment that these people would follow Marvin to their deaths, stopping at nothing to win this battle for God that Bob had so eloquently laid out before them.

CHAPTER 18
Battleground

Jim had just dropped Bob off at Ginny's. He hoped making the plans for the upcoming march would keep Marvin occupied for a while. He walked into the office, his thoughts still in Campbell's Creek. He didn't even notice that, except for June, the office was empty.

"Jim, he called again."

"Who?"

"That man." His thoughts focused on her and the present. "He said this was the last time he was going to warn you. If you don't get out of the protest immediately, he's going to blow up my car."

Jim was in no mood for it.

"If he calls back, tell him I'll provide the match," he said flippantly over his shoulder as he disappeared through the door to his office. (The man did call back a third time, and June gave him Jim's message). He did not take the threat seriously, and he dismissed it from his mind. He sat down at his desk and went to work.

There were no other cars on the road as Larry Stevens, accompanied by Melvin Dickinson, drove toward Delbert Rose's home to pick him up. It was 2:45 AM and pitch dark. The date was October 22, 1974.

Delbert was waiting out front for them when they pulled in. He got in the car without a word passing between them. They headed for Campbell's Creek.

"Where is it?" Rose finally asked when they had been driving for several minutes.

"In the trunk," answered Stevens. They drove on the deserted roads in silence. No lights showed in any of the houses as they passed, going their unobtrusive way as quietly as possible.

Finally, Rose said, "There won't be anybody around at this time of night, will there?"

"You afraid of gettin' caught?"

"I'm not crazy about the thought, but that wasn't what I meant. I sure don't want to hurt anybody."

"Neither do I," said Stevens. "Naw, there won't be anybody around."

Melvin Dickinson sat in the backseat, making no comment. They passed Midway Elementary School, and the tension in the car was electric. They drove on. There were no cars or evidence of life. About a mile above the school, they came to a fork in the road, stopped, and turned around. When they got near the school, Stevens turned off the lights and the engine. The car coasted to a stop just a few yards from the school. All three got out of the car.

Stevens went to the rear of the car and opened the trunk. He reached in, got an object, and closed the trunk lid. He handed the object to Rose. Rose stood there for a moment while Stevens walked down the road and Dickinson walked up the road, all according to a prearranged plan. Stevens and Dickinson were to make certain no innocent passersby would be caught in what was about to take place.

When Rose was satisfied that they had each gone far enough, he walked toward the school building a short distance away. Both the other men were anxiously watching in his direction.

They saw a match flare briefly, then the spewing of sparks. That signaled that the fuse had been lit. The slight tinkle of glass breaking was heard, and then the sparkling of the fuse disappeared. That meant the bomb was inside the school and they had exactly five minutes to get to the car and get out of there. They didn't waste a single second. All three hit the car at a dead run at about the same time. The doors had been left open on purpose, so it was just a matter of firing the finely tuned engine; it started on the first turn. The wheels were turning before the doors were closed, starting with the lights off so as not to arouse anyone too soon. Two minutes had passed, and their speed had picked up to forty-five miles per hour.

"You think it'll do any good?" asked Rose to break the tension.

"Can't hurt," answered Stevens as he pressed the accelerator harder. The speedometer was climbing to sixty.

"Not unless we get caug ..." The rest of Rose's remark was drowned out by the thunder of the dynamite bomb going off. With caution of no further use, Stevens pressed the gas pedal to the floor. The car roared out of the mouth of Campbell's Creek, careened left, and headed upriver, away from Charleston. That's where the police would be coming from.

The crickets were chirping peacefully in the predawn hours of the community of Campbell's Creek. The young frogs, called "rick racks" by native West Virginians (this nickname being earned by the sound they make: rick rack), could be heard from the creek, running the full length of the hollow, about twenty-seven miles. The name of the creek was applied to any small town, village, or row of houses in the entire area, so if you lived anywhere in the twenty-seven-mile range, you lived "in Campbell's Creek."

While the frogs and crickets were heralding that calm night of '74, it suddenly sounded as if Armageddon had come instead. The quiet of the wee hours was shattered by a blast that deafened the people close by and brought sleepers tearing out of their beds as far as three miles away, both up and down the hollow. It had been a tense time for all of Kanawha County ever since Alice Moore had made the initial announcement about the books several months before, and the natives slept light these days, some with guns by their beds.

The blast was over as quickly as it had come, the echo still rumbling up and down the hollow.

"My God, what was that?" exclaimed Winfield Pickens, scrambling from his bed, just two doors up from the Point Lick schoolhouse. He didn't take time to put his shirt and shoes on—just his pants, pulling them up as he went running out the door and down the road.

The distinct odor of dynamite hung thickly over the little

school building; Winfield and most of the "creekers" were familiar with the odor from working in the coal mines. The front door, or what was left of it, was half leaning against a tree across the road. All the windows of the front of the building were gone, only slivers here and there remaining.

There were people gathering around the school from all directions. Some came boldly, not stopping to think; others, closer to the battle that had been raging, came more cautiously, peering ahead in the blackness. They milled around in the schoolyard, a few courageous souls going inside to inspect the damage.

"Marvin's done it this time," somebody muttered from the crowd.

"Shut up. That's dangerous talk," said another voice. The crowd was growing, and soon it included news reporters and law enforcement officers, both state police and deputy sheriffs from nearby Charleston.

The red lights flashing from their vehicles lent an ominous air to the scene; the flashlights they carried darted here and there among the crowd; and the shattered buildings were reminiscent of London during the German blitz of the Second World War.

Winfield moved about listlessly, trying to comprehend it all. This couldn't be happening—not here and not to him and his neighbors. This was the very school where he had learned to read and write, and so had most of the people in the crowd, except the police, of course.

He looked numbly across the road at the shattered door. His initials were still etched there, along with those of a little blond-haired girl he had long since lost track of. Many times he had climbed the tree the door leaned against, happy and carefree during those summers that lasted forever.

No, this couldn't be happening here; this was Campbell's Creek. These were his friends and neighbors, not invaders from some foreign country come to do him harm.

He heard the law enforcement officers talking among themselves, and he went closer so he could hear them.

"This will bring the federal government into it now," the state police leader was saying. "The Bureau of Alcohol, Tobacco and Firearms ... and probably the FBI will become involved as well."

Hearing this, Winfield eased toward the edge of the crowd in the darkness. He didn't want to be questioned. He wasn't in the mood for it and didn't know anything about the situation, except what he couldn't tell without incriminating his neighbors, especially his good friend Marvin.

He made it to the edge of the crowd without being noticed, so he decided to try getting away. He walked away casually so if he was caught, he could say he was just going back home to finish his night's sleep.

If I get caught? What is happening? he asked himself. *I'm walking away from the school where I spent my childhood, going to my own home, and I feel like a criminal—even thinking like a fugitive. This can't be real.*

CHAPTER 19

The Alliance Struggles On

Homer Loveday (yep, that was really his name, and it fit) was the most unassuming and lovable protestor in the whole movement. He would do anything he could, short of breaking the law, to help the cause, no matter how slight nor how time consuming. He was constantly calling the Alliance office, asking Jim's opinion of his latest idea and whether he should carry it out. He never made a pest of himself, always apologizing for taking up Jim's time. He was the epitome of the composite Christian: meek, mild-mannered, humble, soft-spoken, and a willing tool to be used in any acceptable fashion to accomplish God's work.

He appeared to be in his early fifties, was of medium size with a build that could have fit any height, and had a countenance that said the soul was compatible. The soft brown eyes, even in their mildness, spoke of an unshakable determination.

The most memorable event concerning Homer was the day he called and asked, "Mr. Farley, do you think it would do any good if I picketed the chamber of commerce building with a sign saying ...?" and he went on to explain what he had in mind. I was delighted at his plan since the chamber had just come out with their critical article, but even better, the Committee of 100, who had been most worrisome to us, was also housed in the same building.

Jim could still see the image vividly in his mind: Homer, in his low-key aggressiveness, stolidly carrying the sign, scrawled neatly in his own style of print, which read: intercepted message: 10/10/74 dear ken: the good news is the books can stay. the bad news is the schools have to go. yours, george. ("Dear Ken" was in reference to Dr. Kenneth Underwood, Superintendent of Kanawha County Schools).

Amidst all the hatred and violence, occasionally there came a muted explosion of mirth, some genuine, some bitterly satirical: "Fudge, fudge, call the judge. Mama got a newborn baby! It's not a girl, and it's not a boy, it's just a newborn baby! Wrap it up in tissue paper. Put it on the elevator. One, two, three, and out goes she!" (This is not out of context; that's it—the whole rhyme).

Marilyn Hill lent realism to the nonsensical rhyme she was reciting to the congregation of the Marmet Methodist Church. Marmet was one of the many small towns in the upper part of the valley, on the opposite side of the river from Charleston. Marilyn's facial expressions were befitting a little girl jumping rope. A barely perceptible curtsy here and there as she spoke, the pleated skirt with sweater combination, the large dimple in her wide-eyed girlish face, and a speech impediment in her teenage-sounding voice all added to the realism. (Marilyn was thirty-four.) Jim wondered if the people around him could almost see, as he could, the full-color photo of the tiny white-haired baby that was at the top of the page that contained the rhyme. Its mouth was wide in a howling cry; the desperate pleading of its soul came clearly through the stark terror of its blue eyes. An opaque droplet of saliva clung precariously on its tender chin. The fury within him flared anew.

The rhyme was from one of the supplement books of the controversial curriculum material, and it was called *Jump Rope Jingles and Other Useful Rhymes.* Useful for what? Jim wondered.

They were here at the church because of an idea that had come to him a few days ago because of all the valley ministers coming to the office looking for information about the books.

Instead of depending on each individual minister to deliver his interpretation of scant (and usually the lesser pertinent) information, why not set up speaking engagements at the various churches and have different members of the Alliance, the ones qualified and willing, give talks and illustrate what they were up against.

He discussed it with several of the people in the office, and everyone, including Elmer this time, agreed it was a good way to inform the populace and enlist their support.

Marilyn and Mick were the first to volunteer to participate actively, and Larry Freeman said that he would also be available if needed. Marilyn was the wife of Cephus Hill, one of the first people Jim had approached with the plan to organize the Alliance. Cephus had eagerly agreed to become a part of it even before it was formed. He had put out excerpts and leaflets in his store early in the fight.

Jim looked around at the members of the congregation, observing them in an attempt to evaluate their reaction. They were all attentive and appeared shocked and incredulous at what they were hearing.

His mind jumped ahead to the next evening, when he and Mick were scheduled to speak at a church in Dunbar. At least, Mick was scheduled to speak; Jim just went along for moral support, remaining as always, in the background. He withered in front of an audience.

He was explaining this to Mick on their way to the meeting. "Mick, I can do fine one-on-one, but if you put me up on a stage, speaking platform, or any elevated position in front of a crowd, I can't even tell you my own name. I'm just not cut out for the spotlight."

Mick smiled, still looking straight ahead into the night. "It's a heady thing," he said, making it obvious that he enjoyed it.

"Look out, Jim," Mick said suddenly.

Jim turned his attention from Mick to see a car coming down the hill from a side street—straight at them. He swerved the wheel just in time.

He had been so absorbed in their conversation that he hadn't seen the oncoming car. Grinning sheepishly, he muttered to Mick, "I think I had better concentrate on my driving."

Mick smiled, saying, "Yeah, that might not be a bad idea." Jim felt foolish.

They arrived at the church and sat in the front row, listening to the pastor giving his explanation as to who we were and why we were here.

"It is our privilege to have with us the head man of Alice Moore's screening committee, Mick Staton." Mick was watching the pastor closely as he listened. "Mr. Staton will give a brief talk to explain what's causing the uproar in our schools, giving us as much information as he can in the short time we have. From what I have heard, I understand some of it is dynamite."

Mick pulled his searching gaze from the pastor, leaned over to Jim, pseudo-wincing, and said out of the corner of his smile, "I wish he hadn't used that word."

"I know," answered Jim. He smiled and shrugged.

Saturday morning was quiet at the office. Except for Jim and June, Marilyn Hill was the only person there. Jim was glad for the quiet time that allowed him some much-needed rest, yet the sense of urgency this controversy had instilled in him wouldn't permit it.

He wanted to make use of the time in a constructive way. Bill Hamb's office was in plain view on the second corner up from their building. He considered going up and talking with him, but then, for reasons he couldn't explain, discarded the idea.

The phone in his office rang, and he went to answer it.

"Jim, Al Marino. How are things going?"

"Well, kind of slow this morning, Al. How's things with you? Still chompin' at the bit to get in the fight?"

The fire of exuberance that had been in Al's voice the last time was strangely absent. Instead, he was cool and businesslike. "Jim, I've been talking to people from both sides of this thing, and I'm not sure who to believe. Maybe I went off half-cocked. Would it be possible for you to bring some of the books by Monday evening and let me see for myself?"

Jim was puzzled at his change of attitude but, thinking of Marilyn being so handy in the next office, said, "Sure, Al, no problem."

"Good, how about seven thirty?"

"Fine. We'll be there."

He hung up the phone and sat there for a minute, reflecting on his conversation with Al's wife in their shop a few days ago. She, like Al, had felt so strongly about the books. That day, she told him of her father, who had come over from the old country with such strict moral principles. Jim had told her he would like to do a story on him to use as an example to people. He got carried away and told her about some of the businesspeople who were afraid to get involved because of what it might do to their business. Some of them also feared the violence.

Jim couldn't help but wonder if the conversation had anything to do with his change of heart. He shrugged, decided to give him the benefit of the doubt, and headed for the outer office to talk to Marilyn about going to Al's on Monday.

"Marilyn, I've booked you another speaking engagement," he said lightly.

Marilyn looked away from the window that she and June had been staring out of, smiling at him. "Oh, you have, have you? What's my big show this time?"

"You've hit the big time. It's at Al Marino's house."

Unexpectedly, Marilyn's smile faded. You'll have to get someone else."

"What?"

"I won't go to Al Marino's."

"Why not?"

"I'd rather not say. I just won't."

His commitment to the cause was so total that anything less in anyone else always took him by surprise. He didn't know what to say to break the stunned silence. Marilyn sat looking at him, unflinching. He walked to the window and stared up the boulevard. Maybe he should have gone to talk to Bill Hamb after all. Why did it have to be this way? Why did he have to spend more time persuading his "comrades" to fight than he did in the fighting itself?

He turned from the window to look at Marilyn. "Okay, Marilyn, I won't ask your reasons. I can't force you to go. I'll handle it myself."

Mondays seemed to be hectic for everyone. This Monday in the office certainly had not been an exception. He was glad it was mercifully ending. Then he remembered. Al Marino.

The cumulative weight of all the decisions, problems, and frustrations of the long day suddenly crushed him down into his chair. Resentment toward Marilyn for not going to Al's was mixed with envy of her easy decision not to go.

You're crazy, he told himself. Absolutely nuts! If you had any sense, you'd close the doors of this ridiculous office, get a six-pack, go home, and go to bed. But something deep down inside him wouldn't let himself do it. It wouldn't let go, nor would it let him let go. What is it that keeps me in this thing? He asked himself. Christian convictions? I'm not even a Christian. True, I've always had deep religious convictions, but I've never committed myself. So why am I so committed to this? The snarling face of Glen Roberts floated through his mind. Is that what I've become? Have I turned into a fanatic, fighting blindly long after I've forgotten the reasons for fighting? Or is it the fact that somebody is trying to cram something down my throat? He had always rebelled violently whenever anyone attempted to force him to do anything.

Then he thought of the plan—and visions of what the world, his world, would be like if it were not stopped. He had his answer.

He forced himself to his feet, trying to forget the countless voices still ringing in his ears, and headed for the front office. "June, let's lock it up. I've got to be at Al Marin's in twenty minutes." She looked up from the copier they had rented, started to say something, and then put the half-finished copy of the splinter group's review report aside.

"I've got to stop for gas," she said.

This irritated him. He was already going to be late. It was his opinion that punctuality was vital to running any business. He didn't like the thought of June going home alone due to the threats they had been receiving. Although he didn't put much credence in the threats, his family's safety was all important to him, yet he didn't have the time to stop for gas and then follow her to their house before going to Al's. Not for the first time, he wished they were able to travel back and forth to the office together, but he was constantly on the run and didn't want June stuck at the office waiting on him after everyone else had left for the day. His stomach churned as he debated over what to do. Time was ticking and tension mounting. This plan, like so many others that he had put so much effort into, was beginning to fall apart. He could see all his work on this one going down the drain.

Desperation overrode judgment. "All right, I'll follow you to the gas station and then go on to Al's. You'll be all right from there." It was only a mile or so from the station to their home.

They went to their cars, and he stayed on her bumper until she pulled into the service station lot. He gave two short beeps on his horn, meaning "good luck," and she returned it with one short one as a "thank you." He drove on past and headed for Al's.

Al was listening patiently, making an effort to be attentive, or at least appearing to. Jim was pointing out the underlined passages in "Androcles and the Lion" when the phone in the other room rang. Al glanced at his wife, who then got up and went to answer it.

Jim was always in a hurry, and now was no different. There was so much to do, so many people to reach, and so little time. He was becoming agitated at Al's obvious lack of comprehension of what he was showing him.

He restrained the feeling, instead trying to appreciate the courteous, tolerant look Al wore.

"Al." Al and Jim looked up at Mrs. Marino, who was standing at the door. "Excuse me; Mr. Farley is wanted on the phone." She had a strange look on her face.

"Me?" Jim asked, perplexed. Who would be calling him here? June and Marilyn were the only ones who even knew where he was. Maybe Marilyn had relented and wanted to come. He excused himself, got up, and followed Mrs. Marino to the other room. She pointed to the phone and hurriedly left. Jim figured she wanted to allow him privacy.

"Hello."

The voice coming through the phone was quavering so that he couldn't make out the words at first.

"What?" he asked.

"James, they burned my car."

His blood froze. "They what?"

"They burned my car." The trembling voice was June's, and she was crying hysterically.

"Who burned your car? What are you talking about?

"They burned my car." That's all she could say.

"June, calm down. Where are you? Where did they burn your car?"

The voice was only a squeaking croak, barely audible. "I'm home."

"Where's your car?" There was a long pause.

He thought he could hear faint sobbing sounds. His insides were trembling, his hands shaking, but he tried to keep his voice level. "June, who's there with you? Is anyone with you?"

"Yes," she croaked.

"Who?"

"The family."

"Who else?"

"Gary and Diane." Gary was his cousin, and Diane was his wife. They lived three doors down from Jim and June.

Jim was relieved she was not alone.

"June, put Gary on the phone."

There was silence, sounds of shuffling, and then Gary's voice. "Hello."

"Gary, what happened?"

"Jim, I'm not sure. I wasn't here when it happened. They called me after it was already burning. They said they were here in the house, in the living room talking, when they heard an explosion and the sky lit up. Jud ran outside and saw the flames like a bonfire right beside the house. He thought at first the house was on fire. He rushed back inside and called the fire department. When he got back outside, he saw that it was June's car burning. The flames were going up above the roof. It lit up the whole house. In fact, you could see clear up the driveway, plain as day."

"Did you see anybody?"

"No."

"I'll be right there. Keep an eye on June."

He hung up the phone numbly, stood there for a moment trying to compose himself, and then walked back to where Al and his wife were waiting. They looked at him expectantly. By their expressions, he knew that Mrs. Marino had told Al about the sobbing voice on the phone.

"Al, before you make your decision on getting involved in this thing, I'd better tell you. My wife's car is burning right beside our bedroom at this very moment."

They looked at him in stunned silence.

"Excuse me, Al. I've got to go." He scooped up the books, grabbed his briefcase, and headed for the door. Al started to get up, but Jim didn't wait. He just left.

As he pulled into his driveway, he saw the flames leaping and dancing like a bonfire, illuminating the whole side of the house, showing clearly each individual stone he had laid with his own hands. It gave an eerie daylight scene to the drive and parking area.

Abruptly, it was pitch black. Then he suddenly realized the whole scene had been in his mind's eye. In reality, the fire was already out, and everything was dark. He saw a flashlight come on, flitting over the pitiful remains of June's charred little Pinto.

He parked his car and started walking toward it, hearing voices. Only then did he remember he had passed a fire truck parked up the street, its red light flashing a warning to passersby.

As he got closer to the voices, someone apparently heard him coming. The spot of the flashlight found his face, and a voice said, "Here he comes now."

The bearer of the flashlight walked up to him and asked, "Mr. Farley?"

"Yes," Jim answered numbly.

"I'm John Breeden, fire marshal. Do you have any idea who might have done this?"

"Not specifically," answered Jim.

"Generally?"

"Anybody who's in favor of these books."

The marshal looked at him curiously but didn't comment. "Do you know anyone from Georgia?"

"No."

"We found this receipt from a company in Brosia, Georgia, in your driveway."

Jim thought a minute and then asked, "Is that near Stone Mountain?"

"I don't know," answered the marshal. "We can check it out."

They loaded their gear and left. That was the last he ever heard from them.

The next morning, a man identifying himself as Earl Benton, a photographer for the local paper, came out and asked if he could take a picture of the car.

Jim was always ready to use any opportunity to get their side of the fight out to the public, so he agreed. The name Earl Benton struck a chord, but he dismissed it.

"It would add realism and impact if you were looking in the car when I take the picture. Would you mind?"

Jim said he wouldn't and leaned down to look through the

shattered window of the gutted Pinto. Benton snapped the picture, thanked him, and left.

When he was alone, Jim wandered aimlessly around the car. When he got to the back of it, something caught his eye. He looked closer. Through the rear window could be plainly seen the charred remainder of Kelly's Bible, which she never went anywhere without.

Suddenly, he knew why the name Earl Benton was familiar. He was the same photographer who had gone to great lengths to dramatically display the sight of Old Glory on the classroom wall of Wetbranch Elementary School, through the broken panes of the window that had been shattered in the dynamite blast of persons unknown, assumed to be protestors. The connotation was obvious. Why did he not go to the same pains to take a picture of Kelly's Bible through the exploded windows? Why?

DONALD MEANS SURVEYS RESULTS OF THREE THREATENING CALLS

Burned Car Believed Link To Means' Work In Textbook Dispute

CHAPTER 20

The Alliance's Slate

When the slate came that morning, he didn't even look at it. He didn't want to know what the results of Elmer's decision was. Elmer had sent it up via the Nitro taxi, which he always used for errand boys and pony express. It was only one of the unique ways that Elmer had of doing things. Good or bad, he wasn't average.

Due to his narrow tunnel through life up to the beginning of the protest, Jim spent more time in learning the ropes of where, how, and who you went to in order to get something done than in the doing itself. This occupied almost as much of his time as the convincing of the various aspects and approaches of the protest to his comrades.

How do you go about getting a slate printed? he asked himself. Where do you start looking? He leaned back in his chair, straining hard to come up with something. The drone of voices from the outer office was distracting him. He got up and closed the door. While walking back to his desk, it came to him. His cousin ran a print shop! Of course, here was the obvious again. Why was that always the hardest thing to see?

He hurriedly picked up the phone and dialed the number. He got lucky.

"Hello."

"Buck, this is Jim. I need a rush job done."

The abruptness of it caused Buck to hesitate. Then he said, "I don't know, Jim. I'm pretty busy. What do you need?"

The two of them had a least partially the same blood running through their veins and came from the same background. Jim was sure that once Buck knew it was to fight these books, he would drop everything, stop the presses, and get right on the slate. He was wrong.

When he explained what it was all about, Buck hedged. In an irritated, resentful tone of voice, he said, "Jim, I've got regular customers whom I depend on to make my living. They don't care about these books! They just want to make a buck, and to do that, they have to have their printing finished on schedule."

Jim couldn't believe what he was hearing. Never would he understand the attitude of these people. He thought of how little his own business going to pot concerned him. It was the first time it had crossed his mind. Couldn't these people understand what was happening?

The bottom line on the little pamphlet containing "The Dusseldorf Rules for World Conquest" flashed through his mind: "Your greatest enemy, however, is the disregard for the danger signs." Amen, thought Jim.

"Okay, Buck, what would it take to make this important enough to take priority over what you're doing? There was silence on Buck's end of the phone. The almighty dollar always gave incentive.

"How many do you want?"

"That depends a lot on how much they cost."

The impatience showed in Buck's voice. "The cost per copy, Jim, depends on how many copies you want. You should know that by now." Jim occasionally had Buck do printing for him.

"Ten thousand. Let's start with that. Have you ever done a slate before?"

"Of course," came Buck's weary reply. He mulled it over a bit, apparently doing some figuring on the other end. "All right, if you want ten thousand and if you're willing to shell out six hundred dollars, I'll get started on 'em just as soon as you get the original to me."

"You've got it. I'll have it there in half an hour. How long will it take?"

"Give me three days."

"I don't have three days. I need them by two o'clock

tomorrow."

Buck yelled, "Jim, there ain't no way! I'd have to work all night."

"Then sleep all day tomorrow. Buck, I need them tomorrow." Jim ignored Buck's cursing, waiting for the only answer he would accept, gearing up for more persuasion if necessary.

"Oh, hell, all right. Get the damn thing out here, and I'll have it ready by two o'clock tomorrow."

"Thanks, Buck." He hung up the phone with a huge smile.

As Buck had promised, Jim was able to pick up the ten thousand copies of the slate the next afternoon at two o'clock.

When Jim awoke, he thought he was still asleep. He must be because everything was strange; the bed had an unfamiliar lump, there was traffic noise outside, and the occasional light flashing dimly into the room showed furniture he couldn't remember.

If it was a dream, he couldn't understand what it was all about. The traffic sounded real, the furniture looked real, and nothing eventful happened the way it usually does in dreams. No shrieks, sudden faces, or strange, loud noises.

Then his groggy mind began to brighten a little. Now he remembered; they were in their son's apartment, three blocks down from the school board, of all places. He reached over and felt June's body beside him.

No, it was no dream; they had decided it prudent to leave their own home for a few nights after June's car had been blown up right beside their bedroom.

Jim had asked for police protection from the Charleston city police. He was told politely that it was out of their jurisdiction. When he reminded them that Dr. Underwood had been given round-the-clock protection just by receiving threatening phone calls, they made excuses and suggested calling the sheriff's department.

He did. They said the sheriff was at a party, and they didn't have the authority to send the men out. Try the state police.

When the state police declined, expressing their sympathy but claiming a manpower shortage, he gave up. They moved out.

He could tell by the traffic pattern that even though it was still dark outside, it would soon be morning. He and June were supposed to meet Patsy McGraw at daybreak in Shoney's lot on the Boulevard to deliver the slates for the Cabin Creek precinct. He nudged June. She groaned a little and began to stir. They were both exhausted.

They got up, dressed, and taking their morning coffee with them, left the apartment to meet Patsy.

When they pulled up in Shoney's lot, Jim thought of the day he had met Marvin here. It seemed like another lifetime ago.

He saw the dark, outdated Cadillac Patsy had described to him. Although he had talked to her on the phone several times, he had never met her. A large woman extracted herself from the Caddy and walked toward his car. She leaned down.

"Mr. Farley?"

"Jim."

"Okay, Jim. I'm Patsy McGraw. Do you have them?"

"Yes, they're in the trunk." Jim got out of the car to retrieve them for her.

Why do I get the feeling that I should ask for some kind of identification? he wondered. Maybe he had seen too many war movies when he was a kid. The bombing of June's car, the hiding out at their son's apartment like spies behind enemy lines, and this clandestine meeting were making him paranoid.

He grunted as he lifted the first box of the slate out of the trunk of his car. It was heavy. Patsy opened the trunk of her car without a word. A man was sitting in the front seat of her car, but he gave no indication that he was aware of anything happening.

He stared straight ahead.

When the last box had been transferred, Patsy closed the trunk, and the man still didn't turn his head. Jim wondered why he hadn't offered to help. Patsy never acknowledged his presence. She nodded to Jim without a word, got into the car, and drove off.

Jim stood there, looking after the Caddy as if trying to convince himself it had been real. Then it was gone. Had it been real?

He climbed into his own car and started it. When it roared to life, he headed up the boulevard toward the ominous darkness that was the Alliance building looming out of the morning fog.

CHAPTER 21
School Board Bombed

Jud sat bolt upright in his bed. He wasn't sure whether he was awake or having a nightmare. Something had startled him. While he was still trying to sort out sleep from reality, he heard the rumblings of the echo of the blast that had jerked him out of his sound sleep. Little tingles covered his body as he thought of all the bizarre happenings that had been taking place in the valley lately. With his father a key figure in the protest movement, he felt anything was possible. Had someone set off a bomb outside the apartment to warn him? Or maybe they thought his father was staying here again, as he did for several nights after they'd bombed his mother's car.

Jud was in his apartment, a few blocks down from the Board of Education office building. Thinking of the nearness of the board, he wondered if that might be it. Had someone blown up the Board of Education? Lord knows, enough threats had been made about doing it. Maybe somebody had carried out his threat.

Unknown to Jud, that's exactly what had happened. At that moment, Clark Fletcher, the eighteen-year-old computer operator employed by the board, was lying flat on his face on the floor of the school board building, waiting for the second blast he felt sure was coming. The next one would destroy the building completely and take him to oblivion with it. Many things ran through his mind while he waited. He regretted not taking heed of the warning given him by a service station attendant on Campbell's Creek, where he lived. The attendant had told him he had heard strong rumors the school board was going to be blown up. Clark hadn't taken it seriously. He wished now that he had.

He had felt the blast when it came—like nothing he had ever heard in his life—yet it was so quick. He hit the floor so fast that he wasn't sure whether he had done it on his own or was knocked there by the blast. Right now, he didn't care. He just wished he were somewhere else ... anywhere else.

It seemed as if he could hear a ticking; maybe it was the timing device for the second bomb. A wave of terror swept over him. He almost panicked and ran, but he forced himself to lie where he was. He thought that would be the safest place ... unless he was right on top of the bomb! The ticking continued ... forever. Then he heard the most beautiful sound in the world: human voices.

At 11:07 PM, only twelve minutes after the blast, the police arrived, accompanied by the fire department, but to Clark, the time between the blast and the sound of voices coming to help him seemed like a lifetime. Relief brought by the knowledge that he was safe eased the tension, and he shook weakly.

The police and firefighters began to assess the damage. The blast had been so forceful that it had lifted a three-ton air conditioner off the roof and turned it completely around. Many windows of nearby homes had been shattered.

Mrs. Goldie Farley (no relation to Jim) found her hubcaps blown off her car in front of her home at 1611 Franklin Avenue, two blocks away. Mrs. Catherine Grimm left her home at 1607 Franklin to stay with a friend. But the most massive damage was sustained by the home of Evelyn Callaghan at 1608 Franklin Avenue. All the windows on the front of her house were completely gone.

School Superintendent Underwood was called to the scene to inspect the devastation. He walked gingerly through the wreckage, wearing a look of stunned disbelief. As he looked around glassy-eyed, he was heard mumbling, "My God, where will this go before it ends?"

One can't help but wonder what went through Underwood's mind at that moment. Did he regret ever putting the books in the schools? Was he entertaining the idea of withdrawing them permanently? It was obvious by his remark that specters of more violence and destruction loomed in his mind. And they would come.

The Charleston Gazette Thursday, Oct. 31, 1974

DETECTIVES SURVEY damage late Wednesday at the Kanawha County Board of Education offices on Elizabeth Street where an explosion ripped out a gas meter and shattered windows in the building. Detective Harvey Bush (right) is inspecting the area where the gas meter was before the blast.
(Gazette Photo by Jack Kern)

CHAPTER 22

Failed Plans

Jim looked up from his desk as the door to the Alliance office opened. He was used to it flapping back and forth like the swinging doors on a saloon of the Old West during regular hours, but since it was this early, it caught his attention.

A short man stood there; his owlish eyes blinking from behind thick glasses set in a ruddy face seemed almost ludicrous. He looked more like a life-size version of a comic character than a real person.

"I'm Gary Baker, and I'd like to speak to the one in charge, please." The voice quivered but had a certain ring of confidence that suppressed Jim's impulse to wave him off.

"Well, I guess that would be me. What can I do for you?" Baker came over and sat down on the long leather couch, motioning Jim to join him. Betty Rogers came through the door, gave the stranger a hard, searching look, glanced at Jim, and then disappeared into the back office.

Baker pulled a newspaper from his coat pocket. Jim thought he was going to unfold it to show him an article, but instead, Baker just sort of waved it around as he talked, as though Jim already knew the contents.

"On the plane in from Washington," he said grandly, "I came across this article about Elmer Fike. I sympathize deeply with your cause, and I would like to do my part. Help in my own way."

"What do you have in mind?"

"How well do you know Mr. Fike?"

"We're pretty close."

Baker grinned, his complexion growing redder and his eyes more owlish. "I would like to do a complete character profile on the man. Go into detail; really acquaint the public on both sides about what kind of man they're dealing with. What do you think?"

Jim sat looking him over in silence.

"I'm sorry," said Baker. "I know what is going through your mind. You're wondering what gives me the right to waltz in here and make such a grandiose proposal. Forgive me; let me fill you in on my credentials. I've been in public relations for over thirty years. I've just completed an extensive layout for the Snowshoe resort in a promotional campaign." Snowshoe was a brand-new exclusive ski resort at Canaan Valley, in the mountains northeast of Charleston.

Jim still looked at him in silence. He was wondering whether he had a nut on his hands, looking for some sensational headlines, or a bona fide benefactor who was who he said he was.

Baker was staring at him, patiently waiting for him to sift through the information and make his decision.

After due consideration, Jim concluded that he didn't have much to lose. Let him interview Elmer, write the article, and proofread it—then I'll make my decision.

"Okay, when do you want to go see Elmer?"

"The sooner, the better."

"Right now soon enough?"

"Couldn't be better."

Jim caught a movement out of the corner of his eye and turned to see Betty standing at the door between the two offices. She saw him looking in her direction and furtively motioned him toward the back office.

"Excuse me, Gary. I'll be right back." He followed Betty into the other office. She walked to the farthest corner before turning to face him.

"Jim, I don't think you should be talking to that man."

"What do you mean, Betty?"

"I don't like his looks."

Irritation tempered with incredulity flooded through him. “Betty, if we only talked with or dealt with people whose looks we liked, we’d be in bad shape in this fight.”

“I mean, I have the feeling that he’s a spy for the other side. I don’t think you know what you might be letting yourself in for.”

The irritation grew into outright resentment. “Look, Betty, I may appear to be naive, but believe me, I’ve got the world’s biggest microscope in my head, through which I examine everybody. I know exactly what I’m doing. If anybody wants me, I’ll be at Elmer’s office.” He turned to lead Gary Baker out the door to the elevator.

Jim turned the car into the now-familiar driveway to Elmer’s plant. He pulled sharply in front of the office, spewing cinders up on the wall. The receptionist looked up as they entered the building, saw Jim, and immediately called Elmer. Elmer came down to the waiting room to talk.

“Elmer, this is Gary Baker.” Elmer reached for Baker’s outstretched hand, looking the man over.

Jim filled in the background of Gary’s credentials and told him why they were there. Elmer stood blinking, not speaking.

“Well, what do you think?”

“Oh, I don’t know, Jim. Come up to the office. There’s something I want to show you. Excuse us, Gary.” That last remark made it clear he wanted to be alone with Jim. Gary took the hint.

They climbed the stairs and went into Elmer’s office. Elmer turned and said, “Jim, Betty Rogers called me and said for me to keep an eye on this man. What’s going on?” Jim felt the bitter resentment in his mouth. “Elmer, Betty is paranoid. She has some notion this man could by a ‘spy’ for the other side. It’s the most ludicrous thing I ever heard.”

Elmer blinked the wise old owl blink. “How do you know he’s not?”

Jim couldn’t believe he was hearing Elmer say that. “What difference would it make if he was?” he asked impatiently, his voice rising. “The way I see it is we let him lay out his program, proofread it, every word .... and then make our decision. How could he hurt us?"

Elmer blinked again and said. "Well, I don't guess he can if we do it that way," he finally answered.

"Well, I'm glad you agree," said Jim. "Now maybe we can get to work putting this thing together." He tried not to notice the frown of skepticism still clouding Elmer's face. He turned quickly and left the office before Elmer could change his mind again. He hurried downstairs, got Gary, and headed back to the Alliance office. Gary chattered all the way about how he was going to do Elmer's profile.

Jim only half listened. He was trying to come to grips with the problem of internal friction within the protestors' ranks. He had accepted the fact that the three leaders were always going to be at odds with each other, but now it was beginning in the Alliance; and it was supposed to be comprised of intelligent, reasonable people. We spend more time fighting each other than we do the enemy, he thought bitterly.

He pulled the car onto the parking lot.

"Jim, if you'll let me out here, before you park the car, I'll get up to the office and get started," said Gary, obviously excited.

Jim stopped and let Gary out. He looked around for a space and maneuvered the car into it. He then headed for the office, taking the steps two at a time.

He opened the Alliance office door and stopped short. A loud voice was hurling angry threats and orders at Gary Baker, who was backed into a corner. Shock and fear had drawn his features almost unrecognizably tight. He was totally cowed by the suave man, dressed in a Saks Fifth Avenue suit, that the voice belonged to. The man, who looked Lebanese or Jewish, was chewing Gary out proper.

"You little pipsqueak!" he yelled. "We give you a chance to make a comeback and what do you do? You go out and get on a crusade with a bunch of Bible-thumping preachers and stupid hillbillies. Well, you can stay out there on your stump spouting off your harebrained opinions. You're fired." The man turned on his heel and left, followed by a second man Jim hadn't noticed. Gary stood quivering.

Jim walked over, put a hand on his shoulder, and asked gently, "Is there anything I can do, Gary? Who were those men, anyway?"

Gary composed himself enough to stop his teeth from chattering as he answered. "They were my superiors from Snowshoe. I can't imagine how they knew I was here. They should have thought I was still in Washington.

Jim was about to comment when he looked over Gary's shoulder to see Betty Rogers standing in the doorway leading to the other office, her expression showing bitter triumph. "Excuse me, Gary. I think I may have the answer to that." He started toward Betty, who darted into the office. Jim started to follow Betty and then changed his mind.

"Gary, I'm sorry about this—and especially about you losing your job." He wondered about the man's remark about the comeback but considered it none of his business. He had a feeling that Gary had been on the skids—that this was his one shot to be somebody important, and he had just lost it. "What will you do now?"

Gary was still trembling slightly but managed an answer in a quivery voice. "Oh, don't worry, Jim. I've got a little money saved." He paused, grimaced bitterly—the pockmarks seemed to be more pronounced—and said, "After all, what would a man like me spend his money on except to eat?" Gary dropped his head and stared at the floor; Jim, embarrassed, looked on in silence.

Finally, without a word, without even looking up, Gary Baker shuffled out the door that was still open. Jim watched him go with compassion and a pity he had never felt before.

After the debacle of Gary Baker's superiors firing him, Jim was sure he would never see the little man again. But he didn't know the man's tenacity, which, as it turned out, was far greater than his physical stature or the shadow that he cast.

It had been about three weeks since the belligerent big shot from Snowshoe had tongue-lashed Gary with a whipping that sent him out of the office with his tail between his legs. Jim had seen him only once since then, darting up Virginia Street and furtively disappearing into a doorway in that peculiar hop-saunter gait of his.

The telephone on his desk rang, and when he answered, the unmistakable raspy croak came over the wire: "Jim, Gary Baker. How've you been?"

Jim sat stupefied for a moment. After a long pause, he answered, "Just fine, Gary. Where in the world have you been?"

"Oh, I've been here and there," answered Gary. "Say, Jim, the reason I called is that I've got an idea that might interest you. I think it will let you accomplish the biggie you've been reaching for.

Jim was curious but cautious. Could it be that Gary had thought of a way to overcome what Jim felt was the biggest obstacle and was also Jim's fondest hope of somehow getting the message of what was going on here in Kanawha County out to the rest of the country.

"What do you have in mind, Gary?" he asked when it became obvious the other man was waiting until Jim asked before continuing. Jim could just see the grimace grow wider and the watery blue eyes sparkle in spite of their watering. Gary was enjoying this, and he was going to milk it for all it was worth.

Finally, when it was obvious that Jim wasn't going to press for more and the silence became embarrassing, Gary began to speak, and then he stopped in the middle of a word, saying, "Jim, this is too good to waste telling you over the telephone. I'm only a few blocks away. Hang in there. I'll be right up."

Jim was a little irritated at hearing the line go dead after being brought so close to the climax, but he shrugged, hung the telephone on its cradle, and sat back in his chair, watching the door and waiting for it to burst open, which he knew would happen.

It seemed like hours, and he wondered if Gary was deliberately making him wait.

Finally, the door burst open, just as he expected, and the

diminutive body of Gary Baker came hurtling through.

"Hi, Jim. How are you?"

Jim only nodded. Gary pulled up a chair across the desk and sat down, still grinning. He looked into Jim's eyes for a long time and finally said, "Jimbo, this time I've got the answer for you. You've been trying to get the message out to the world, right?"

Jim acknowledged with a puzzled nod.

Gary became dramatic in his gestures and as animated as he was capable of, building up for the big moment. "Picture this," he said. "We call a press conference of national news reporters. I can arrange that through my contacts." Jim knew this would be no problem; these days, all the national (even some international) reporters were clamoring for anything they could get from Kanawha County on the textbook situation. "We hold the conference in the West Virginia Room of the civic center." He paused, smiling broadly. "Get it?" he asked with a meaningful twist of his head. "Then we show them what we are objecting to right out of the books themselves." He sat back, waiting.

Jim felt a great sense of letdown and a small amount of disgust. "But, Gary, we've tried that with groups here locally, and it just won't work. There are too many books to take around to each person, and if you try to quote them, you're accused of taking the quotes out of context. You show them excerpts and you get the same comment. It just won't work."

Gary's grimace grew bigger. His eyes ablaze, he stared at Jim with relish, still leaning back.

Abruptly he lurched forward, coming halfway across the desk. Triumphantly, he almost shouted, "But picture this: all the national newsmen sitting there, a captive audience, their attention focused forward on a large screen while we flash page after page of the objectionable material on it in foot-high letters." The grimace was at its widest at the look of puzzlement on Jim's face. "What do you think of that?" he asked.

"Well, it sounds great, Gary, but just how do you propose to accomplish it?"

"With an overhead projector."

"What's an overhead projector?"

"It's like a movie projector, except it can take a single sheet of paper and projects it over the heads of the audience, onto a giant screen in foot-high letters."

Jim felt Gary's excitement start to spread to himself. This had been his big frustration; he knew too well what was contained in these books—the definite plan that was there—but how did one get it across to other people, especially the outside world—the world beyond the boundaries of the hills surrounding the valley?

Jim thought bitterly of the interview the national TV news had taped of him at the Holiday Inn. When they had asked him to do it, his excitement knew no bounds. Here was the perfect opportunity to broadcast the message from coast to coast. His hopes were crushed by their cutting him out altogether.

"Well, what do you think?"

Gary Baker's raspy, shrill voice jerked him back to the present. He looked at Baker thoughtfully. "Why not? We've tried everything else. Let's go with it."

Gary's excitement was still running at a fever pitch when they got to Elmer's office. He paced up and down in front of the desk as Jim began to explain to Elmer what it was all about.

"Elmer, are you familiar with an overhead projector?" asked Jim.

"Yeah, I know what they are," said Elmer patronizingly. He waited patiently, ignoring Baker's pacing.

"Well, Gary came up with the idea that will finally enable us to get the contents of these books out to the rest of the world."

"How's that?" asked Elmer, smiling skeptically.

"Don't you see, Elmer? We project each page onto a movie screen with the letters showing up twelve inches high for all the national news reporters to see for themselves."

"How do you know they will come?"

"Oh, come on, Elmer. You know as well as I do that anything pertaining to these books will bring them on the run from all over the country; no, from all over the world."

Elmer thought this over while glancing up at the still-pacing Gary.

"Well, even if they do, what will that prove?"

Jim was becoming exasperated. "Elmer, don't you understand? The reporters can't refuse what they can see with their own eyes. They can't argue with cold facts in black and white."

Gary Baker didn't say a word, just kept pacing. He likely figured his credibility had been damaged to the extent that he had best stay out of it.

"Oh, all right, Jim. Get it set up. In the meantime, I'll give it some more thought."

They left Elmer's plant and headed back to the Alliance office, Gary Baker sitting silently beside him in the front seat of the car. Neither of them spoke until they were out of the chemical stench of Nitro. When the car climbed up onto the interstate and into fresher air, they both looked to their right at the attractive residential section of Nitro and Dunbar, almost a hundred feet below the interstate.

When he got back to the office, Jim started making the calls necessary to put the plan into action. He couldn't wait to see the reporters' faces when they saw the evidence of what the war was all about flashed on the screen in one-foot-high letters. He felt a tremor of excitement run through him at the expected headlines across the country and the world: WAR IN KANAWHA VALID; HIDEOUS PLAN UNVEILED.

His fingers trembled as the tempo of his calls picked up. He called the civic center first. "This is Jim Farley at the Alliance office. I'd like to reserve the West Virginia Room for November fourteenth ... all day." He listened impatiently while the man on the other end droned on about the fee and the deposit. "Yeah, yeah, I know all about that," he broke in abruptly. "We are ready and able to meet your terms. Just put it down for that date, tell me the amount, and I'll send a check."

He hung up, running a mental balance sheet of the money he had already spent out of his own pocket, knowing the check he would send would be his own. The donations had been painfully sparse and slow. His appeal to The Heritage Foundation for financing assistance had been deftly parried by McKenna into the wastepaper basket—called file thirteen—to indicate a dead issue.

So far, the Alliance had been run entirely on his money. He didn't know how much longer that would be the case, but he had secretly committed every resource he had to win the fight—whatever it took.

Three days passed after he had done all he could to prepare and expedite the details necessary for the big day of the overhead projector. He sat at his desk, drumming the top of it with his fingers to release his nervous energy. He would have preferred to vent it in more constructive ways, but he had been thwarted in every way he tried. Something had to break soon ... or he would.

The West Virginia Room was reserved; Gary was on standby, ready to flash the word out over the wires to all major networks to advise them of the event so they could dispatch their reporters; the books they were going to use were spread on top of his desk; and he was chomping at the bit to get started. Why didn't Elmer call to give permission to proceed? That was all that was holding them up. He stared at the phone, mumbling things at it that would have done "the books" proud. Why didn't it ring? Suddenly, it did; or had his desire for it to happen caused him to hallucinate? He reached for it.

"Hello."

"Jim, this is Elmer."

Jim's heart leaped.

"I've been thinking over your idea about the overhead projector, and I think we'd better scrap it."

"What do you mean, 'scrap it'? Elmer, do you have any idea what this could do for us?" The choking sound came from Jim.

"Oh, I don't know, Jim. I am in charge, as the president of the Alliance, and I've decided against it—and that's the end of it." The phone went dead.

He sat there stunned. What kind of Frankenstein had he created? What had prompted Elmer to make such a decision, and why the abrupt finality? He would never know. The world would never know. The books on top of his desk stared at him in smug silence, their secret—"the plan" in its entirety—still safe ... still secret. It was unnerving.

Jim was exhausted as he lay on the couch in the Alliance office. It had been a hectic day and he was trying to unwind and get a little rest before the gang showed up to wait for the election results. Carol or Ginny had suggested it, and everybody agreed that it was a good idea for everybody to meet at the office and watch the telecast. They were all coming: Alice Moore, Mick, Roger, Carol, and the rest. He hoped they wouldn't come too soon because his mind was spinning like a top. When he closed his eyes, he could still see the sea of faces swirling before him, faces of people who had paraded in and out of the office all day. Their voices still hummed in his ears.

He had rested only a short time when he heard the office door open and heard Roger's voice joking, "Man, you're some fearless leader. What are you doing there?"

Jim got wearily to his feet, cracking back, "What in the world did you get me into, anyway?" He was waving his arms in mock exasperation.

Roger laughed and then asked how things were going. They both got serious, and Jim explained some of the events that had taken place. The rest of them started trickling in, first Carol and then Ginny, followed by Bill Seaman and Herb Smith. Somebody turned on the TV and added to the noise of the room. Jim slid back into one corner as far as he could for a little privacy. The voices and TV blended into a consistent roar, and he didn't even hear the door open. If he hadn't been looking at it, he wouldn't have seen Mick come in, followed by Alice Moore. She was even prettier up close than she was at a distance. Jim was almost awed by this woman; he admired her so much. He had never seen a woman who could stick to a point in the face of dissenters the way she could. She was speaking to each one of the people here, smiling her sweet smile all the while. In the middle of all the greetings, Mick stopped her long enough to introduce her to him, saying, "Alice, this is Jim Farley."

Jim watched her nod to him casually and start to go on to the next person, when the name suddenly registered as the man she had been talking to on the phone so much in the last several weeks—a man she had never seen. She looked back at him with interest, her smile widening, her eyes sparkling.

"So you're Jim Farley," she said, studying him. It was evident that she had wondered about the face that went with the voice, wondered about the man himself. She had heard so much from this man, so many plans, ideas, and suggestions that were a welcome relief from the inane and grandiose ones that she had heard from so many others before. She had felt compelled to agree with the others for fear of losing much-needed support too soon. But she had to admit it was refreshing to find someone she heartily agreed with in reality. A little embarrassed to realize she was staring, she finally pulled her entranced gaze away and glanced, a little red-faced, around the room.

"I'm glad we finally get to meet ..." He started to say "Mrs. Moore," but he stopped and said instead, "I hope you don't mind if I call you Alice."

She chuckled with tinkling laughter. "Not at all. Everybody else does."

"I know. That's why I would feel like I was talking to someone other than 'Sweet Alice' if I called you Mrs. Moore." Her demure blush heightened the image. She smiled.

The affinity between them was felt by both but was mentioned by neither. She turned to the rest of the room and went on with her amenities. He returned to his corner. They did not converse anymore the rest of the evening.

CHAPTER 23
Interview with CBS

Jim Kincaid, a reporter from CBS, had come by the Alliance one day and asked Jim if he would sit for an interview.

Jim only had twenty-four hours to prepare for it, and he made the best of each one of them, right up to when he was on his way to the taping. He made a last-minute stop to call Bill Hamb to ask him how far he could go in his statements and stay within legal bounds.

When he finally pulled up in front of the Holiday Inn, where the taping was to take place, he was more nervous than he had ever been in his life. He wasn't sure he could to through with the interview. He cringed when he thought of making a fool of himself in front of the whole country. Worse, he would have to live with facing his friends and family. Jim had promised himself when he was a boy that if he ever had a family, he would always be somebody they could be proud of.

He sat in the parked car, wanting to start the engine and get out of there. He took a deep breath, braced himself, and got out of the car.

He took the elevator to the third floor, found the room number that Jim Kincaid had given him, and knocked.

A man he had never seen before opened the door.

This was the big chance he had been waiting for—probably the only one he would ever get (maybe the only one that he would need if he did it right)—and he had to make sure he conveyed the full implications of what was happening here and alerted the rest of the country. He had to get as many pertinent facts across as he could in the terribly short time he would have.

He had deliberately wound his nerves tight for full concentration, but then when he thought of sitting in front of that camera, which was in effect sitting in front of millions of people (he had made it clear to Elmer, Mick, and all the rest that he was not a public speaker), he became nervous in a way that he did not want. The more he thought about it, the more nervous he became, and the more nervous he became, the more fear he developed that he was going to jumble it, until it became a self-feeding neurosis.

He hoped the two traits in his makeup that had always served him well would not fail him now. The first was already working, maybe too well. He had always said about himself that his brain was like a steel spring—leave it alone, with no necessity for making decisions, and it would just relax like a loose coil. But the more pressure applied to it, the faster and more clearly he could think. Compress the spring with pressure and it snapped back efficiently.

The second trait was what he was depending on now: anytime he was subjected to a crisis of any kind, he relaxed to a dead calm. It was like someone throwing a switch: he'd turn off his emotions completely, and his brain would take over. The more deadly the emergency, the calmer he got—until it was all over ... and then he fell apart. He hoped it wouldn't fail him now.

And it didn't. By the time he stepped into the room with all the reporters and equipment, he was like a mechanical man, the cogs of his brain whirring objectively and efficiently, totally removed from emotion.

Jim Kincaid, the CBS reporter who had invited him here, came to greet him, his hand extended. "Hello, Jim," he said. "Glad you could make it. I'm Jim Kincaid."

The self-introduction was unnecessary since Jim knew Kincaid's face as well as the man next door because of the many newscasts he had watched him deliver.

"Yes, I know," said Jim. "I've been an avid fan of yours lately." Kincaid smiled understandingly. He introduced him to the rest of the men in the room, all of them part of the team that would be doing the taping. Jim didn't bother trying to remember names or duties.

He sat down in the chair that Kincaid motioned him to and waited.

"Feel like a rehearsal?" Kincaid asked pleasantly, plainly trying to put him at ease.

"Sure," he answered. "In fact, I think I need one. I had better warn you, Jim, that I'm not a public speaker, and that thing,"—he pointed to the camera—"scares me to death."

Kincaid smiled and said, "Don't worry about it. It scares everybody."

One of the crewmen in back of the camera said, "Let me tell you ... I've been on this side of the camera for over twenty years, and I've filmed a lot of footage of other people, so you would think that I'd be right at home in front of it. One day, I went to a shopping mall in my hometown to pick up some things for my wife. I was elbowing my way through a crowd on the sidewalk when I looked up to realize that I was staring into a TV camera. They were doing one of those 'man on the street' interviews. I have to tell you, I froze. I couldn't even tell him my own name. Talk about being embarrassed!"

He told it in such a sincere way that Jim knew it was true. They all had a good laugh and relaxed. Jim felt much better.

"These are some of the things I'll be asking," said Kincaid, going into the rehearsal. He aked questions and listened to Jim's answers, nodding occasionally.

When the rehearsal was finished and Kincaid was satisfied, he asked Jim, "Are you ready for the real thing?"

Jim took a deep breath and said, "About as ready as I'll ever be, I guess."

"Okay, here we go," said Kincaid, nodding his head at the cameraman. A little light came on above the beady, threatening eye of the lens, and Jim's throat convulsed. He swallowed hard.

The camera swung to focus on Kincaid. "This is Jim Kincaid, *CBS News*, in Charleston, West Virginia, or more specifically, Kanawha County, where the interest of the world has been focused in the last several weeks. We are here now to interview

Mr. James Farley, a leading figure of the faction protesting many of the controversial textbooks selected last May by the local school board.

"Mr. Farley's wife's car was firebombed beside their home, in what was thought to be retaliation for Mr. Farley's part in the protest."

He turned to Jim, and the beady-eyed gaze of the camera followed suit. Jim tightened up and then suddenly went dead calm.

"Mr. Farley, can you tell us what got you involved in this protest?"

Jim was amazed at the professional clarity and authority in his own voice as he responded. "To answer that, Jim, with any measure of understandable accuracy, I'll first have to explain that I'm 'from Missouri,' as the saying goes. When Alice Moore first brought what she considered objectionable material to the public's attention, I was very skeptical. I went to one of her book showings and was unimpressed. Then, later, I went to one of Marvin Horan's rallies and, among other things, listened to a tape of "Diary of a Madman," based on the article of the same name by Guy de Maupassant.

"The way the subject was presented in the tape made my skin crawl. The voice narrating it drooled lovingly over the word 'kill' as it extolled the virtues and desirability of killing. It disturbed me to think that such material was being used in our schools, but I still wasn't convinced.

"When the boycotts on the schools were called, I requested that the third-grade books of my young daughter be sent home so that I might examine them. I skimmed through her Communicating reader by the D. C. Heath and Company and saw nothing. I began to read it again, and one story caught my eye. It was called "The Cow-Tail Switch." It was a story set in India, telling of a tribe that, in effect, took the bones of a cow and performed the miracle of resurrection, of breathing life into the dead body of a cow. I thought this a little unusual, but by itself, not startling. But then I dug further, in light of what had struck me in the one story, and I saw more of the same nature.

"Jim, suddenly a definite, diabolical plan leapt out at me from those pages. It scared me more than I have ever been scared in my life, and the feeling increased each day as I uncovered more and more of the plan threaded throughout these books."

"What exactly did you see, Mr. Farley, that you're referring to as 'the plan'?

"It is a cleverly constructed plan to continually use the substance of various stories in the Bible for the basis of stories under the headings of MYTHS and FABLES, thereby suggesting to the child that the stories he will find in the Bible are mythical in nature."

"Don't you feel that's being a little paranoid, Mr. Farley?"

"I thought so at first, Jim. But then I got hold of a third-grade reader and discovered even stronger evidence. Take the story of 'Androcles and the Lion,' for example. It is a direct parallel to or takeoff on the biblical 'Daniel in the Lions' Den.'"

"Well, the writers of these stories have to get their material from somewhere; why not the Bible?"

"I asked myself the same thing, Jim, but then I read further. Even if that were the case, why would they refer to a mythical god with a capital G—as 'a God'? That happens in a story on page 143 of the third-level Communicating series.

"And why would writers and publishers who claim to strive to be in step with the times, accentuating 'relevancy' and 'now', stressing the 'real' world, use fables so profusely in the first place? And in the second place, why would they draw their material from the age-old Bible? The proclaimed theme is 'relevancy to now; do not hang on to yesterday.'

"Furthermore, the Bible, along with prayer, has been banned from public schools with the approval of these very people."

"In your opinion, Mr. Farley, what do you feel will be the ultimate result of this so-called 'plan,' if it does exist?"

"I am convinced of the plan's existence, and if it is left unconfronted in our schools, exposing our children to its devastating influence, I see no doubt that it will deteriorate their belief in the Bible to near atheism ... or possibly total atheism."

"Don't you think that's a bit strong?"

"I wish I did. No, I'm afraid it's stating the facts as they are."

"Concerning this valley of Kanawha itself, Mr. Farley, it has been torn apart by this controversy. Do you think it will ever by the same again?

"No, I don't," answered Jim. He paused long enough for the camera to pan over and register the attentive, expectant perplexity on Kincaid's face, and then he went on to conclude, "I think it will be much better for the experience. I think this will make them aware of the problem we're facing, and I think they will address it." He smiled warmly and said, "These are good people here in this valley, and I think this will draw them closer together."

The camera went back to Kincaid, who said, "Thank you, Mr. Farley". Jim Kincaid paused for effect and then said, "Is Mr. Farley correct in his analysis of the plan and the problem? Perhaps we will have to wait for history to make that judgment. Jim Kincaid, *CBS News*, Kanawha County."

Author's note: They cut this interview out—kept it out of the news. They banned it. Is this not censorship? Or would they call it selectivity?

CHAPTER 24

The Old Irishman

"Jim, you want to go down the street and have a cup of coffee?" Jim looked up from his desk to see George Tucker's smiling face. George always smiled with true mirth, yet his eyes and mouth never quite matched in their degree of enthusiasm. That, plus looking like an overgrown boy, an outdated man about campus, good looks and all, gave George a unique charisma.

"Ginny, can you stay here with June?" Jim asked.

"Sure." Ginny never wasted words or expressions. Either she gave you that serious, searching look, as though she were weighing everything you said, along with its consequences, or she smiled faintly. Jim had only heard her laugh aloud once.

Walking down Capitol Street beside George, who hadn't stopped talking since they left the office, Jim was only half listening. He was observing the people they were passing, automatically wondering about each one. Where did he or she stand on the textbook issue? Friend or foe? Or worse, uncaring. Apathy and ignorance vied for first place as the worst enemy of the protestors' struggle.

As they approached the sparkling new MacDonald's restaurant, with its huge gold "M" hovering over the business district, he was saddened more than a little by the changes that were taking place in his beloved town. He still thought of it as the relatively small town he had grown up in, but it was rapidly turning into a modern city, and its growing pains hurt him. It made him feel as if someone had taken the classic old home place down on the farm and remodeled it, added to its size, and turned it into a commercialized motel, erasing all the memories. He and George entered the restaurant, ordered their coffee and found a secluded seat.

His resentment at the change made him wonder about the

book advocates' accusation that the protestors' chief objection to the textbooks was that they were against change, that they wanted to hang onto yesterday. Was that his real reason for joining the fight? He had always tried to be honest with himself, constantly analyzing his own motives, feelings, judgment, and so on. He was never quite sure if his answers were correct when they came, but he tried his best with all he had. That's all anybody can do, he told himself.

"He and I were 'playing hooky' buddies." George's remark startled him back to the present.

"Who?"

George smiled accusingly, knowing Jim had not heard a word he had said.

"Bill Pauley, the mayor of Marmet."

"What about him?"

George smiled broadly. "I was telling you about the excerpts from some of the books he said an old Irishman he knew had. Bill said they were dynamite."

Jim's interest was instant and intense. "Who is he ... and where can we find him?" The crowd and the city faded as he focused in totally on George, eager for his answer.

"I could call Bill and ask him."

"Do it, George, do it."

George was clearly amused and pleased at Jim's excitement. "All right, all right. I'll call him."

Jim and George went directly to the closest telephone booth. While George was making the call, Jim paced up and down outside the booth. He had never been as fired up in his life as much as he was over these books, or rather the plan in them. Normally, he was a moderate person, even low-key, taking no stand at all on most issues, preferring harmony to discord.

George came out of the phone booth, and Jim turned toward him eagerly. "Well?"

George looked at him in mock seriousness. "I'll trade you the answer to that for a ride to Marmet. I left my car there and came down with Ginny this morning."

"You've got it. Where do we meet him?"

"In Marmet City Hall."

"Let's go."

On the way back to the parking lot to pick up his car, and also during the twenty-minute drive, Jim thought of the far reaches of the isolated valley he had made trips to whenever he had even a glimmer of hope of acquiring bits and pieces of evidence about the adverse contents of the textbooks.

He had the feeling that George was feeling him out. There was a lot of talk between them, but occasionally George would insert pointed questions, such as the ones he was asking now: "How far would you really go to stop these books, Jim? From what I've seen, you've gone all out. But do you have a stopping point? Just how far are you willing to go?"

Jim looked at him guardedly. He had developed a suspicion of everyone, bordering on paranoia—especially since the bombing of his wife's car.

"What do you have in mind, George?"

George became evasive. "Oh, I don't know. Just speculating, I guess. It's just you are more fired up about these books than anybody I know. I know for a fact that you haven't worked a day since you really got involved."

Jim grew silent, thinking about the nights he had lain awake, the structure of George Washington High School looming large in his mind. It was the elite of the progressive educators' edict as well the most modern building in the school system of Kanawha County. To top if off, it was located on South Hills, and the majority of the student body came from the wealthiest families of the valley. Some called them spoiled brats. More infringements of rules were tolerated there than at any other school in the system. Alcohol (bottled, not moonshine) and drugs were in abundance, sometimes with not too much effort to hide them.

While he had lain awake, he had methodically worked out

various plans in his imagination, including slipping through the woods from his house to the school (they were in sight of one another, on opposite hills, separated only by a valley), carrying a homemade bomb of dynamite. He could see himself carefully placing the bomb in a strategic location in order to do the maximum damage. A thrill of satisfaction would run though him as he envisioned bricks, glass, and wood flying in all directions. He told himself the only thing that kept him from it was the fear of injuring human beings, innocent or otherwise. At times, he tried to convince himself that if he set the charge at two o'clock in the morning, there would be no one around. But then, he thought, with my luck, some drunk will run his car into the ditch and come staggering up to the front door of the school looking for a phone just as the whole front of the school explodes in his face. No, he couldn't take that chance. (He doubted that he would ever carry out such a plan anyway, but it was satisfying to think about it).

"You decide not to stop at City Hall, Jim?"

"What?" George's remark brought him out of his thoughts.

"You passed it three blocks back." The amused smile on Tucker's face told him once again that George had been rambling on, and he had not heard a word.

He shrugged sheepishly, wheeled the car into a side street, and drove up the alley to City Hall. They parked between a fire truck and a police car, both of them new.

"Well, Jim," George said, "this is where I leave you. Go through that door, up the stairs, and it's the first door to your right."

"You're not going up?"

"Nah, I think the Irishman would be more relaxed and receptive if only one man showed up."

"You don't know him?"

"Never met him in my life."

Jim gave him a puzzled look. A twinkle in George's eye was added to the amused smile. He seemed to delight in keeping a person guessing. "Go on. It'll be all right. He's waiting for you." He got out of the car and began walking away, turning the corner out of sight. Jim sat watching him go, the feeling of mystery deepening. He got out of the car.

He stopped at the top of the stairs and listened. Nothing. The second floor of city hall was as silent as a tomb. He wondered if George was playing a prank on him. He shrugged. I'm already here—might as well see it through. He looked at the closed, unmarked door that George had indicated. If there was to be a joke on him, he might as well get it over with. He opened it.

A lone figure sat in the far corner. It was a man, looking straight at him. Even though his shoulders were slumped over the long conference table now, they were broad and muscular. The mass of gray hair suggested wildness yet wisdom. He did not move, nor did he speak. Each of them waited for the other to acknowledge the reason for being here.

It was Jim who finally broke the silence, becoming embarrassed by the length of it. "Are you the man I'm supposed to meet here?"

"You Jim Farley?"

"Yes."

"Than I'm the man."

The old Irishman's history was written in his personality. His anguish and failures were stamped plainly on his face for all to see. A life wasted in barroom brawls, drowning himself in a sea of whiskey to escape the dreary drudgery of the endless hours in the mines ... The first drink was to cut the black dust from his throat; the dust he knew would end his life too soon. The second drink was to relieve the nagging pain of the physical—his torn and overworked body. The third drink was for the soul, to drive the cold winds out of the vast cavern of emptiness inside him. From there on, it was drink for the sake of drink. Pour it down, drink after drink, until it becomes a fiery river, searing body and mind to numbness, finally dropping into an abyss of darkness, only to wake up in hell the next morning.

He told of the night he stumbled into a tent meeting of a Pentecostal revival, unable to control the trembling of his body, caused by a weeklong drunk. The alcohol leaving his body was flogging his soul, screaming through the corridors of hell, the caked blood showing through the dirt of his unshaven face, testifying to the beating he had taken. The swollen, cut fists proved he had given some of what he had received.

He stood there in the center aisle, just inside the tent flap, swaying uncertainly back and forth, a horrifying sight to the shocked faces of the congregation, which had turned toward him. The services had been frozen, the preacher stopped in mid-gesture, the piano stilled. He continued to sway ...

Suddenly, the preacher outstretched his arms in an inviting gesture, and he broke down into uncontrollable sobbing and lurched forward in a stumbling run for the altar. He fell to his knees, and the preacher dropped beside him, followed by a surge of the entire body of the church, until he was smothered in a mass of praying bodies, joining him in his fervent plea to God for relief from hell. And the demons in his soul went out, screamingly, until he was clean and pure and at peace.

"I took up the banner of the Lord that night," said the old Irishman, "and I ain't laid it down since."

He looked at Jim levelly, neither bragging nor apologizing, just stating a fact. His gray eyes were clear and intelligent. They looked at Jim with interest now, waiting to see where the conversation would lead.

Mesmerized, Jim sat silent. The buildup of the sense of intrigue by the sequence of events leading up to this moment set the stage of his emotions, and the dramatic speech just delivered by the old Irishman stunned him. Forgotten were the books. The man before him was a wonder, he sensed.

Jim's greatest asset, one that he had relied upon heavily all his life, was an instinct about people. That instinct that had served him well in his business was telling him now in a loud voice that he was in the presence of a most unusual man, a potpourri of intelligence, wisdom, experience, and above all, understanding. As the conversation progressed, this impression of instinct would be shored up by facts.

Jim suddenly realized that he was staring into a face that was still unflinching. The old Irishman's expression hadn't changed; he showed no impatience but was waiting for the right time for the talk to resume.

Jim pulled himself together. "Bill Pauley sent word that you had some strong excerpts from the books."

"Dynamite," said the old Irishman quietly. He reached into the inside pocket of his worn tweed coat and came out with a fistful of ragged papers. He handed them over and sat watching with the same curious, unflinching gaze as Jim began to read.

Jim was sure he had long ago gotten past the point of being shocked by anything he would find in these books. He was wrong.

When he reached a particular point in his reading them, his head snapped up to look at the Irishman in disbelief. The Irishman nodded slowly in understanding and confirmation. Jim went back fearfully to his reading. He didn't finish. He couldn't. He didn't want to.

He slammed the papers to the desk. "I can't believe this is actually in children's textbooks."

"It's there, lad."

"Are you sure?"

"If you look, you'll see the name of the book and page number where each passage can be found. It's in them, lad." The voice was quiet, unemotional. There was no indignation at having his word questioned.

"Who would do it? Why would it be allowed?"

"As to your first question, I won't name names, but I have watched the same influence at work in the United Mine Workers, the UMW, for years. I've even kept an eye on it since I retired. It's there, and it's real."

Jim studied him warily. "Do you mean who I think you do?"

"Remember, lad, I said I won't name names."

"But if it's true, what would keep people in high places who are against it from recognizing it? And doing something to stop it?"

He studied Jim thoughtfully. When he was satisfied, he answered. "For a lot of reasons, to start with, lack of understanding."

"How could anybody not understand that?" Jim said angrily, pointing at the excerpts.

The Irishman showed expression for the first time. He smiled tolerantly. "In a time when the Supreme Court can't tell the difference between art and pornography, even with all their education, wouldn't it have to be a lack of understanding? I ain't never had much book learnin', but the good Lord did give me my own brain to think with. I always wanted an education," he said wistfully, "but when circumstances force you to go to work in the mines at eight years old, there's not much time for goin' to school. I've studied life, I've studied people, and I watch the news all the time. And I study it.

And, of course, I read my Bible. That's my rock, the Bible. It's kind of like this—if a man is out in the water, it all looks alike. He can step a little to this way or that way, be swept to and fro by the water itself, and after a while, he don't really know where he is ... or how far from the shore he's drifted. But if he'll occasionally climb back up on that rock, he can get his bearings. Then he can start out again. That's kind of the way life is. Without the rock of absolutes or guidelines, we drift a little at a time, until we don't know where we are. The Bible is my rock."

Jim studied the face before him, without trying to hide the fact that he was doing it. He knew the Irishman wouldn't take offense. The Irishman's eyes were crystal balls of wisdom. In all the marks of weariness, there were signs of eternal youth. The man seemed to be the confluence of the ages, the symbol of the textbook controversy itself.

"What do you intend to do about these books?" asked Jim.

"I'll do what I can do in my own way," answered the Irishman quietly.

A myriad of thoughts ran through Jim's mind at what that might be, but he asked no questions.

"Well, I really appreciate your meeting me here and the use of the information. I've got to be getting back." He got up; the Irishman didn't move. They shook hands in that position, looking into each other's eyes for a moment, but neither spoke. Then Jim turned and walked out of the room without looking back.

He started his car, looking around. No sight of George. It was as if he had never been there. He pulled out into traffic and headed downriver toward Charleston.

Suddenly, something struck him: he didn't know the old Irishman's name.

CHAPTER 25
Steps Taken Against the School Board

Glasgow City Hall was dark as Jim pulled up in front of it. It was an unpretentious one-story cinder block building painted light gray. He had passed this way many times before, but he had never really noticed it, so he didn't know which part of the building the police department was in. He was supposed to meet George Tucker, Marvin, and a lawyer named Hizerman at police headquarters—to plan the arrest of the members of the school board. Tucker's brother was the mayor. When Tucker had approached him this afternoon in the office to set up the meeting, the reason for all the mysterious questions on the way to see the old Irishman became quite clear.

It felt strange pulling up to a police station to plot something having to do with their side of the fight. The police had all been on the other side. He was uneasy as he walked toward the dimly lit doorway. He wondered if he was becoming paranoid. The vision of his wife's burning car illuminating his house wiped that thought out of his mind.

He stepped through the door and into a hallway. He heard voices coming from one of the rooms and went in.

They were all sitting around a long table talking. There was Marvin, Tucker, a man Tucker introduced as Eddie Hizerman, a man who was currently a state policeman but wouldn't give his name, and a man sitting on a chair in the corner, whom nobody bothered to introduce. Tucker's brother, the mayor, sat at the head of the table.

Eddie Hizerman had the floor, and he was saying, "Tucker asked me to come up here for some kind of clandestine meeting. He wouldn't tell me anything, just asked me to trust him. Okay, I trust him—here I am. Now tell me what this is all about."

George Tucker looked straight into Hizerman's eyes while he spoke to the other men in the room. "Eddie and I were in the army together. Eddie had been a captain in the CIA before he joined my outfit. His intelligence background made me think he could help us in what we have in mind. On top of that, he's a good lawyer as well as a good friend."

Tucker looked to be in his midthirties, with boyish good looks and a shock of unruly sandy hair. Hizerman was almost totally bald, wore glasses, and looked at least twenty years older than Tucker. It was hard to imagine the two of them being in the army together.

"That's a flattering introduction, George," said Hizerman, "and it makes me nervous. What are you setting me up for?"

Tucker looked him straight in the eyes again, growing extremely serious. He took a deep breath and said, "Eddie, we want to arrest the members of the school board."

Hizerman sat stunned. "You want to what?"

"We want to arrest the school board," repeated Tucker.

Hizerman looked at him as if he were seeing a madman. "Do you know what you're saying? Arrest them on what charge?"

"Contributing to the delinquency of a minor. Can it be done?"

The lawyer looked at him and then looked away for a long time. Finally, he said, "It could be done, but it's not quite that simple. First off, who's going to be crazy enough to sign the warrant?"

Tucker turned to the inconspicuous little man in the corner who had been completely forgotten. "Mr. McDaniels here said he will."

Hizerman looked McDaniels over and turned back to Tucker, wearing an incredulous look. "Come on, Tuck, they'll never buy it."

"He has a child in the public school system."

"That's not what I mean, and you know it. Can he qualify as a taxpaying citizen? Does he own anything or work anywhere?"

Tucker beamed. "He owns his own home, even if he doesn't work."

"You're reaching, Tuck."

Tucker got serious again. "We're desperate, Eddie. You know what's been going on, what we're up against. Jim here had his car blown up right beside his house. This is not a game, Eddie."

"The last time I saw Jim, he had books under each arm, swinging both fists in the fight," laughed Marvin, a twinkle in his eye.

Hizerman looked at the floor for a long time, then slowly brought his gaze up and stared at each person. He finally began to speak. "If you'll take my advice, you'll forget the whole thing. The board will be back on the street an hour after you arrest them."

Jim hadn't taken part much up to this point, but he could hold his silence no longer. "Mr. Hizerman, when you were in the CIA, didn't you ever get involved in a mission where you did one thing to accomplish another?"

Hizerman looked at Jim as if seeing him for the first time. "Yes, I suppose I did," he answered, "but what does that have to do with this?"

"Everything," said Jim. "We're not interested in sending these men to jail for a long period, although if it were possible, we probably would. What we're interested in right now is having it splashed coast to coast on the six o'clock news that the members of the school board of Kanawha County have been arrested. Period. Of course, it would have even more impact if the media chose to throw in a picture of them being led away in handcuffs." Jim's persuasive powers were on full force, his eyes blazing with emotion. Hizerman was mesmerized. He looked at Jim intently.

Jim continued. "Right now, Mr. Hizerman, the tide is against us, thanks to the media. Think what it would do with the headlines coast to coast screaming: SCHOOL BOARD ARRESTED IN KANAWHA COUNTY. How can they possibly distort that to go against us? It's bound to get us favorable attention. Besides, we will get the fringe benefit of rattling their cages some more. It can't do anything but help."

"In other words," said the lawyer, "all you want and expect out of this is the headlines."

"Now you've got it," retorted Jim, banging his fist down on the table.

Hizerman still appeared skeptical, but Jim got the impression Hizerman was impressed with Jim's persuasive argument. His eyes became glassy shields, hiding his thoughts. His mind seemed to whir like a computer, sifting through the information and options at hand, looking for the right one.

Finally, expression returned to his eyes as he glanced around the circle of tense faces looking at him, waiting for his answer. It appeared the old warhorse of his CIA days must have stirred in him, for Jim could see the admiration for the boldness of these men and their plan as he said, "It will work. You have the grounds."

The circle came alive with jubilation, and he raised a hand in warning to temper their enthusiasm. "I will take no part in the execution of this. Can any of you type?"

They all looked around at each other. George asked, "Jim, can you type?"

"Not me," said Jim.

Finally, George, after no one else spoke up, said, "Well, I guess I'm elected. I'm strictly a hunt-and-peck kind of guy, but I can eventually get it with two fingers."

Hizerman rose to go. "Well, that does it then. Tuck," he said with a smile, "although officially, I still advise you to forget the whole thing, let me unofficially offer you my best wishes and the best of luck in doing this. I hope you pull if off."

With that, he smilingly shook all their hands and took his leave. After thanking Hizerman for coming and seeing him to the door, Tucker retired to a room across the hall to painstakingly type the warrant.

Jim and Marvin took turns pacing the floor nervously.

"What do you think the results of this will be, Jim?" asked Marvin.

"I don't know the exact results, but I can't see where anything but good can come from it."

They turned expectantly as George came bursting in. "How do you spell delinquency?" he asked. When Jim spelled it for him, Tucker popped back out of the room to continue the agonizingly slow typing. Jim and Marvin returned to their pacing, trying to ignore the long spaces between each of the tap-tap of the typewriter.

It reminded Jim of a scene in the movie *Tora! Tora! Tora!* The story was woven around the Japanese attack on Pearl Harbor, and in this particular scene, the Japanese envoy to Washington was nervously pacing the floor while he waited for the only person he could find on a Sunday morning in the Japanese consulate to type his government's ultimatum to the United States. The message was to have been delivered an hour before the attack on Pearl Harbor was to take place. Due to the lack of a typist and the time it took the man with no experience to do the job, the attack was delivered forty minutes before the message, consequently changing the complexion of the attack and the history of the world. He didn't feel that tonight's typing of the warrant would be that earth-shattering, but it was no less nerve-racking. At least time was in their favor.

Finally, it was finished. After last-minute details were discussed, Jim left the building and walked to his car. There was little traffic this time of night, so he had the opportunity to reflect on tonight's events as he drove back to Charleston. The fog rising from the river running parallel to the road looked fresh and bright in the moonlight. He felt like it was an omen of the results of their evening's work. He got a grim satisfaction from the image in his imagination of the Matt Dillon–type state policeman delivering the warrant to the shocked members of the school board and slapping handcuffs on their wrists. He smiled.

Jim's interest in the struggle of the textbooks had intensified daily. What had looked at the beginning to be a simple matter, taking only the outcry of public indignation to resolve the situation, had developed into a complex, frustrating, sometimes seemingly hopeless battle. When he had become involved, he had thought it entailed only a few misguided schoolbooks. He realized now that the 164 books were but a droplet of water in a sea of oppression, threatening the apple pie way of life that he, along with millions of other Americans, had always loved so much.

"America, America, God shed his grace on thee ..." Jim could hear the strains of the beautiful old song wafting out from the little one-room frame schoolhouse he had attended periodically for his first six grades of education.

The great American dream was still alive then.

When the magnitude of the total scope of attack became vivid to him, it shook him to his very roots. It scared him more than he had ever been scared in his life. Then he got mad—first at the attack, then at the ones behind it, then at himself and his contemporaries for letting it happen while they slept.

Now, at this point of the struggle—no, at this point of the war—all this had combined to cause a resolve in him, bordering on fanaticism.

Each time he was thwarted, he got madder and fought harder. With all this in mind, his feelings about the upcoming arrest of the members of the school board were understandable. He looked forward to the event with anticipated relish. All the board members had become hated enemies, except "Sweet Alice." She was the only one excluded from the warrant they had so laboriously typed.

"Jesus loves you." Jim had dialed the telephone number of Karl Priest—or at least thought he had. The voice answering at the other end in this manner surprised him and made him wonder.

He decided to take a chance. "Karl?"

"Yes." (He would come to realize that this was Karl's customary fashion in answering the phone. He always answered this way, no matter who called.)

"My name is Jim Farley, and I was told that you don't particularly like the textbooks that are in our schools now."

"That's true."

Karl Priest was a reticent man who smiled little, and then only weakly, but he was a dedicated born-again Christian. He took this role seriously, as he did his part in the textbook controversy.

"I wonder if we could get together and discuss an organization that I'm putting together."

"Certainly. When do you want to do it?"

"How about tomorrow morning at ten?" Since today was Friday, he figured Karl would be free the next day.

"Fine. Where do you want to meet?"

"How about in the office that my organization has rented? It's in the Union Building. As everybody is fond of saying, it's the only building on the wrong side of the boulevard."

"Yes, I know the one. I'll be there."

Karl was the first active schoolteacher he had approached. He hoped to get several eventually, maybe even enough to form a teachers' group within the Alliance. He felt this would give them an inroad into the educational system, provide inside information, and do wonders for their credibility.

CHAPTER 26

Strange Happenings

He and June were alone in the office. It was long past their normal quitting time, but they dreaded going home, and there was always more paperwork to do than they could take care of during the day. Because of the two reasons, they were still at it even though it was past ten o'clock. The telephone startled Jim when it rang. It sounded loud as a fire alarm. He answered it.

"Alliance for Better Textbooks."

"Is Mr. Farley there?"

"Speaking."

"Mr. Farley, this is Katherine Messingale. I'm quite sure that doesn't mean a thing to you, but I feel I know you like a good neighbor down the street. Although you're not aware of it, we have a lot in common. We're even partners of sorts."

Jim was puzzled. What was she talking about?

"I saw your picture looking in at your burned car on the front page of the Portland newspaper, so I even know what you look like."

The information was coming faster than he could absorb it. He mulled this over, waiting for her to go on. When there was silence from the other end, he said, "You mean the picture of me was on the front page clear up in Oregon?"

"Oh, you're front page news, Mr. Farley—not only in Oregon ... but headline news across the country. Didn't you know that?"

"Well, I have heard about other parts of the country showing interest in our problem, but I didn't realize it went that far."

"Oh, yes ... You're the focal point of the nation."

"Well, I have had people that I know give me a few reports.

My cousin, for example, who was in Pennsylvania on business, called his wife to ask her what in the world was going on down here in Charleston. He said the textbook controversy in Kanawha County was all that was on the news there."

"It's the same all over the country, Mr. Farley. I follow it. Which brings me to my reason for calling. I'm the head of a national women's organization, and we've been dedicated to fighting this for longer than you would believe. We have offices in practically every major city in the country, at least one office in each state.

"I've been following your struggle there with keen interest from the beginning, and although I admire you very much for the stand you are taking, I'm sorry to tell you, Mr. Farley, but you can't win. 'They' will beat you in the end."

This rankled Jim's hillbilly ire. "Well, we're sure gonna give it a good try".

"Don't misunderstand me, Mr. Farley. I'm on your side. I wish I could be as optimistic about the outcome as you are, but believe me, I know them. They are well organized, well financed, and totally committed to their cause. You know, when I first saw these people moving into West Virginia, I knew they had a fight on their hands."

"Why is that?"

"It's because West Virginians are a special breed of people. Take your state motto—'Montani Semper Liberi' sums it up. 'Mountaineers Are Always Free.' You hillbillies have a singular quality about you that is missing in the rest of the country. Some people would call it narrow-mindedness and backwardness, and they do call it that. But I see it as pride, backbone, and unswerving dedication to your beliefs. The topography of West Virginia is part of the reason for this. You're separated geographically by the hills. The people in one hollow are a world apart from their neighbors just a mile or so away, sometimes less, because they are cut off by the mountain or hill in between.

"To reach one another, you sometimes have to travel as much as twenty or thirty miles or more, which of course, you never do.

When you do come 'out of the hollow,' or 'holler,' as some of your people put it, it is to take care of necessary affairs in one of your small towns or the capital city, Charleston. Consequently, your lives seldom touch, except those of the few people in the same area. So, therefore, you're definitely rugged individualists. And you're clannish. But overlaying this diversity, there is also a common bond. You're all hillbillies."

Jim listened with his emotions in neutral. Usually, what the woman was saying would offend him because, as a rule, it was intended to be derogatory. But the admiring tone in her voice made it clear that she was paying homage in a complimentary fashion. Besides, she was right. He thought of the year of the state's centennial, 1963. He had gone with a group of schoolchildren that included his oldest daughter, Carmella, and a niece of his to East Bank, one of the small towns several miles upstream from Charleston. The children were there at a high school, dressed in colonial days' attire to perform in a celebration marking the birth of the state one hundred years before.

An incident that happened while they were there gives credence to the chopped-up geography the woman was referring to. While waiting for their turn to come, they were asked by the woman in charge where they were from—in other words, what school. Jim's six-year-old niece shyly answered, "West Virginia." Because of the long drive, weaving around and over hills, she thought they had traveled to some other state.

The woman continued. "Although you're not aware of it, Mr. Farley, my organization has been working with you, or rather in conjunction with you, all through your struggle. I want you to know that if we can be of any help in a more direct way, don't hesitate to call on us. You already have my name. Let me give you my address and phone number as well."

Jim found a pen and paper and was writing down her address and phone number as she recited it. Then the line went dead. He waited a while time for her to continue before he realized that it was dead. What had happened?

He thought about what the woman from Oregon had said. She evidently knew a lot about West Virginia and its people, as well as the terrain. He wondered if she was familiar enough with the diversity of the population—educationally, financially, intellectually, and socially—to consider the same thing he had thought of many times. He had wondered if that was why the people behind this, whoever they might be, had decided to use Kanawha County as a testing ground—these people who were so diverse that they were almost like a cross section or a sampling of the population of the nation as a whole. Almost any type could be found somewhere within Kanawha County.

Why had the phone gone dead? He knew she hadn't hung up. She was right in the middle of a word when it happened. Why did it go dead? Why?

He stared out into the dark night, thinking of the burning of his wife's car. He still couldn't quite grasp the reality that some faceless creature had brassily walked down his driveway and arrogantly thrown a firebomb in the backseat of his wife's car. His mind wouldn't accept this.

He had built the driveway himself, on property that he had played on when he was a child. It had been his own private world all his life. He had built his house with his own hands ... raised his children there.

And now some unseen force he couldn't identify had caused his wife's car to explode right beside their bedroom window like a munitions cache in a war. It lit up the whole house as it burned.

Thinking of the car burning, he thought the light flickering briefly in the parking lot below was in his mind's eye. Then he saw it again. It went out again. Icy fear of the unreal chilled him throughout. His body tingled, and his mind went numb.

He focused his attention, concentrating on the spot where he thought he had seen the light. It was at the rear of the second car in front of his own, parked on the public lot beside the building. The Alliance office was on the third floor, so he was looking down with a clear view of all the cars there, except he could only see the outlines in the darkness. The light went on again, stayed on briefly, and then went off.

He tried to convince himself that some child was playing with the brakes while waiting for a parent to return from shopping. But the stores had closed over an hour ago. Besides, no child would be left alone this late. The light came on again.

What bothered him was the rhythmic sequence it followed. It went off again. A week ago, he wouldn't even have noticed it. He remembered his flippant remark to his wife about "providing the match" to the caller who said he was going to bomb her car. He had never believed for a minute that it could really happen. Now he was ready to believe anything. The light went on again.

Was it some kind of signal? If it was, who was the signal intended for, and for what reason? Was someone waiting for him and June to leave the office, the way he apparently did the night the car burned? Maybe the person waiting was nervous, his foot inadvertently hitting the brake pedal as he fidgeted around.

He watched the lights of the cars going up and down the expressway across the river, and he felt very lonely. It was as if he and his wife were totally alone in their plight and the rest of the world was bustling on its busy way, uncaring, not even knowing they were there.

For the second time since he had taken up the fight, he wondered if it was worth it. Those people out there, driving blissfully up and down the streets and highways, were the ones he was trying to protect, and right now they didn't seem to care. He could put his daughter in a Christian school and forget it. Maybe that's what he should do. He was tired ... very tired.

Staring for so long at the spot where the car was parked, his vision blurred. He looked away to rest his eyes for a moment, and when he looked back, the car was gone. Just like that, it was gone. He looked closer to make sure. It truly was gone.

He told himself that now he could relax and forget it. It was just a coincidence. But that was the eerie thing about this whole happening. Nothing was ever clearly defined. It was like a fog, solid, immovable; look again and it was gone—then back again, in a different place and a different form. It was nerve-racking and disconcerting. He knew it would be hours before he would stop waiting for an explosion, or for a bullet, to come crashing through the window. At every sound in the hall, he expected the door to come crashing off its hinges.

This is silly, he chided himself. Then the grisly picture of his wife's little Pinto, gutted by fire, the charred remains of Kelly's Bible in the back window, filled his mind and the foreboding fog returned.

He had gotten his little .22 single-action revolver from his son yesterday. His son had borrowed it to do some target shooting. It wasn't much of a weapon, but it would at least make some noise and maybe slow an assailant down. He didn't want to kill anybody. He slid open the desk drawer where he kept it and closed his hand over the butt of the gun. It felt good, reassuring, having the cold, hard steel of the weapon fill his fist. He squeezed it, knotting his jaw as he looked down on the parking lot again. "Come on, boys," he muttered through clenched teeth, "Come on. Let's get this over with." He almost wished the door would burst open so he could see and come to grips with the enemy.

He looked around himself at the empty office, feeling foolish but filled with a new resolve. H– no, he wasn't going to quit. They had done made him mad. Nobody was going to come into his private little world, kick anything he wanted to apart, then blithely go laughing on his. No way ... By golly, he was going to do some kicking of his own.

He took the gun from the drawer, put it in his belt, and went to tell his wife they were going home.

CHAPTER 27
School Bus Attacked

Sam Barnett's mouth was dry as he dropped the clutch and sent a big yellow bus, with the black words KANAWHA COUNTY SCHOOLS on its side, lurching out into traffic. He was leaving the bus garage at St. Albans, heading for his usual destination of Dawes Elementary School at Alum Creek. It was a long drive and most of it over lonely roads, the last leg being a three-mile section of secondary Route 214.

Sam was understandably nervous. In all of his eighteen years of driving a school bus, he had never found a situation like the one that confronted him now. In the raging war over the controversial textbooks, there had been schools dynamited, bullet holes put in state police cruisers, and even people shooting arbitrarily into the air. He couldn't get the thought out of his mind of what an easy target the big yellow bus made. The fact that his buddy George Ashby was directly behind him in his bus (they had been instructed to travel in pairs for safety) was some comfort ... but not much. After all, whether his superiors knew it or not, bullets could come out of the brush from anywhere on the sides of these hills; they could rake two buses as easily as one, and the joker or jokers firing the shots could be long gone before any kind of police help could get to the scene. The people fighting these books were hillbillies, born and bred; some of them were as familiar with these hills as with their living rooms, from their many years of squirrel and deer hunting ... Deer hunting ... Sam wished he hadn't thought of that. Deer hunters meant deer rifles, powerful guns with very long range, more than enough range to effectively kill a man from the top of any one of these ridges.

He was leaving most of the houses behind now, and as he downshifted for the long, steep hill into Alum Creek, his nervousness grew. He had almost reached the bottom of the hill—the school building would be coming into view around the next bend—when suddenly, it happened. He saw a flash from an oncoming car and heard an explosion. Steam hissed from his radiator, ruptured by the shotgun blast. Sam swerved the wheel hard right, heading deliberately for the ditch, at the same time throwing himself to the floor. The bus hit the ditch with a sickening crunch, throwing him up under the dashboard. Pain shot though his shoulder and neck.

He lay still, waiting for the sound that he didn't want to hear: that of additional shots coming. Nothing. Not even the sound of the car that the shot had come from. Either it had stopped and its occupants were heading for the bus to finish him, or they were long gone. He wondered what had happened to George. Still no sound except for the hissing steam ... and even that was diminishing. Finally, total silence. Where in blazes was George?

After what seemed like an eternity, he screwed up enough courage to peek cautiously over the dash and through the windshield. George was parked down the road about two hundred yards—well, his bus was. There was no sign of George.

A wave of panic swept over him. What if George was dead? He jerked his head around in the direction the car had gone. Nothing but the lonely stretch of road met his eyes. The wind whistling through the crack in the door had an ominous sound. He breathed a little easier. He figured he had better check on George, like it or not.

He got out of his bus and headed reluctantly in his buddy's direction. His feet felt as if they had lead weights tied to them. He walked cautiously around George's bus. Two side windows were shattered. The gaping holes where the windows had been, and the many pockmarks on the side of the bus, left by the shotgun pellets, totally unnerved him. He was trembling all over as he inched his way to the front toward the driver's seat. The eerie silence didn't help.

Suddenly, he felt like yelling with joy as he saw the unmistakable hulk of George's form come tumbling out of the door of the bus, landing on his feet, very much alive.

Sam rushed toward him. George looked up, fear in his eyes

until he recognized the familiar face of a friend. They were so happy at seeing each other and being alive that they simultaneously grabbed each other in a bear hug, almost dancing in their relief.

When they regained their presence of mind and became a little calmer, Sam said, "George, I don't know about you, but as far as I'm concerned, as of now, this big yellow monster belongs to Underwood, and he can come and get it if he wants it. I'm gettin' out of here."

"I'm with you," retorted George. They lost no time in putting distance between them and the two big yellow vehicles lying ignominiously in the ditch. The first path leading up into the woods off the road offered too much lure to resist, and they disappeared from the road.

CHAPTER 28

Media Blitz

Jim glanced sideways at the national news reporter as he waited for a break in the traffic. The man had come to the office looking for directions to Ginny's house. He had been assigned to cover the meeting that was to take place there today. Jim knew that with its winding streets cutting back on themselves, the short blocks, and the confusing bypasses, an out-of-towner could never find his way up through South Hills. He had known people who had lived in Charleston all their lives to get lost up there for hours, winding around and around until they eventually wandered off the hill back down into the valley and recognized a landmark to tell them where they were.

Thinking of this, he figured somebody had better drive the man, so he volunteered. He was one of the people who was supposed to be interviewed, and he had to go up there anyway. He didn't plan to stay for the taping of the meeting, but he did want as many reporters there as possible.

The protest movement was bogged down in the morass of tar-paper shacks, complete with moonshine-drinking, tobacco-chewing miners that the media had been flooding the news with.

Ginny's house was a modern contemporary nestled in one of the new subdivisions that had been developed around the valley for the upper middle class, not stately but comfortable. The house itself and the nice neighborhood it was in should help their image considerably, but the most important factor was the address: South Hills, the citadel of the pro-book forces, at least according to the media.

Jim was finding more and more people there every day who were secret protestors, appalled at the philosophies contained in these books, but they would not come out in the open for fear of what their neighbors would think of them. That was the most frustrating thing of all to Jim. He knew firsthand that there were people all over South Hills, as well as in other parts of the valley, who were adamantly against the books, but they were sitting idle, simmering in silence because they were under the conviction that all their neighbors were in favor of them. The negative backwoods image perpetrated by the media was very effective.

Kanawha County became the focal point of the world—the vortex for social, religious, and political differences—the whetstone for nearly every known faction in the three categories to grind their axes on. Eventually, representatives from each surfaced. Some came; some were already here. Some had voices like thunder, rolling across the rugged hills, reverberating up and down the hollows like the voice of doom. Some bleated their plaintive claims in voices so weak that one had to strain to hear, and then faded back into their catacombs of obscurity from whence they had come. Some walked softly, some furtively. But some came with solid and steady strides—and stayed.

Jim thought of the reporters who had come to the Alliance office from all over the world—France, Canada, Australia, and Japan, to name a few. He himself was interviewed and filmed for Japanese TV viewers. (Someone who happened to be in Japan at the time and saw the report on their news told him that it mirrored our own media in its slant, completely against the protestors.)

The Gablers were interviewed by the Japanese February, 1982. They showed the textbooks that were being protested. The Japanese stated they were having similar problems with their textbooks.

Kanawha County was front-page news around the world.

Everybody was hearing what they thought was truth. They were being given distortions, vagaries, and (inadvertently or intentionally) outright untruths.

Alice Moore's tiny voice, drawing impetus from its strong resolve, became a living metaphor for the first act of the Civil War at Concord Bridge: the "shot heard around the world." Only hers was the shout heard 'round the world. Its echoes rolled, not only over the hills of Kanawha County but around the world.

That's why this interview at Ginny's, with national coverage for television, could be a turning point. The primary importance was sending the new image to the world. Not only was it an inroad into the heartland of enemy territory, but it would alert the silent protestors that they were not alone. In addition, it would give heart to the wretched protestors of the street to know there were, after all, some of their own among the elite of "Snob Hill."

They were out in the traffic now, moving across the South Side Bridge. Jim had been waiting for the reporter to break the silence, but the man remained in his own world, wherever that was.

"Ordinarily, you're the one asking all the questions, but this time I want to ask you a couple," Jim said.

The reporter only partly pulled himself out of his reverie. "Okay, go ahead."

Jim was twisting the steering wheel back and forth, concentrating on the curves ahead as they wound up the hill toward Ginny's.

Jim related his observation of this very thing happening at the rally at Watt Powell Ballpark just recently. "Why is it that all you reporters, when you come in here on this issue, look for the seediest-looking character you can find to interview, making sure you get a close-up of the tobacco juice trickling down his chin, recording his most asinine comments in his dumbest vernacular, when there are well-dressed, obviously well-educated people in abundance all around them?"

The reporter seemed to come into total awareness of his present surroundings and what Jim was saying. He thought a moment and then answered, "What you're saying is sad but true. We reporters tend to look for stereotypes to depict the locale and subject that we're covering." He looked around at the hills and the city below them, taking up the entire valley except the part occupied by the river.

"This is my first trip to West Virginia, and frankly, I fully expected to come in here and find a moonshine still on every hill, with hillbillies in bib overalls and black tattered hats stirring the mash while they puffed on their corncob pipes. That's the way the rest of the country sees this state, I'm afraid. You can blame Hollywood for that, I suppose."

Jim didn't quite accept the statement as total truth but chose not to press the particular point. He decided instead to improve the percentages of getting some camera shots of the attractive and expensive neighborhood where Ginny lived.

"I can understand when you put it that way, but why do you travel over rough roads and go to an awful lot of trouble taking pictures of tar-paper shacks and never show any of the nice houses like Betty Rogers's, for example. She lives in as fine a home as you would find in any neighborhood in New York, and yet you never see a picture of it on the news or in the paper. And Betty is one of the most outspoken protestors I know ... and one of the strongest supporters of the movement."

The reporter half nodded in agreement, and Jim hoped he had created a favorable frame of mind that would still be there when the reporter gave his cameraman his instructions at Ginny's. They were already in the neighborhood and nearing the house. The reporter was taking in the houses and yards as they passed through.

"One more question," said Jim as they turned the last corner. "Why does the media keep hammering away at the phrase 'Violence does not settle anything'? I'm not an advocate of violence myself, but if it is not an effective instrument and settles nothing, how come our biggest single expenditure in the federal government budget is for defense? Why do policemen carry guns and billy clubs? Of course, there are those who say it's as a deterrent. But if they are to be used as a threat and nothing more, and everybody knows it, then they lose their effectiveness as a deterrent."

The reporter stared through the windshield thoughtfully, then said, smiling wryly, "That's a good question. You do have a valid point."

They pulled into Ginny's driveway.

As they got out of the car, Jim noticed that Ginny's house was already bustling with people. Bob Dornan rushed forward with his usual effective flair to extend a warm hand to the reporter. Then he introduced him to the rest of the people there. Karen Hill, the attractive leader of her particular group in the protest, had long, flowing blond hair; blue-gray eyes; and full, ripe lips. She caught people's attention, and the soft, almost whispery voice with that Southern language enhanced her image into a magnetic mystique that captivated almost everyone. Her followers adored her. Then there was Ginny, of course, with Mick Staton, John Wilshire, and an assortment of others in the background, who would not be interviewed but were there for support.

The reporter brought in his crew that had followed Jim's car here from the office. They set up the lights and camera and began testing.

As Karen answered a question—"When I realized these books and the plan in them would undermine and eventually destroy the faith of my children in that Bible ..."— she glanced at a Bible lying on the coffee table in front of her.

Bob Dornan, although looking outwardly calm, was clearly urging silently, fervently, Pick it up; pick it up! He was surely thinking of the emotional impact it would have, seeing this attractive young mother, a genuine tear trickling down her cheek, with the Bible in her hand, explaining to the TV audience across the country the damage these books could do to their children. She never did pick it up. The camera never did record it.

When the interview was finished, the camera crew moved outside and gave them an overlay view of the neighborhood. The camera and the rest of the people followed. The supervisor looked around and directed them to set the camera up on the bank on the opposite side of the street from Ginny's house. It began recording all the modern middle-class homes.

Smiling grimly, Jim said, "I wonder how they will make tar-paper shacks out of these houses."

"Yeah," said Dornan, neither of them taking their eyes off the street.

Later, they were to find out how: they cut them out altogether. The houses were never shown!

In our complex, pluralistic society, there was no way we were going to get accurate, unvarnished, and unbiased truth from the media, Jim thought. Take a good look at the people reporting the news. They run anywhere from young and inexperienced to old and tired, simpleminded to sadistic-minded, leaving some to doubt their ability to report in an unbiased fashion. They are motivated by different things, so their priorities are diverse. Some may be good, dedicated, capable, and knowledgeable people, but they have their own unique problems as well. They run into opposition from their editors, maybe enduring communications gaps, policy differences, and pressures from the top.

Then there is the problem of communication. We hear that President Reagan chops wood on his ranch for relaxation. Someone writes to *Parade*: What kind of ax does he use? Back comes the answer: He uses a chain saw. How do you "chop" wood with a chain saw?

What do we have here? A lie? No, this was not deliberate. This is one of those times that a breakdown in communications occurred. Some editor delegated a cub reporter the menial task of finding out what kind of axe the President uses; the reporter asks whomever he thinks is in authority; the man he asks is preoccupied or doesn't fully hear or understand the question, or doesn't really care, and it goes something like this: Reporter: "What does the president cut (not chop) wood with?" Busy executive, with much more important things on his mind: "A chainsaw." The cub reporter jots it down, rushes back to his typewriter, and proudly types up the story. The general public goes around asking themselves and all their buddies, "How do you chop wood with a chainsaw?" Is this story anything to blow up the TV station about? Hardly. But it is only one small example of the thousands of things, and in no way the least of them, the media gets distorted—some inadvertently; some intentional; most of them terrible.

CHAPTER 29

The School Board Is Arrested

Elmer stood at the Alliance window, looking up the boulevard at the impressive St. Luke's Methodist Church as though trying to decide whether the magnificent spires were like fingers reaching for God or man's symbol of praise to himself. Elmer was a Methodist.

His interest was directed toward this particular church because of the meeting that was to take place there today. He had persuaded Bishop Wertz, the Methodist leader of the state, to preside over a conference between the protest leaders and school board members in hopes of reaching a compromise. If this was accomplished, it would end the war once and for all.

He turned from the window to look at Jim, who was seated behind his desk watching him. "I just hope Graley and Hill don't turn it into a shouting contest." His brows came down above the gray eyes in concentration as he stared at Jim. "I've always felt that Marvin was the most intelligent of the three. Don't you think his is?"

Jim smiled inwardly but kept a straight face. "Yeah, I would have to agree with that."

"I think he is," said Elmer. He glanced at his watch and bent down to pick up his briefcase. "Well, I've got to get up there. It's almost time." He briefly looked up at the church again. He appeared to be preparing himself. He turned to leave, saying, "Well, Jim, I hope something good comes out of this."

Jim only nodded, feeling like a traitor. Something will, Elmer, he thought, but not what you're expecting.

It made him feel even worse when Elmer added over his shoulder as he went out the door, "I've always had a great deal of respect for Bishop Wertz." With that, he disappeared from view.

Jim physically sank down into the chair. He swiveled his chair around to stare at the spires of the church with conflicting emotions. This was brought on by his knowledge of what was really going to happen at the meeting Elmer was attending. The entire school board, except Alice Moore, was going to be arrested! His guilty feelings were intensified by the fact that he had been instrumental in preparing the warrant that the constable of Cedar Grove would be serving on the board in less than an hour. Elmer knew nothing about this plan. He had never liked doing this behind Elmer's back, but he knew it was necessary because Elmer would never have agreed to it. No member of the Alliance knew about his involvement—not even Ginny, who had first introduced him to George Tucker.

But then, in contrast to his guilty feelings, the exultation flowed profusely. With great anticipation, he saw in his imagination (he wouldn't learn the actual unfolding of the drama until years later, when Elmer told him) the events that were taking place about now in the church.

All the participants were seated at a long table in the conference room: the board on one side, the protest leaders on the other, with Bishop Wertz at the head. Elmer sat at Wertz's left; Marvin next to him; then Avis and Ezra.

Dr. Underwood, the school superintendent, sat at the right of Wertz, then Russell Issacs, then Kinsolving, Stump, and Dr. Standsbury. Wertz had just called the meeting to order.

"Elmer," said Bishop Wertz, "this was your idea, so I'll start with you. What are your suggestions as to what can be done to bring this madness to an end?"

Elmer, always the moderate, gave Bishop Wertz one of his rare smiles and said, "I think madness is a strong word, Bishop. And I think that's our problem. We're all going to extremes on both sides, in words and action. That's why we formed the Alliance; we had hoped to provide a middle-of-the-road venue for people to come together in compromise. It hasn't worked that way.

"The moderates who could provide balance with the street protestors won't come forward in large enough numbers, and emphatically enough, to accomplish that. I thought perhaps we could in this meeting today."

The men seated around the table had mixed reactions. Marvin's penetrating gaze bore into Elmer as he spoke; Hill was attempting a skeptical attitude; Graley, trying to appear authoritative, looked more like a big lovable dog waiting for a command. The members of the school board looked on with expressions ranging from mild interest to total boredom. Underwood led the boredom.

"Dr. Underwood, what do you th—" Bishop Wertz was stopped in mid-sentence by a sudden movement at the entrance. He was the first to see the uniformed figure, seeming as out of place as a swastika in a Sunday school.

All the men in the room, clearly wondering why he had stopped talking, turned to follow the Bishop's stunned stare. They all focused on the constable standing in the doorway, looking like Barney Fife with a scowl. It may have been illusory, but Elmer could have sworn the man had his chest thrust forward to form a bulge under the badge that read C. L. TUCKER – CONSTABLE – CEDAR GROVE. Time stood still. The scene looked as if someone had stopped a movie mid-frame, with all faces in frozen shock—that is, all but Elmer. He sat looking at the figure in the doorway like a hoot owl that had been startled by an unexpected noise and was trying in his owlish wisdom to determine whether it was a fox or rabbit.

The constable, seeming to sense that he had milked all he could out of his moment of glory, broke the stunned silence, by saying, "I have a warrant for the arrest of the school board superintendent and all board members present."

The wise old owl decided it must be a fox and the room was full of quail because they suddenly flushed, bursting in all directions, looking for telephones to call their lawyers. The constable, though startled by this, stood between them and the outside.

"Elmer, did you know about this?" asked Bishop Wertz in an outraged tone.

"No, I didn't," answered Elmer, beginning to recover from his bewilderment.

"This is outrageous," said the bishop.

Elmer the owl was following the scurrying figures around the room with interest. "Well, Bishop, you've wanted to get this thing into the courts. Maybe this will get it there."

CHAPTER 30
Enlightenment

The arrogance of power was never epitomized more than in the simple headline in the November 8, 1974, issue of the *Charleston Daily Mail*: BOARD RETURNS ALL BOOKS TO SCHOOLS.

Against all the parents' protests, against polls showing clearly that the majority of the citizenry of Kanawha County were opposed to these controversial textbooks, against all logic and reason, the school board had voted to put all the disputed books back in the classroom. Save one, that is: Sweet Alice. The tenacious woman was still sticking to her guns. She was a remarkable woman.

As Jim read the accompanying article, all the resentment came flooding back. All the wearisome rallies, all the struggling, all the planning, and above all, the frustration of the fight began to seethe and rumble in him like a volcano. It all built into such a rage that the volcano erupted in a fury he had never experienced before. He reached for the phone, jerking it angrily from its cradle. He knew John Wilshire's number by heart.

"Hello," said John.

Jim didn't bother to identify himself. The inner circle of the hard-core protestors had become like a family, constantly in contact, so he had no doubt John would recognize his voice immediately.

"John, how long would it take to get enough of the really raunchy stuff out of the books together to make up a full-page ad?"

John paused, obviously wondering what he had in mind. "Oh, it wouldn't take long if the whole group worked on it. What do you have in mind, Jim?"

"We're gonna publish it in the *Charleston Daily Mail* for

everybody to see."

There was a longer pause. "How do you know they'll publish it? There's some bad stuff there."

"They'll publish it," Jim said through clenched teeth.

John was still skeptical. "Maybe you ought to check with them first, Jim, just to be sure. It's going to be a lot of work putting it together."

"You get it together, John. I'll get it printed."

There was another long pause, and then John finally said, "Okay, if you say so, Jim. I'll call Mick and the others and get started on it. It will take us a couple of days." The tone in Jim's voice convinced John that somehow he would get it published.

"How about tomorrow?"

"Oh, come on, Jim. That's asking a lot."

"There's a lot at stake, John."

The silence at the other end of the phone lasted so long that Jim was beginning to think the connection had been lost.

Finally, Jim heard John let out a deep sigh and say, "All right. Tomorrow." John hung up.

Jim dialed the familiar number of the *Charleston Daily Mail.* "Al Starr, please.

"Al Starr."

"Al, Jim Farley,"

"How are you Jim? What can I do for you?"

In his business, Jim had done considerable advertising with Al, and he had placed numerous Alliance ads with him.

"We're getting together enough excerpts from the books for a full-page ad, and I'd like to know how soon we can get it in the paper."

There was a deep intake of breath at the other end. "Jim, you don't really want to put that stuff in the paper, do you? Some of it is quite raw."

Jim became furious, virtually shouting into the phone. "Al, do you mean to tell me that this stuff is all right to force-feed our kids in school, but it's not fit for your readers?" If Al had hung up the phone, he probably could have heard Jim just as well, as loud as he was shouting. The newspaper's office building was only a block and a half away.

Al's tone of voice was apologetic and pleading. "But, Jim, we've got a family newspaper. Who knows who'll be reading the stuff you're talking about?"

Jim was incredulous. "They would have to be old enough to read, Al, in order to read it, which means they're old enough to go to school, which means they are reading it. Let's stop kidding each other. The only people who are going to read this stuff in the paper who wouldn't otherwise are the unsuspecting parents and public. Is that why you don't want to print it? Don't you want the public to know what's being taught in the schools their tax dollars are paying for?"

Al didn't answer for a moment. At last, he said, "All right, Jim. Get it together and bring it by. We'll take a look at it."

"That's not good enough. Will you print it?"

"Yeah, we'll print it," Al said wearily.

This was Friday, November 8. John and the group were supposed to work on the material for the ad all day Saturday; and then Elmer, Mick, Larry, and Jim were to meet at Mick's house on Sunday to look it over, making any beneficial changes and editing it.

When he got to Mick's house Sunday afternoon, Mick's lovely wife, Lynn, answered the door. She smiled warmly when she saw him. "Hello, Jim, come on in. Mick and the others are in the kitchen."

"Thank you, Lynn. How have you been?"

"Oh, just fine." She stepped back, indicating to Jim to go ahead. He knew where the kitchen was, so he walked through and saw Mick, Larry, and Elmer grouped around the table with the rough draft of the ad and other assorted papers spread on the kitchen table.

Mick looked up, smiled, and said, "Hello, Jim. How are you?"

Elmer glanced up but said nothing. Larry continued poring over the ad.

Mick pulled a chair out, and Jim sat down. "Here, Jim, see what you think," said Elmer, shoving the rough draft over to him. Jim studied it briefly, Elmer watching him. "Some of that's pretty bad," Elmer said. "I think we ought to cut it out."

"Elmer, that's the whole idea," Jim said patiently, masking his irritation. Elmer was always just a little too moderate for Jim's taste. "We've got to shock these people into taking action. And to do that, we've got to show the worst of it, not pussyfoot around with some milder terms."

"Well, I guess so," said Elmer grudgingly. He still didn't like it; that was obvious.

"But what about this one?" Elmer asked, quoting from the ad: "Is there such a thing as a black human brain? What's that got to do with anything?"

"Elmer, you haven't been to the street rallies like I have and noticed the conspicuous absence of black faces in the crowds. We have to make the black community aware that the people behind the plan in these books are deliberately driving a wedge between blacks and whites in every way they can. That's vital to the final phase of their operations."

Elmer looked at him in that confused wise old owl way and said nothing.

Jim went on. "I first began to be aware of this early in the controversy, when my brother-in-law brought my attention to the fact that there wasn't a single black in the first protest group that I attended in front of the school board building. I've looked for them since at every rally and meeting. None. The other side has the black community convinced this is a racial issue, and we've got to show them the books themselves are racial. We're enlisting others here to accomplish that. Or trying to anyway. The one you just read is from the book *Themes in the Act Play,* page two-oh-five. These two are from the book *African Images.* On page seventy, 'Two deaths for a godd– nigger'; and on page one thirty-three, "the bleary bastard. Bleary black whore.'

"Elmer, you wrote that letter to the editor, commenting on the liberals' accusation that the protestors were attempting censorship and pointing out they were the ones that began the censoring process in schoolbooks when they insisted on taking *Little Black Sambo* out."

Elmer had been staring at him silently, unblinking.

"I remember. Okay, I see what you're saying. They wanted, well, insisted, on taking *Little Black Sambo* out of the textbooks because it just might offend some blacks. It's ludicrous that they would consider something that innocent and cute as offensive to blacks and then stamp their hearty approval on something as blatantly derogatory as this."

"That's right," said Jim.

"Okay, I agree with that, but what about this other stuff? Do you really think it's necessary to assault the public's sensitivity with such things as 'How the boy trembles and delights at the sight of the white excrement of the bird,' from *Man in the Expository Model*"?

Jim smiled. "I don't know Elmer. Is it? It's in the books." Elmer got the point.

"Let me read you this one, Elmer. If you find it too offensive to put in a family newspaper, we're really going to have trouble talking you into the truly raunchy stuff. This is from *Themes in the Act Play*, page two forty-eight: 'What are you doing? (pause) Gilbert? Is that you? (creaking springs) What are you ... no, no ... go back to your own bed and go to sleep. (pause, silence) Gilbert? (pause, creaking springs) Gilbert, we are old people ... This is ... This is ... you shall not. (pause) Please ... Please, Gilbert. (Gilbert grunts several times) How dare you attempt this disgusting behavior!'"

Jim finished reading and looked at Elmer. Elmer stared at him a moment, his expression making it clear that his mind wasn't accepting what his ears were hearing. Then he said, "As bad as that is, Jim, I know what the liberals are going to come back with."

"What?"

"They're going to say that those kinds of things really happen in life."

"I realize that, Elmer, and about that, they're right. I learned about things like this as a young man, just as you and everybody else in this room did. But we learned in bushes and back rooms, out of forbidden books and from older boys, knowing that we shouldn't. Knowing that this was the seamy, animalistic side of life. We were being taught in the schoolroom about a brighter, better side of life, and it was presented to us as the desirable way to live. After all, there are more things in life to enjoy than perverted sex. I've got nothing against sex. It's one the nicest things around. But it's beautiful only when it's an extension of love. Otherwise, it's perverted and prurient and, at best, an animal-like release. There are many enjoyable emotions that a human can experience. These books are portraying life as either one big sex orgy or the alternative of a dreary, depressing existence.

"Take the book *Perspective*, for example. The overall theme of this one is violence, hatred of different races, murder, dope, drinking, disrespect for parents and older people ... Out of six hundred pages, only eighty-seven were used to teach English. The stories in this book were all sad, terrible stories. There were no happy thoughts at all. This is written more like a murder mystery than an English book.

"And rather than being the exception, I'm afraid this is typical of the entire selection, right down to and including the one they have on photography. I wish you could see it for yourself. This is a whole book with nothing but pictures and only an occasional small caption. If you can find one cheery picture in the whole book, I'll eat it, cover and all. Nothing but violence, ugliness, dreariness, and depressive subjects from cover to cover. Is there no longer any beauty in the world?"

Elmer stared at him in silence, with Mick and Larry looking on. They both were familiar with the books. Very.

Larry saw his function as professional advisor, not a judge of what articles to delete, but Mick had strong opinions and voiced them. "Elmer, I'm a Christian and it grieves me to see such things as some of this filth in print, but in this case, I don't think we have any choice. The public has to be alerted."

Elmer, deep in thought, studied Mick.

"Just listen to one more, Elmer. I won't get into the real bad stuff but try this one." Elmer looked at him as he went on. "This is from the book *Compass*, and it's a story called "On Saturday Afternoon." On page one twelve, we have a ten-year-old boy helping a man hang himself. Now there's a constructive idea for ten-year-olds on how to spend Saturday afternoons. And they used to say we were being naughty going to the swimming hole on Saturday afternoons, wasting our time instead of hoeing corn." The attempted added humor did not soften the morbid horror.

Elmer was convinced. "All right, all right. I don't want to hear what you keep referring to as 'the bad part.' I've heard enough. Let's go with the way you have it. But I would like to make two additions, not changes. I would like to include two coupon-type inserts. The first one I would like to have as an application to join the Alliance."

Jim liked that.

"The second one would be a piece of paper that parents could cut out and send to the principal of the school their child or children attend. This paper would, in effect, say, 'I, as a parent, object to the controversial textbooks.'"

Jim didn't like that one at all. "Elmer, I think that would be a bad mistake."

"Why?" asked Elmer.

"Because I know people, and to a great percentage of the parents, this would vent their wrath, and they would consider they had done their duty and promptly forget the whole thing." He didn't admit it to the group, but he was regretfully thinking of the time at the beginning of the controversy when Eloise George had brought the petition around. He had signed it, feeling proud of himself, and then he promptly forgot it.

"No, I disagree," said Elmer. "I think it should go in. It will give the parents an opportunity to express their opinions."

Jim was certain it was a mistake, but he had asked for and gotten so many concessions from Elmer that he was reluctant to push it. He let it go.

He sat back and relaxed, reflecting on Charley Quigley's remarks printed in the newspaper—that a group of businessmen was willing to back him in the fight. Charley, if you only knew, he thought grimly. Nestled deep in his pocket, the check he had written for the full-page ad seemed to burn his leg. Financially speaking, up to this point, he alone was the group of businessmen. He was the only one who had put any money into it. So far, the Alliance was running entirely on his checkbook.

The full-page ad was out. It was on the streets; it was in private homes (including the home of Bert Wolfe—Jim made sure of that by mailing him a copy); it was in the hands of teachers, for and against; it was in churches; and most importantly, it was in the hands of horrified parents.

One such parent called the Alliance first thing that morning. His voice was at once incredulous, suspicious, and seething with anger. "Do you mean to tell me that this stuff is actually in the books these children are reading under the label of learning?"

"Every word," answered Jim cryptically.

"I'm going down to get my son and his belongings out of that school this very minute." He hung up.

This created delightful visions parading through Jim's mind of hordes of similar parents swarming down on the schools, swooping Junior and Jane up in their protective arms and leaving empty schools behind. He wanted the books out of Kanawha County now, and now the rest of the country would know what it really was all about. *Now* was the time to start the stampede, countywide and nationally. He hoped the shock of the full-page ad would set off a tremor that would rumble and grow into a full-fledged earthquake, coast to coast.

Both phones never stopped ringing all day. Jim had seen the office jammed with people many times, to what he thought was full capacity. He was wrong. Today it was full capacity plus. Sardines in a can were like suburbia in comparison, and every hand in the room was angrily waving or shaking a copy of the ad. Rage was on every face. The roar of fury was music to his ears.

CHAPTER 31
Underwood Attacked

The boardroom was packed with people standing all around, several behind the school board members themselves. Jim didn't really like being here because this meant he had to be face-to-face with people with whom he had tried to keep a low profile. He looked around the room uneasily, staying as low in his seat as he could.

A loud, raucous female voice caught his attention across the aisle to his left. His uneasiness increased when he looked over to See Frances McCune. On more than one occasion, she had been known to use the very four-letter words that some of the people were objecting to in the books. Jim's silent hope that, tonight at least, she would behave herself was short-lived. She made some remark that he didn't hear, but he heard the woman next to her say, "Frances, you'd better be quiet or they're liable to throw you out."

Jim cringed as Frances's voice shrieked across the entire room, "I don't care! I came here tonight to have a good time, and by G—, I'm going to have it!" He slumped a little lower in his seat and put his head in his hand, pretending to wipe something from his eyes with his thumb and forefinger. All heads in the room turned in her direction.

Frances gave them all a sarcastic grimace that told them where they could go as far as she was concerned. The board members turned back to the matter at hand, trying to concentrate.

The agenda this particular night included giving three members from each side of the book protest the opportunity to present their views on the textbooks and the controversy arising from them. Each side was allowed to choose their own speakers who would offer different viewpoints on bringing resolution to the protest.

Doug Stump, the acting school board president, sat with Alice Moore to his left and the other board members to his right. Jim thought it noteworthy and significant that Matthew Kinsolving, Alice Moore's onetime staunch ally, was deliberately at her side. Jim learned later that Kinsolving, weak of character, had caved under pressure from the opposition.

Stump called the meeting to order. He had the secretary read the minutes of the last meeting, then delivered a brief outline of the controversy to date. Finally, he announced the first speaker, Karl Priest. Karl gave a short talk in his low-key way, his mild voice so low he could barely be heard at the back of the room.

The next speaker introduced by Stump was the fiery redheaded Mrs. Parsons. She stepped to the microphone with purpose. "Ladies and gentlemen, this is probably the hardest thing I have ever had to do in my life. Right up to the minute that Mr. Stump announced me, I wasn't sure I could go through with it. But deep down, I knew I had no choice. What makes it so hard is the fact that I will be saying things that I know could get me fired, and I can't afford to lose my job. Besides, my big dream in life for as long as I can remember has been to be a teacher. To place all that in jeopardy over principle required a lot of thought. But there is more than principle involved here— and a lot more than a few four-letter words, as the majority of the people think.

"The materials contained in these textbooks that are causing all the trouble is clearly intended to undermine everything we believe in. They will break down what morale our young people have left. They will destroy their faith in God, erode their belief in the Bible, cause patriotism to become a thing of the past, and instill contempt for authority and the police.

"Those are strong words, you say. Yes, they are. But if anything, I'm understating the matter, and keep in mind, ladies and gentlemen, I teach from these very books. Not all of them, mind you; the perpetrators of this sadistic plan are too clever to put the plan glaringly in all books. Besides, they would lose their effectiveness that way. The plan is intended to begin at a very early age and then continue right through high school and beyond."

Mrs. Parsons had been directing her attention and remarks toward the general audience, giving the board members themselves only sidelong glances. But now she turned to face the board squarely.

"I know what is probably going through your minds. You're wondering how a mere teacher can stand here right in front of you and this audience and make such a judgment. Well, I don't mind telling you"—her green eyes were flashing now; her voice, filled with emotion, was rising steadily—"that it takes guts to stand face-to-face with your superiors and tell them they are wrong. These books should never have been allowed in our schools. What forces the courage upon me to say these things is the knowledge of what these textbooks contain and what they will do to our children and our country. When I walk into the schoolyard where I teach with all this on my mind and I look up to see Old Glory waving in the breeze"—her voice rose to a lusty fullness—"then I know I have no choice. I've got to stop these books and their destructive plan at any cost." She finished with a defiant look at each member of the school board.

Stansbury looked away with embarrassment, Stump looked at the table, and the rest avoided her eyes in one fashion or another, except for Alice Moore, who sat smiling at the teacher admiringly. Mrs. Parsons sat down.

After a long, awkward silence, Stump cleared his throat and announced the next speaker. This time it was Robert Kittle, the acting board superintendent since Underwood had resigned. Kittle was a soft-spoken man in his early forties. He walked quietly to the microphone and began giving the school board's view of the situation, along with a financial report. His relaxed manner and subdued tone belied the undertones of tension that were evident.

Kittle was just winding up the financial report, when suddenly, and without warning, violence erupted. The blurred form of a man pushed Kittle aside on his way to the board members. He took a swing, and his fist against Underwood's jaw sent the latter tumbling backward off his chair.

The meaty sound could be heard above everything. Then chaos developed. Two men stepped in to restrain the man attacking Underwood, and four protestors jumped them. Pandemonium reigned as the whole room came alive, most rushing to join the scuffle, some trying for the door. The crowd engulfed the board members. Jim could only see flailing arms and struggling bodies.

Suddenly, the air was permeated with an odor that choked you and burned your eyes. Frances McCune had sprayed mace full in Underwood's face. As Jim pushed his way toward the door, he hardly knew what to expect next. The ear-shattering thunder of gunfire would not have surprised him.

He stumbled through the door, tears blinding him and streaming down his cheek. The cool night air hit him, and he pulled it into his burning lungs, coughing convulsively. Then he became aware of coughing all around him.

At last, the fumes began to dissipate, and the coughing lessened. He was still rubbing his eyes when someone backed into him in the darkness.

"I'm sorry." The melodic voice of Alice Moore was instantly recognizable.

"What in the world happened in there?" he asked her.

"I don't know," she said, laughing nervously.

Coming to Jim's mind was Elmer Fike's remark that "school boards are under attack across the country as never before." He never meant literally, but it had begun!

CHAPTER 32
KKK Enters the War

The crackling flames born of pine and nurtured by the high winds of December leapt and danced high in the air, illuminating the ghostly figures gathered about in their hooded white robes. The huge bonfire could have been from burning textbooks, according to the liberal media, but it wasn't. Its purpose was not to destroy textbooks—not directly anyway. Indirectly? That was a matter of speculation. According to Dale Reusch, the leader of this segment of the Ku Klux Klan, they were in Kanawha County to help the protestors "stamp out these Communist, un-American, nigger-lovin' textbooks any way we can." One had to presume that included burning them. A fiery cross, burning dramatically against the black sky of midnight, gave an ominous impact to his words.

Reusch, who was presently the Grand Dragon of the National Knights of the Ku Klux Klan of Ohio, had just announced his candidacy for the office of the president of the United States. Jim had shuddered at the prospect, remote though it was, when he read the announcement in the newspaper.

Whether it was intentional or not, the Klan could not have been more effective at defusing any accusations directed toward Communism if it had been carefully planned. Their article announcing Dale Reusch as their first candidate for president of the United States said it all; dateline Stone Mountain, Georgia, showed Reusch in a photograph. The Klansman leader, complete with his evil, piercing eyes, appeared humble and was holding his hand over his heart.

Underneath the picture, the article added to the stigma of stupidity that was begun by the Klan's absurd announcement of their "candidate." The Imperial Wizard of the National Knights of the Ku Klux Klan, James R. Venable, said, "In my opinion, it's Communists and Socialists that are trying to destroy the brains"—note the usage of brains in place of minds—adding to the asininity of our children."

Venable said that Klan representatives from Georgia, Alabama, North Caroline, South Carolina, Pennsylvania, Ohio, Michigan, Texas, and Oklahoma had unanimously voted to investigate the textbook situation in West Virginia, saying that a delegate would be sent to its capitol of Charleston. "I've never seen such filth in high school textbooks." This was a clever diversion, once again, away from "the plan" in the lower levels—inadvertent or intentional?

In another article, but related to subject and timing, Dale Reusch, the Grand Dragon (and presidential candidate), in his ostentatious wisdom, offered his final solution to the book problem: "We should have a 'book party' like the Boston Tea Party." Meaning a book burning. Now there's an intelligent suggestion.

Harold Goff was a hillbilly, born and bred. He fit the image completely, as he was a fundamentalist reared in a "holler"; he spoke like Hollywood's version of a hillbilly; and he even lived in a log cabin he built himself. He chewed tobacco too.

Harold had always been a dedicated family man. That's why he was here tonight, a neophyte in the Klan. With scant education, he made his living by cutting the stone out of the hollers and fashioning retaining walls to hold back the West Virginia hills for whoever had the need.

With this background, he had searched out various options, looking for the most effective way he could do his part to stop these books. He and Jim Farley had known each other all their lives. Although not reared together (Harold lived "down on the creek" and Jim "up on the hill"), their paths crossed many times in their teen and young adult years. Harold had worked for Jim in his business for a period after they became men.

Because of this, Harold had become an affiliate member of the Alliance. He supported it generously, financially, and made a few visits to the office observing. He decided he didn't belong there.

When the Klan came to the valley, he had attended one of its rallies, and he felt that's where he would fit. He became a member. Now he stood on the fringes of the hooded crowd, listening to Reusch's gruff voice tell of the threats, plans, and intent of the Klan. He wanted to find out what this was all about and where it was headed.

The cold drizzle of falling rain made him wish he could get a little closer to the crackling bonfire, but the desire for anonymity made him hang back in the crowd. He looked around at the faceless creatures covered in white, head to toe. Their white hoods shadowed their features. Their silence added to the eeriness that hovered over the scene like an omen.

When he found nothing in the crowd that stood out, Harold directed his attention toward Reusch, trying not to notice the armed guards walking the perimeter, their rifles clearly visible.

Reusch stood, feet widespread, on a hastily constructed platform of rough oak, situated on the opposite side of the fire from the crowd, the burning cross at his back. Between the two, his building features were accentuated like a mask. Hands on hips completed the preconceived image Harold had of a Klan leader. Ed Miller stood at his side.

"The people pushing these dirty textbooks can put whatever label they want to on their reasons," Reusch was bellowing, "but we all know where they come from: Communism! We can approach this problem in several different ways. We can burn a few crosses on the right people's yards ... and everybody knows what that means."

Harold wondered about the burning cross—why it became the symbol of the Klan. What was the significance of its origin? Was it supposed to connote Christianity or deride it? He knew, like everyone, what to expect when one was burned. Somebody was going to get hurt.

Reusch was scanning the crowd, naked hatred in his eyes. "We can blow up a few schools and help ease the traffic problem by eliminating a few cars ..." A sardonic smile twisted his face. "Or we could be a little more direct and forcefully take these filthy books from the warehouses and schools and have the biggest bonfire ever seen."

He paused, letting enough time go by in silence to be certain all of this had sunk in.

Then he said in a totally different voice, "Or we can take a completely different path." He looked around.

"We can fight them on their own ground and on their own terms. If a member of the Klan occupied the White House, we could do anything we wanted to. And that includes banning from schools the books that don't meet with our approval and censoring the ones we do allow." He stepped up the tempo. "Now, it don't matter to me, boys; I've fought on the line and loved every minute of it." The cross burned brighter. His evil smile widened. "In fact, come to think about it, deep down, maybe that's the way I hope you decide to go. I'd sure look forward to that. If we choose that path, blood will be spilled, and some of it might be yours. If we take to the political trail, it's gonna cost money, lots of it. Your money. And anybody else's that we can beg, borrow, or steal."

Harold wasn't sure just how much of the last statement was intended as humor, but he didn't like the sound of it. He had never been a man of violence, but the direct approach appealed to him. It's what had attracted him to the Klan to begin with. He wondered just how far the violence would go. Would people be killed? Was the chill he felt truly caused by the rain?

The crowd had been strangely silent through the entire speech, without any movement. It gave Harold the feeling that the sheets covered lifeless forms rather than living bodies.

He shifted his position to get a better look, and his right foot slipped into a mud hole. The icy water filling his boot brought cold reality into focus. For the first time, he faced the truth of what he had become a part of. These people were talking about spilling blood and destroying property, maybe even human life. Was that they way he wanted to fight this thing? What good would he do his children if he wound up a murderer—maybe spending the rest of his life behind bars?

But on the other hand, what choice did he have? He thought of his children and the kind of world they would have to live in if these books stayed in school. Fathers had gone to war for the sake of their families before, sacrificing their own lives so their children might live. Why should he be any different? Maybe dying in some back alley with a knife in your back from an enemy you didn't even know or blown out of your bedroom by a faceless creature some night may not be as glorious a death as dying in a uniform decorated with brass medals, but was the cause or result any different? They put up statues in the town square to honor men that had died for their country, freedom, God, and family. Was this any different? If it was, he failed to see it.

He pulled his foot out of the mud hole and walked boldly up to the roaring fire. He was going to get warm.

He looked up at Reusch in a new light and felt a kindred feeling toward Ed Miller. They were in this thing together—to the death, if necessary. Miller half smiled down at him as though he read his thoughts.

The war was on.

CHAPTER 33

The Big March

The morning broke gray and bleak. Jim was at the office long before the first faint streaks of light announced the arrival of the day of the big march. He wondered how many people would participate.

Marvin was not normally given to presumption or grandiose claims, but Jim couldn't help but wonder if his expectations of ten thousand weren't a result of the desperation bred of the weeks of frustration.

This march was supposed to represent the upper half of the valley only, intended to be a portent of the "big" march of the total valley later. Jim felt the major support would come from the working class, and today wasn't a holiday for all of them. Some had to work.

Traffic was beginning to flow on the boulevard. He could almost tell the time of the morning by the different tempo in the tires singing on the pavement each morning as their owners hurried to their respective places of work.

He tried to force himself to get things on his desk in order before the mad rush of people started to pour into the office. He didn't know how many more days his nerves could stand the constant harangue of endless chatter of the multitude of well-wishers. The office was usually wall-to-wall people, each one with a great idea, a solution to it all. He was the one everybody expected to act as counselor, mediator, and decision maker. Just about all of them ended the conversation with the same thing: "We're praying for you." That finally got to him the other day. A preacher had said it; and exasperated, he looked at the man and said, "Preacher, we've got about all the people praying for us that we can handle; what we need now is help."

The preacher had been shocked by his remark, but Jim had reached the point that he felt if one more person said, "We're praying for you," he would scream.

It wasn't that he didn't believe in the power of prayer; he did. It was just that he was sick and tired of people expecting God to do it all. He felt God would do His part, but He expected a little help from the people themselves.

Jim Stephens was the first to make it to the office, as usual. Jim and June had been there about an hour when he came in, smiling as usual.

Stephens had been one of the most dedicated workers they had, and Jim had been extremely grateful for his help. But when he began the process of trying to fit a face to the phantom that had brazenly sauntered down their driveway, burned his wife's car, and dissolved into the night, Jim had looked at Stephens in a different light. Near paranoia had possessed him, and everyone was suspect.

Stephens had a stoic way about him that didn't quite fit the committed crusader that he seemed to be. Jim thought of the stereotypical Communist agent: cold, unemotional, dedicated to the cause.

Stephens said good morning and went over to the chair across from Jim's desk, where he always sat. He sat down, folding his arms as always, and took turns staring at the floor and looking at Jim. Sometimes it gave Jim the creeps, having him there doing that. Sometimes it was reassuring.

Crazy, thought Jim. This whole thing's crazy. Maybe I'm crazy. Maybe we all are.

He reached for the telephone and dialed information. "Police headquarters, please."

He got the number, dialed it, and the desk sergeant answered. "Sergeant, this is Jim Farley at The Business and Professional Alliance for Better Textbooks office. I'm calling to verify our request for a parade permit for our march we have scheduled for today. Are you familiar with it?" The sergeant said he was. "Has it been approved? I have a man here that I would like to send down to pick it up."

"Well, it's not quite that simple, Mr. Farley. We need more detail than the man who brought the request provided us with."

Defensive resentment automatically welled up in Jim. "Why is it," he asked angrily, "that people for the books can get anything they want, anytime they want, and when we protestors ask for the simplest thing, it suddenly gets complicated?" He was thinking of his request to all three segments of the law enforcement agencies for the protection of his home after his wife's car was burned, to no avail. Underwood had round-the-clock protection by the police until he left town.

The voice on the other end didn't get hostile, but it did get firm. "That has nothing to do with it, Mr. Farley. The request form wasn't filled out properly. We have only a vague outline of the march itself, a sketchy route plan that makes no sense, and the man who brought it didn't even bother to sign it. If you will send down the man you are talking about, and if he can finish filling it out, give us a map of the route and sign it, I'll be glad to issue the permit on the spot."

Jim felt sheepish.

Bob Dornan was at the head of this march, side by side with Marvin. Later, during the actual parade, Carl McCantyre (a nationally prominent evangelist who at that time operated a radio and TV ministry out of a Christian complex in Florida) made the exasperated statement, "Where is the Civil Liberties Union when you need them?"

Jim's heart swelled as he watched the crowd totally obliterate Kanawha Boulevard with their mass of bodies, sidewalk to sidewalk, as they came marching from the civic center toward the state capitol.

The phone rang, and he reluctantly pulled himself from the window to answer it, listening as the person started to tell him of some trivial incident.

He couldn't contain himself. "You wouldn't believe it. There are thousands, and they're still coming." His voice rose to a hoarse shout. "I've got to go! I'm sorry you're missing this!"

He went back to the window. Marvin and Bob led the parade with an unidentified World War II veteran carrying Old Glory in a belt, holding the proud old flag as it flapped in the stiff breeze.

Jim wondered just how many in the parade knew that's what it was really all about—Americanism and the way of life it represented. How many of them thought it was only a few dirty words? How many of them thought it was only the educational system? Only a handful grasped the true thing at stake, he suspected. He felt certain that Bob Dornan, Mick Staton, Alice Moore and himself understood. He wasn't even too sure about Elmer.

There were the usual hecklers, and as the main body of the marchers passed the Alliance office building, one heckler threw a brick at random into the crowd. Jim cringed as it barely missed the head of a little girl, no more than six years old, who was totally unaware of how close her head came to being bashed in.

The incident was so like the fight itself. The children and the next generation were what it was all about, and yet, like the little girl, most people were totally unaware of the consequences if, like the brick, the plan connected and was effective.

As the parade passed the assortment of gala flags ornamenting the sidewalk, including the stars and stripes, he couldn't help but wonder if a year, two years, or five years from now if the American flag would still be used.

It depended entirely on whether the War in Kanawha County would start a whiplash across the nation that would awaken the people and if they took action. If the sea of people he was watching fill the Boulevard from end to end would start a flood to sweep the land.

It was a chilling thought!

Surrounded by protest signs, left, one marcher makes her way along Kanawha Boulevard with several thousand other anti-text demonstrators. Above is a portion of the crowd which stretched for several blocks. The group began its march at the Charleston Civic Center and after filing past the Kanawha County Board of Education offices on Elizabeth Street, arrived at the Statehouse. The group was protesting Kanawha County's controversial English textbooks.—Daily Mail Photos by William Tiernan.

In Conclusion

By 1975, the conservatives and liberals alike were admitting in the press that Macmillan Publishing was forcing its writers of textbooks to show life not as it is, but as they (Macmillan) wanted it to be. They were depicting false situations in sexism, racism, family life, and politics.

Here is a condensed version of a commentary by the most liberal reporter, Nicholas Von Hoffman, in the "Liberal Beacon of the East," the *Washington Post*. In the article dated July 21, 1975, Von Hoffman writes:

HEADING FOR DOUBLETHINK, LITERALLY

> The Macmillan Publishing Company has issued marching orders for its textbook writers. Henceforth, anyone hoping to write for Macmillan had better familiarize himself with a document called "Guidelines for Creating Positive Sexual and Racial Images in Educational Materials."
>
> The preface by Matina S. Horner, the president of Harvard's prestigious Radcliff College, says it's high time for the textbooks to do their share in "our search and struggle for a more egalitarian society (social change). Horner's contention is that said search is a struggle impeded by the "limiting tyranny of the norm." If the Soviets can teach their kids socialist realism, why can't we indoctrinate ours with capitalist realism (or socialist realism)?
>
> Read Macmillan's guidelines and you'll see why George Orwell's 1984 is the most influential book in the English language today:

Accurate portrayal versus ideal situations except in the social studies field, we are more interested in what can be, rather than in the negatives that still exist. "Reality" itself is subject to slanted interpretations. The fact that black persons do not yet hold a proportionate share of executive positions should

> not prevent us from depicting a sizeable number of blacks as executives. Doublethink, no think, black is white, up is down, and now you know how people are ordered to lie without exactly being told to do it. The guidelines are specific about what propaganda line the textbook writers are to take.
>
> They have a great collection of dos and don'ts for the hacks who manufacture this trash. There are minute instructions about how to falsify the condition of every race, color, creed, and ethnic group.
>
> What's doubly infuriating about Horner and Macmillan is that conservatives will rightly pick on this and call it a liberal plot. As if the cause of feminism or the black people has to rest on telling schoolchildren lies. No wonder they're blowing up schoolhouses in West Virginia.
>
> Beneath the flouncy verbiage about realizing individual aspirations, what these people are selling is a depraved egalitarianism in which children are turned into atomized pumpkin people who may serve the manpower needs of government and corporation but certainly not truth or beauty.
>
> Amen, brother.

This article would have been understandably predictable coming from conservatives, but coming from the ultraliberals, it has clout.

On the conservative side of the field, an article appeared in the *Washington Star* the following month after the Von Hoffman commentary. On August 8, 1975, in his column, James J. Kilpatrick said pretty much the same thing as Von Hoffman about Macmillan, the guidelines, and the intended results of both.

Many books have been written about the intended takeover of America by Communist subversion. I will not make that judgment or statement here, but I will make some observations. One of the compilations of information gleaned from these books and from his intensive study of the "Communist conspiracy" in the sixteen years he served with the FBI has been made by Cleon

Skousen, and it appeared in the Congressional Record, January 10, 1962. There were forty-five Communists' goals taken from his book, *The Naked Communist*. We quote from that list, the eleven Communist goals that are certainly carried out in these textbooks we are objecting to, whether intended or not.

1. Get control of the schools. Use them as *transmission belts* for socialism and current Communist propaganda. Soften the curriculum. Get control of teachers' associations. Put the party line in textbooks.

2. Break down cultural standards of morality by promoting pornography and obscenity in books (also in magazines, movies, and TV). Our plan is to promote ugliness (repulsive, meaningless art).

3. Eliminate prayer or any phase of religious expression in the schools on the grounds that it violates the principle of separation of church and state.

4. Eliminate all laws governing obscenity by calling them censorship and a violation of free speech and free press.

5. Present homosexuality, degeneracy, and promiscuity as normal, natural, and healthy. (Like incest, which some students are now being taught is sometimes beneficial to the child.)

6. Discredit the American Founding Fathers. (Like giving George Washington one paragraph in the history book and Marilyn Monroe seven pages in comparison.)

7. Belittle all forms of American culture and discourage the teaching of American History on the grounds that it was only a minor part of the big picture. Give more emphasis to Russian History since the Communists took over.

8. Discredit the family as an institution. Encourage promiscuity and easy divorce.

9. Create the impression that violence and insurrection are legitimate aspects of the American tradition.

10. Infiltrate the churches and replace revered religion with

social religion. (Rector J. L. Lewis was involved in many liberal activities that some considered radical and pro-Communist. The church was St. John's Episcopal in the heart of Charleston—a most prestigious church.) Discredit the Bible and emphasize the need for intellectual maturity, which does not need a religious crutch.

11. And last, but by far not the least, emphasize the need to raise children away from the negative influence of parents. Attribute prejudices, mental blocks, and retardation of children to suppressive influence of parents.

I thoroughly researched the objectionable textbooks in question and found that they fill completely the requirements of all eleven of the above goals. Whether this was intentional to fulfill the Communists' goals, I will not qualify. I will leave that up to the reader's judgment.

I drove down Washington Street, the main artery through Charleston, on October 19, 1982, and was stunned by the sight of a bookstore openly advertising Communist material just four blocks away from the school board building where the war in Kanawha County started eight years before. He learned from Carol Banks, one of the first people he encountered in the beginning of the war, that the owner of the store was running for the U.S. Senate. Were the protesters too late?)

FAREWELL TO CHILDHOOD INNOCENCE, the article was headlined in the October 1981 issue of *Reader's Digest*. It had been condensed from the *New York Times*. The subheading at the top said, "Something has changed in the timetable of growing up. Social upheaval, family breakdown, TV, and movies have helped make too many kids too worldly before their time."

Then the writer of the article goes on, stumbling vaguely through the fog of reasoning, looking for the answer or answers. A finger is pointed haphazardly at everything from improved nutrition—that's right, improved nutrition (this is supposed to cause them to mature faster—to women's lib, breakdown of the family, and a few other issues, with the forerunner being TV and the upheaval of the 1960s coming in a close second.

People, people, when are you going to see the obvious! You're looking at the symptoms, not the cause. Hitler was right when he said the average person tends to overlook the obvious. But now we're talking about more than the average; we're talking about the educated elite. Also, we're talking about the political and civic leaders.

The article continues as follows:

> Once, children read books about fairies and animals, about other children engaged in the innocent pleasures of childhood. Today, children read about different subjects. Steffie, a beautiful girl of 14, runs away from a small town, where her father is a barber and her mother is a laundress, to seek her fortune in the big city.
>
> A handsome man who befriends her, turns out to be a pimp and compels her to become a prostitute. At first, she is appalled. Soon, out of love for her protector, she becomes one of his most successful hookers, which arouses the jealousy of the other girls. One of them introduces Steffie to a man who puts LSD into the heroine's soft drink, and she has a bad trip. Finally, after many adventures, she enters a rehabilitation center for runaway children. There she gets therapy and prepares to return home — sadder but wiser.
>
> Books such as this one, Steffie Can't Come Out to Play, by Fran Arrick, is widely distributed and read by 10-, 11-, and 12-year-olds. George A. Woods, children's book editor of the New York Times, describes with amazement recent submissions for review: "It's not just sex that defines the change. I've got books coming in on children with harelips, epilepsy and insanity, as well as ones about alcoholic parents, drug-addicted children, child beaters, divorce and death."

Charlotte Zolotow, vice president and associate publisher of Harper Junior Books, defends this new genre. "We can't protect our children anymore from all that we would like to spare them." (Thereby admitting that our rearguard actions are becoming weaker and more desperate.) She says, "We can help them form their own judgments and defenses by being honest in the books we write for them."

This last remark brings up two interesting points. What is being honest? What is truth? Is there no longer anything in life but perversion, hate, misery, sex, lust, suffering, and hopelessness? Have we already reached Norman O. Brown's euphoria of despair? Is it too late to look for a small ray of hope? Is there no longer a bright side of life to show our children?

The second point is this: If we are to help them form their own judgments and (get the next word) defenses, why do we insist on bringing them down to the juxtaposition viewpoint of depression to make that judgment?

Anyone knows that when a person is in a bright frame of mind, things look completely different, and consequently, judgments and decisions are made differently than when one is in a foul mood. (Take Norman Vincent Peale's *Power of Positive Thinking*. That's not to say that we use his book as a guideline, but millions of people do, apparently quite successfully.)

Watch a karate expert for a while. He huffs and puffs, contorts his face, and goes into total concentration, almost trancelike, in a particular frame of mind. He has to go in on the right level of thinking, at the right slant, from the right point. What if the point he went in from was negative, as being advocated by Ms. Zolotow and these books? What would happen to the hand when it came down on a brick?

Once there was an Age of Innocence, when children believed that adults were good, that the adult world was bigger and better than their own. Children were expected to treat adults with respect.

Now, according to Annie Hermann, an early-childhood expert, "We want our children to know very soon that adults are not as wonderful as they think. We feel it is unfair to let children have false illusions about adult omnipotence." She is concerned about this trend, believing that a child is often not developed enough to absorb the realities of life that are foisted on him. He *needs* to feel dependent on the adult, to believe in parental omnipotence. That belief helps develop a basic, life-giving trust in the child.

Child psychoanalyst Peter B. Beubauer, director of the Child Development Center in New York, sounds another warning: "Children pushed into adult experiences do not become precociously mature. On the contrary, they cling to childhood longer, perhaps all their lives."

But Dr. Neubauer goes on to say, "We cannot reverse the changes in the family, or woman's liberation"—were we back to Norman O. Brown again?—"and we mustn't idealize children's happiness in the past. Remember high infant mortality and child labor?"

Isn't the avoidance of this at the expense of the moral and psychological damage like throwing the baby out with the bathwater?

Michael I. Cohen, chairman of pediatrics at Albert Einstein College of Medicine in New York, thinks today's children may turn out to be better than our own generation, "because they are getting better information."

Yet as we make the transition from an era of protection of children to one in which children are incorporated early into a less-differentiated society, reports of child abuse, child neglect, and child exploitation are on the rise. For many children, childhood is difficult and dangerous. Says a fifteen-year-old girl who looks back on a past that includes a parental divorce, experimentation with marijuana from the sixth grade on, and a troubling experience with sex in the eighth grade: "All the kids I see are in a rush to grow up, and I don't blame them. I wouldn't want to be a child again."

The last paragraph in the article reads: "Will our changing concepts of childhood prove beneficial or damaging to children and society as a whole? Unfortunately, we will know only when a generation of children without a childhood begins to raise children of their own."

Remembering Spock's remorse at his "having ruined a whole generation" and "I will devote the remainder of my life to rectifying this," isn't that a scary thought?

We have come across many observations and remarks by prestigious men, such as the one by James Michener in the October 1981 issue of *Journal*, which coincided with his concept of what was happening in the schools.

It was titled, AMERICA IS WORRIED ABOUT ITS SCHOOL, Michener said, "If I had a child today, I would send him or her to a private school for the sake of safety, for the discipline that would be enforced, and for the rigorous academic requirements. But I would doubt the child would get any better education than I did in my good public school." (Mr. Michener is stating two things here, whether that was the intent or not. One, he recognizes the fact that public schools in his time were good, or at least much better than now. Two, that the private schools are at least as good now as the public schools were then.) "The problem is that good schools are becoming pitifully rare, and I would not want to take the chance that the one I sent my children to was inadequate," he says.

But again, like so many of his contemporaries, even though he recognizes the problem and acknowledges it, he falls short of the mark as to the cause. "I know all the reasons for this sad decline," he goes on: "automatic promotions, court interference so that principals can no longer discipline, the seduction of television, and a rising level of violence in our national life and a lessening of our teacher dedication."

I have to agree with the first three, especially the one dealing with television, as it was possibly the biggest cause in his list and a contributing factor to his next cause. The last, teacher dedication, I can agree with in part, but not in the way that Mr. Michener intends the meaning. I think some of the teachers are dedicated, but to a different end than the public thinks and expects of them.

In his book *The Naked Ape* by Desmond Morris, the author vaguely pinpoints the real root of the problem when he says, "We are teaching barbarism in our schools and are appalled at our own success."

In his book *The Schools and American Society*, Daniel Selakovich, of Oklahoma State University, reflecting on the thesis that school curriculum tends to cater to middle-class interests and is oriented toward middle-class values, says, "The most notable of these include the observations that the curriculum is designed to prepare students for college ..." If this is true, which it should be, why are more and more colleges bemoaning the fact that students come to them lacking the basic qualifications needed to enter college?

He continues: "The program is designed in a way that encourages order and conformity"—he didn't read the same books I did—respect for law and order, good manners, hard work and so on."

The only explanation that I can think of for Mr. Selakovich's statement is that his book was first published in 1967, and that perhaps then, maybe these things were true.

But no more. If others, including Mr. Selakovich, would take the time to examine the books in question, the ones in our schools that we are presently objecting to, they would discover that just the reverse of his thesis is true: that these books teach and encourage disrespect for law and order, that good manners are passé, or a matter of opinion at best, and that work is a four-letter word.

And, of course, they go much further; they tear and rip at our national image. We're not against relevancy—perhaps George Washington is outmoded—but couldn't they have found someone more positive and productive to be relevant to than Marilyn Monroe, whom they dedicated seven pages to, while allowing George Washington a scant paragraph? Speaking of relevancy, what is *Anal Eroticism* relevant to? That was one of the books almost adopted before Alice Moore raised the furor.

They subtly, almost imperceptibly, loosen the roots of faith in the Bible in the elementary levels, clearing the ground for the seedbed of contempt for Christianity that is amply sown in the secondary levels.

Then, and only then, is when the four-letters are brought profusely into play. This is where the brunt and the bulk of the controversy is directed on both sides—erroneously. By this time, the real damage is done. The four-letter words are only the candle on the cake, in addition to being a diversion.

Mr. Selakovich goes on to quote a fellow author, H. Otto Dahlke, who says in his book *Values in Culture and Classroom*: "A current interpretation of the public school is that it merely reflects and upholds middle-class values. The norms apparently support this idea, but continuity of school and middle-class norms is incidental. Many of the norms and even value emphasis occur not because of middle-class influence, but because the school is a group. Emphasis on work, punctuality, getting the job done, control of aggression, avoidance of conflict, and being relatively quiet are necessary conditions, if any group is to persist." (Looked in a schoolroom lately, folks?)

There is a common saying that the first prerequisite to being a politician is to be able to talk all day without saying anything. The same rule could be applied to liberals, except they have the knack to accuse everybody else of what you yourself are doing, without ever giving them the opportunity to argue the point.

I thought of this as I watched Mary Calderone, the co-founder of Sex Information and Education Council of the United States or SIECUS, on *Sixty Minutes*. At the same time she is scurrying around the country via jets, espousing her philosophy (Question: "Mrs. Calderone, do you think it's all right for a child to masturbate?" Answer: "Of course it is. I can't believe God would make something that beautiful, then not expect us to use it ..." What can I say, dear reader), her fellow liberals and disciples are bemoaning the Moral Majority of Jerry Falwell imposing his views and beliefs on the rest of us. Where's the difference? I wonder.

As to Mrs. Calderone's position on and method of justification of children masturbating, wouldn't the same rule apply to other things? (If it applies to anything, that is.) Such as rape? All the required ingredients are there just as much as in the case of masturbation. Involves another party, you say? That makes the difference? What about the members of the child's family? They are other parties.

I wonder if Mrs. Calderone ever heard the words discretion or restraint or self-denial or self-discipline ... or a lot of others.

It's no wonder we need the Bible.

How could Mrs. Calderone believe God exists if she doesn't believe the Bible to be true? Who is God? Without the Bible, who decides?

To believe in God, you have to believe the Bible. And if you believe the Bible, all you have to do to explain why Mrs. Calderone is totally wrong in her thinking (on masturbation, for the time being) is to read in the story of the beginning about God putting the delicious, appetizing, enjoyable fruit in the Garden of Eden and telling the first man and woman not to eat it.

Sadistic torture? Or a test of love, obedience, restraint, self-denial and self-discipline?

Decide for yourself. Mary Calderone has decided for herself.

An editorial in the *Charleston Daily Mail*, dated June 20, 1974, comes closer to making sense than anything I've read yet, beginning with this bold headline:

come now, discrimination is far from censorship. It reads: "The argument that censorship prevails unless sixth graders are instructed in pornography is tantamount to saying that their freedoms are violated unless the hot lunch program includes a choice of alcoholic beverages.

"The public has decided that it does not wish to encourage social drinking in the lunch hour. It prefers to put its money into a nutritious diet. It can as easily decide what it wishes to include on the literary menu in the interest of a wholesome mental and moral development."

Feed them sewage, you only make them sick for a time, physically. Feed their minds the material from these books and you destroy them forever!

"Everyone has twenty-twenty hindsight." How many times have you heard this? Hindsight is merely sifting through events that have already taken place, fitting the pieces together that are now solid and well defined in retrospect—the same pieces that were so vague and obscure in conjecture. Theory is fine; speculation is fine; both are necessary ingredients to life and living and to experimentation. But as the nuclear scientists admitted when they pushed the button to set off the first atomic explosion at Oak Ridge, even after all their theorizing, speculating, calculating, and planning, they did not know what was really going to happen once the button was pushed.

How can we ask innocent, impressionable children to make up their own minds on subjects that they have absolutely no experience with, by simply giving them two ways to choose from? And when the two choices are presented as being equally good? And how do we present two sides of anything with perfect balance? And if they are not perfectly balanced, if one is a little heavier than the other in its persuasiveness—or biased, if you will, have we given them a fair choice? And what about teaching evolution in schools (whether it is taught as fact or theory is irrelevant) without teaching the alternative of creation. Are we being fair and impartial?

Giving children two choices of the unknown, without pointing them in any direction, is tantamount to giving a traveler in a strange country a road map without names of destinations or route numbers, only lines indicating the different ways he can travel.

A wise man once said, "The past is a road map to the future." Why are we banning their road maps?

The liberals who advocate free thinking are, once again, bouncing their words off the wall and back onto their own heads. Their thesis for this is the philosophy that progress dictates—that we must stay abreast of the times, discarding yesterday and becoming relevant.

In yesteryear, freethinkers were much more necessary than now; they were also more efficient. The reason for the former was that we did not have nearly as many tested events as we do now. But the second reason is even more important and relevant and that is because in yesteryear there was ample time, all the time you needed, to think something through and make your own decision, based on the facts you had available to you.

In this day of high speed in everything we do, decisions have to be made much faster, most times split second, or the opportunity is lost. The freethinker could flounder.

To consummate an effective student in out high-speed society, that student has to be programmed. Then, and only then, when two or more choices come at him, does he have the basis to bounce back a rational choice.

This is not to say that the student should be a robot with no thought process of his or her own. Far from it. Simply put (I do hope I'm not accused of being too simplistic), for those who still don't understand, we need guidelines; what guidelines and who chooses them are the two big questions, ones that we will not attempt to answer at this point.

Aren't we guilty of what the liberals are against—namely, telling the children what to think by giving them only material selected by us? By omitting the material that they might come across in their own travels, are we not guilty of censorship?

"There are no pat answers."

"There are no absolutes."

Sound like the same thing? Apparently, it does to a liberal. I have had a basic belief in absolutes all my life. I also acquired from experience and observations the conviction and philosophy that there are no pat answers in life. Sounds like a contradiction, doesn't it? But it isn't. This is where I finally got the handle on where the liberals are confused and are doing their best to drag the rest of us along with them.

Situation ethics. This is the ineffectual attempt of the liberals to bring the problem into focus. (One could transpose the term progressive educators over the word liberal here.)

It is a doctrine (or non-doctrine, if the liberals prefer), claiming that ethics can and must change to fit each situation. What is right and proper one time is wrong another.

This is correct! Or rather, it's almost correct. Or rather, it could be correct.

Confusing, isn't it? Take all three of the above versions—imagine them as three images in a camera lens, sitting in a row, side by side—and you'll see why I chose the phrase, bringing into focus, to describe the problem. Let's merge the three, thereby bringing them into focus.

I think most people with any thought will generally agree that heredity plus environment is a big contribution in what makes up who a person becomes as an adult. Heredity instills traits in each of us, some of which can be changed and others that cannot. If the ones that cannot are negative, we can at least learn to control them if we are aware of them and want to.

The traits that can be changed make up the area that is vulnerable to persuasion. This is where the educational process comes in.

Taking the basic qualities of heredity, the teacher—whether it be the parent from day one of birth, the professional teacher of the first grade or twelfth grade, or the college professor—molds the character like a sculptor molding clay into the finished product. In the case of a real person, unlike the statue of the sculptor, the form is never finished. We have a never-ending process as long as life is there.

But let's pick a point as the zenith of education and head for it. Starting with the basics, the human computer controlling the brain and emotions has to be programmed to react to certain situations in order to make decisions. (You wonder why I did not use the term rational decisions? Because, in any case, decisions will be made, rational or not.)

A soldier is taught—or programmed, really—to react to orders; he must respond immediately, without having to think, to be an effective solider. The same holds true for the thought process of a child. Contrary to the thinking of the liberals, it is not an absolute. It must be programmed. This process will take place regardless. The only things left optional are the direction it will take. This, of course, will be determined by the outside stimuli the subject is submitted to or exposed to. This can come in the form of regimented classes (formal education), complete with professional teacher, or from the kid down the block (peer pressure).

To allow a child, as a student, to seek out his or her own basis or guidelines for the decision-making process is absurd. Also, a child (and this trait stays with us throughout life) reaches out for boundaries. When she suddenly realized that she would be a seventeen-year-old in just a few days, my daughter decided it was time to assert herself. The problem was that she didn't know what that meant, exactly. As the two of us sat alone at the dinner table one evening, just two weeks from her aforementioned birthday, I was a little shocked to watch her arrogantly throw a piece of bread across the table at the bread plate. This was totally out of character for her, so it registered with me vividly. I called her attention to it, telling her that I never wanted to see her doing that again (thereby establishing a boundary: "That's as far as you can go, kid."). I also recognized that the assertive process had begun.

This is a natural phase of growing that we all have to pass though if we are normal. Without boundaries, a child keeps pushing (the thrown slice of bread becomes a cup, then a knife, and so on) until somebody or something finally sets a boundary or stopping place. If no boundaries exist, the subject floats in endless space and limbo; resistance is needed for substance of reality.

A child needs boundaries, not only for guidelines, but more importantly, to give structure to his or her life.

We humans use pretty much the same method as the bat in a cave to find our way through life. We send out feelers, or signals. If they go away, unanswered, we go straight on. If they hit an obstacle or barrier, we veer to avoid it. These signals and feedback from obstacles or guidelines are what determine a child's pathway to adulthood and through life. So the programming of our sending and receiving ability is extremely important.

One word explains the problem: vague; one word explains the solution: clarify. We need to clarify some boundaries between teacher and scholar. We need to clarify the distinction between informative and obscene. We need to distinguish between art and pornography. The absolute used for setting the definitions will vary. For example, the criteria for dividing scholar from teacher would have to be that one is paid to teach what his employer wants taught and should stay within guidelines of achieving the desired result. The scholar, on the other hand, is out to learn, so he had the right, under the Constitution's freedom of speech and academic freedom, to say anything he wants to anyone who will listen. The distinction here consist of two things: in the one case, we have a paid employee teaching and, molding a captive audience, captive under the compulsory law of the land. In the second case, we have a free citizen who, if someone says something to him, can disagree, rebut, or just simply walk away. Freedom of speech and academic freedom prevail.

How do you define between informative and obscene, or between art and pornography?

The definition of each of these would have to come from the reaction of the recipient; if it "turns on" the person, it is pornography. If it is received and analyzed objectively, unemotionally, it is art. Therefore, what is art to one will be pornography to another. This being the case, unless some genius of a liberal has come up with a way to gauge emotional reaction on a device such as the Richter scale, why should we not use the only sensible process available to us: selectivity.

(I have just come to realize something, dear reader. I have been exercising the liberals' criteria all my life and didn't know it. I have made a study of all the people whom I have encountered, a generous cross section of society, with no preempting guidelines set down by my predecessors. Using only inherent intelligence, unhampered by the education of yesterday, I have sought out and found my own conclusions on the human race.)

First to sixth grade: obviously no one will suggest four-letter words here (yet), so it comes down to basic philosophies: Christianity or Humanism? (They chose a philosophy very cleverly. Humanism is not even defined as a philosophy.) Can't choose? Then remain neutral. After all, the liberals are always screaming about separation of church and state. The Founding Fathers began the public school system to teach the Bible. They wrote the law separating church and state specifically to prevent government from interfering with this teaching of Christianity.

As a Supreme Court judge stated, "We have turned the meaning of this law completely around."

But if we cannot agree, teach no religion in school to a captive audience. Webster defines religion as "a way of life as incumbent on true believers, declared by authoritative teachers."

You have two choices to answer the question that Henry David Thoreau asked himself in his deep meditation down by Walden Pond: "Where did we come from and where are we going?"

We will assume that he never found the answer since everybody is still wondering about it, so the first choice is evolution. I think you would have to be a gibbering idiot to believe that a slimy amoeba somewhere in place and time started wiggling and decided to better himself, and from that ignoble beginning, Einstein was the end result. Especially when common sense and science agree that all evidence goes against the theory.

The second choice, the Bible, on the other hand, spells it out clearly from start to finish—where we came from and where we are going. Science has attacked it, as many adversaries have over the centuries, but it stands. Napoleon said, "The Bible conquers all that oppose it." Sir Isaac Newton said, "There are more sure marks of authenticity in the Bible than in any profane history"; and modern science is uncovering more and more of these marks as time goes on.

You choose as you will between the two. My choice is made.

The four-letter words are the beginning only in the sense of the desensitizing process. The "plan" is cleverly designed to correspond to the categories of normal advancement already established in the educational schedule.

The gentle, subtle, yet effective, dislodging of the elementary school child's faith in basic Bible beliefs and Christian principles is the real beginning.

In the secondary school, the second phase takes place, that being the introduction of the four-letter words. We will recognize at this point again that the student will eventually be exposed to these four-letter words. We all have in the past, clear back to

George Washington and beyond. But, again, we repeat that it is the respectability given these words being included in the school curricula, plus being force-fed to the child, that leads the forefront of our objection. But the desensitizing effect is the real damage, beginning in the first six grades.

The plan is culminated right on schedule, synchronized with the schedule of established education.

There were those who claimed that in no way could a book corrupt. If this were true, how could a book possibly have any social redeeming value or any beneficial purpose? If it cannot degrade, how can it possibly uplift? That defies the first law of physics itself: "For every action, there is a reaction."

What young man who read *Treasure Island* didn't acquire the burning passion to wrap a bandana around his head and go find a sailing ship? An avid reader doesn't read a book; he lives it. It flows through his mind and nervous system like an electric current, charging the memory bank of his computer with the thoughts and emotions irrevocably connected with the subject matter in its particular slant.

Whatever happened to the thesis that you were being cultured when you read Shakespeare ... or the conviction that you were learning a moral and a good lesson when you read *Ten Nights in a Bar Room*?

Who can argue that heredity plus environment equals the adult, and we contend that each book is an environment. After all, what is teaching? Is it not instilling the thoughts, ideas, concepts, and experience of others? Can you not instill the bad of these equally as easily as the good?

Doctor Underwood himself was photographed at a point in the controversy, carrying a sign that read EDUCATION IS A JOURNEY, NOT A DESTINATION. A journey takes one somewhere, up or down!

Stud Turkle, defending his book to objecting parents in Girard, Pennsylvania, in February 1982, said, "A few words do not make a book bad."

Although not occupying the same status as Shakespeare,

Mickey Spillane, the author of the Mike Hammer detective stories, would emphatically disagree. In one instance, he argued with his editor about changing his words in the book he had written. When the editor wouldn't relent, Spillane sent him a finished (almost, anyway) manuscript, with the exception of one word ... the very last one. The last sentence in the book went like this: "Juno was a ____."

It drove the editor up the wall. He called Spillane, virtually screaming in frustration. "All right, all right, what was Juno? What's the last word, for crying out loud?"

Of course, the last word was the key to the whole plot of the book. The last word was man. Juno was a man. Throughout the story, Juno had been posing as and living the life of a woman!

Do words—or even one word—not make a difference?

The favored fallacy of well-meaning parents is putting their trust in the proverb from the Bible: Train up a child in the way he should go. Even when he is old, he will not depart from it.

"If a child is exposed in the home daily to the family reading of the Bible and sees in the parents a conviction of God's reality and the need for a righteous life through Christ, no textbook, regardless of its content, will easily remove the child from deeply rooted beliefs," parents told themselves.

How right they might be, were it not for three factors. The first and foremost factor is found with the key phrase deeply rooted beliefs. In this day of preoccupation with making money and the allure of television, just how deeply rooted are those beliefs?

The second factor is that the parents are forgetting the generation gap that exists nowadays between parents and children; that gap being widened by the contents of these books, giving teachers priority.

The third factor, and the dynamite that will blast the other two to kingdom come, in such a soft way as to fulfill Kruschev's promise to "bury us so silently, we won't even know we're dead," is the plan in the books themselves, which tears at these very roots of belief.

Proponents of the books always focus in on the four-letter words, making it clear that children will read or hear them eventually anyway. The truth of that compels us to ask the obvious question: Why in heaven's name spend the taxpayers' hard-earned money and devote so much of the students' lives to teaching them something that they are going to learn so ridiculously easily on their own? This can be likened to expending the same money, time, and effort to teach them the sun will rise in the east every morning. That is to say nothing of lending respectability to these four-letter words by including them in the school curriculum.

And therein lays the embodiment of our entire objection to these books.

We recognize the reality of their learning the words, regardless, so this is not our concern; but rather the aforementioned waste and the label of respectability given them. We do not object to Mark Twain as an author; but rather that out of all his cheery, beautiful works, the one drab piece he ever wrote was the one chosen to be included in these books. We do not object to black authors; but rather that out of all the good black authors (I personally was inspired in my youth by a recounting of Booker T. Washington that I still remember to this day), they chose an avowed Communist black author who has openly, in his book, bragged of raping black women until he gained enough expertise in this endeavor to cross the tracks and defile the white man's woman with the same degradation.

We do not object to "Androcles and The Lion" being presented as a myth, as was reported on the national news by Walter Cronkite, trying feebly to suppress a smile in the telling (I personally called Mr. Cronkite's office in New York to clarify this, even though I knew it would do no good), but rather we object to its being told in direct correlation with, and in direct parallel to, the story of "Daniel in the Lions' Den" from the Bible, presented under the bold heading of MYTH. Furthermore, if this were the only instance of this, we could have easily overlooked it. In fact, that one story alone would not have even caught our eyes. It is when it is told in sequence, with a long line of parallels, with stories from the Bible under the label or heading MYTH that we object. And strenuously!

George Washington said this about the Bible: "It is impossible to rightly govern the world without God and the Bible."

Napoleon said, "The Bible is no mere book, but a Living Creature, with a power that conquers all that oppose it."

Ulysses S. Grant said, "The Bible is the sheet-anchor of our liberties."

Andrew Jackson said, "That book, sir, is the rock on which our republic rests."

Sir Isaac Newton said, "There are more sure marks of authenticity in the Bible than in any profane history."

Johann Wolfgang von Goethe said, "Let mental culture go on advancing, let the natural sciences progress in even greater extent and depth, and the human mind widen itself as much as it desires: beyond the elevation and moral culture of Christianity, as it shines forth in the Gospels, it will not go."

Horace Greeley said, "It is impossible to enslave, mentally or socially, a bible-reading people. The principles of the bible are the groundwork of human freedom."

There are those who will say these are staid thinkers, fossils of the past, skeletons to be perhaps preserved in a museum for curios, but not to be taken seriously or put to a plow. But have any of these contemporary wise men come up with a better set of guidelines than the Ten Commandments?

So there we have it, folks: the combined wisdom of the ages, both secular and religious. Want more proof? Check Revelation in the Bible and then read the headlines in your daily newspaper. Read McGuffey's outline for stability and sanity of civilization; compare the results of their time, when it was taught and in vogue, with what we see around us today as a result of the new generation's do your own thing and their free (nothing's free) sex, dope, and amoral thinking in general. Throw off the bondage of the chains of guidelines. Be free ... Interviewed any of them lately? Have you listened to some of the comments (admissions, really) of even the advocates of this line of thought, admitting that everything is not well?

Feel like you're in turmoil? Mixed up? Don't know where you're going and don't know what you're going to do when you get there? For that matter, don't even know where you are now? Or sometimes not even know who you are? Standing on a swirling quagmire of instability?

Would you like a rock under you? How about a rope to lead you to solid ground permanently?

After complex complexity, the only answer is simplicity. The answer to all these problems is one (simple enough) word: Bible!

The apex of verbal asininity is shared by two terms in their misuse. The two terms are academic freedom and censorship. Anytime an educator, especially a teacher, particularly a progressive teacher, wants to push anything through the educational system and someone balks or objects, they immediately begin screaming academic freedom at the top of their lungs, not unlike some of the characters I have seen in children's cartoons. (One such teacher at an NEA rally in Charleston, representing that ostentatious group, was asked by Bob Dornan, in the middle of her speech on the subject, if that freedom included a teaching saying the four-letter word f– in front of her class. The teacher literally screamed the reply, her face contorted with rage, "That is her right!") Is no ground sacred or forbidden to the plowshare of academic freedom pulled by the horse of progressive education?

William F. Buckley, in his book *God and Man at Yale*, points out that the scholar may perform two distinct functions. His is a teacher, and he is a seeker for truth. As a seeker, he enjoys academic freedom, and he promotes his viewpoint without interference. It is only by free expression that new ideas, deeper truths, and ultimately a better consensus are established. Academic freedom is essential to the process.

When the scholar teaches, his job is to promote accepted truths that are laid down by the organization that hired him. A math teacher would not be allowed to teach that two and two are five. In the field of social studies, the truth is not so clear, but certainly there are some values that cannot be denied. (I'm not convinced that there exists such clarity of distinction. I read of a man who had devoted his entire lifetime to the study of mathematics, and at the climax of that life, he could not be convinced that two and two are four, nor that the shortest distance between two points was a straight line)

Censorship is another loaded word that is often misused to create a false impression rather than to express the truth. There are so many books and other materials available that some selection must be made. As surely as some books are selected, others must be rejected. When is the choosing of one book and the rejection of another a legitimate selection process, and when is it an undesirable censorship? Too often the answer is that if you agree with the choice, it is a legitimate selection; if you disagree, it is censorship. Used this way, the word censorship becomes propaganda in the worst way.

"Jack be nimble, Jack be quick. Snap the blade and give it a flick. Grab the purse. It's easily done. Then just for kicks, just for fun, plunge the knife and cut and run." This is a selection from a nursery rhyme book entitled *The Inner City Mother Goose*, used in Philadelphia public schools in 1973. An attempt to get this book removed was being contested by the Civil Liberties Union as censorship.

Why did they not consider it censorship when they did not select a book in its place, such as Duncan Williams's *Trousered Apes*? This book became a best seller in England in spite of the fact that the literary establishment ignored it (perhaps they even tried to censor it). Few critics ever reviewed it, and no wonder—it condemns much of the current literature that the critics praise so highly. Furthermore, it traces the breakdown of values in our society to the literature that is being written today.

"Let he who is without sin cast the first stone." Christ's profound words, concerning the harlot at the well, have never been expounded in the way of improvement.

It's a shame that L. T. Anderson's education was retarded by the boundaries of secular textbooks and did not reach the realm of real understanding of life that can be found only in the Bible.

The *New York Times,* in an editorial, concluded that the present fad for pornography (this editorial appeared in early 1973) is just that—a fad. "It will spend itself in the course of time; people will get bored with it, will be able to take it or leave it alone in a mature way, and in some, we're being unnecessarily distressed about the whole business.

"In the end ... the insensate pursuit to shock, carried from one excess to a more abysmal one, is bound to achieve its own antidote and total boredom. When there is no lower a depth to descend to, ennui will erase the problem."

Let's begin at the beginning, at the root of the problem, or better put, at the germination of the root itself. Why spray a little insecticide on an oak tree that is already thirty feet tall and four feet in diameter? How much effort does it take, on the other hand, to uproot a tender shoot just pushing its way through the soil growing from an acorn?

We must begin our examination, as well as our cure of the problem, at its very base, in its basic form. The word basics, implies the foundation for learning or teaching and starts in kindergarten or the first grade. Grades one through six is where the groundwork is laid and the real damage is done.

Let's consider for a moment what the American people as a whole (the majority of them) have been preoccupied with for the last twenty or thirty years. The first thing that comes to mind, of course, is making money. This is true, but I'm thinking of their leisure time. What takes up their evening time?

If you had been called into as many homes as I have on business, at the request of the owner, and if you had tried to discuss that business between words and glimpses at the television, you would know the answer.

Let's consider, hypothetically, the generation of children who come out of their homes with the tube being their predominant time consumer and teacher. Their parents, also engrossed in the television, are too preoccupied to instill the old-fashioned values, principles, absolutes, and morals into their offspring.

Consider further (still hypothetically) what would happen if these same children are sent, with no firm standards, into the elementary schools, where they are taught from books that are programmed to deliberately destroy their belief in the Bible, treat God as a myth, hold Christ in ridicule, undermine parental authority as well as other kinds of authority, such as police, undermine their patriotism, and in general instill the basis for an amoral society, attacking everything we hold dear as the American way?

We intend to prove on the following pages that this is exactly the case. (When I interviewed a teacher, a devout Christian and a loving parent, who had taught in Charleston High School at the very time the textbook fight was at its height, who had no knowledge of the contents of the books, I asked her what her reaction would be if this were true. Her face paled, and she looked off in the distance and muttered, "God help us.")

"If you can induce a community to doubt the genuineness and authenticity of the scriptures, to question the reality and obligation of religion, to hesitate in deciding whether there be any such thing as virtue or vice, whether there be an eternal state of retribution beyond the grave, or whether there exists any such being as God, you have broken down the barriers of moral virtue and hoisted the floodgates of immorality and crime. I need not say that when a people have done this, they can no longer exist as a tranquil and happy people. Every bond that holds society together would be ruptured; fraud and treachery would take the place of confidence between man and man; the tribunals would be scenes of bribery and injustice; avarice, perjury, ambition, and revenge would walk through the land and render it more like the dwelling of savage beasts than the tranquil and happy abode of civilized and Christianized man."

Whether or not you subscribe to this is up to you (I can't understand how any thinking person of any measure of intelligence could avoid accepting it), and this is of no consequence. You may say that this couldn't happen—that these things are a matter of opinion and have no bearing or are not relevant.

What is important is the fact that this was written in 1854 in the McGuffey reader. Can any man, woman, or child argue that these things have taken place? For the cynics, I admit I wasn't alive in 1854, but there are history books and records, and the comparison of conditions then and now, the conditions described in the article are irrefutable, no matter who does the interpreting.

Ah, the interpreters. Therein lays the crux of the real problem. No matter what the subject, no matter what the event, everyone has his own rendition. That is precisely why we need absolutes.

Try to imagine a world where everyone makes up his or her mind about everything based on his or her own feelings.

Start with a traffic signal; no set rule applies, so Joe pulls up to the red light, decides that it is an infringement on his rights by the establishment to tell him when he can or cannot drive his own private car. He feels like doing his own thing and goes on through, immediately broadsiding the car driven by Pete, complete with family, who has followed the absolute of the traffic law, killing all the occupants.

A world without absolutes is a world without sanity. Man's adaptability is, at once, his greatest asset and his greatest liability. Submit him to terrible circumstances for a while, and he will adapt. He will get used to it.

Example: Poverty-ridden people living in squalor adapt to it; they don't even see the loose boards on the porch, don't smell the stench of the outhouse or the pigpen. Beans and potatoes taste quite good when you're used to them ... and with the sauce of hunger poured over them.

Now, in theory of logic, if these people find these conditions tolerable, almost pleasurable at times, if they were moved into slightly better circumstances, with better food, they should remain happy for the rest of their lives. Right? Wrong. Why? They adapt. Or, as we more commonly put it, they adjust.

They are happy for a time, but when the adapting process is complete, they are once more dissatisfied, usually even more so than they were in their previous, much poorer circumstances. This is partly due to the adapting process but more so because now their appetite has been whetted for better things, or the good life.

Hubert Humphrey once said, "Poverty-ridden people in the ghettos have accepted their lot, have resigned themselves to their fate. But give them the slightest ray of hope, of improvement and they become frantic in their pursuit of hope to get out."

There is nothing wrong in wanting to improve one's condition. Our point is that the subject in question has adapted. His endurance of his former state was an example of his adaptability being an asset; the second phase was an example of his adaptability being a liability. Had he not adapted to his second condition, he would have been forever happy. We need absolutes for an anchor on the sea of adaptability.

What squirrel hunter has not sat in the woods after shooting one squirrel, waiting for another to come along, marking the spot where the first squirrel fell by one particular tree; then, the longer he sits there, the more the other trees around that one begin to look alike, until he can't tell one from the other?

Without absolutes to come back to, like a tall tree, to get our bearings from, our trees blend together until we can't distinguish one from the other. Then any old tree will do.

The battle cry (or bleating) of the liberals—"If we let them start, where will they stop?"—could also be taken up by the conservatives, could it not? The favored tactic of the liberals is to accuse everybody else of what they are doing themselves. Did they not begin the censoring process when they insisted on taking the story *Little Black Sambo* from children's books?

The battle cry could apply generally, but in this case, we're thinking specifically of censorship.

Think of the absurdity of it, dear reader. A favored classic that has endeared itself to generations of people, numbering in the millions, is struck from the records forever, never to be read again by anyone for the simple reason that it might, just might, offend a small number of a minority group. And the liberals see no hint of censorship in this. (Do they not give blacks credit for having a sense of humor? The majority of the blacks I've been privileged to know have the ability to laugh at themselves.)

But then, when the vast majority asks their children not be

submitted to shocking profanity, disgusting vulgarisms, assaults on their religion and their country, the liberals are up in arms, screaming censorship.

Hitler knew people well. It has been documented that his philosophy was, tell the people a big enough lie and they will believe it; that seems to apply to absurdities as well as lies, Adolph.

If we are to be realistic, we cannot go to either extreme. Censorship, unchecked, is abhorrent. But we could take up pages and volumes of examples of words and topics that do not belong in certain places; we're not talking about just textbooks. There is a time and place for every word and subject in the English language.

It is not a question of censorship, dear reader. It is a question of selectivity—what belongs where, and for what purpose. We are not even advocating favoring the majority over the minority. (Although most people seem to feel this is what a democracy is supposed to be all about, that the majority rules. We are aware, dear liberal, of the eleven instances in the Constitution where the majority does not make the choice.)

In the particular that we are dealing with now, education, first we have to come to a consensus concerning the definition of the word educate (or education).

Webster defines it, quoting verbatim: "to rear, bring up, educate; to bring up (as a child or animal); rear 2a: to develop (as a person) by fostering degrees the growth or expansion of knowledge, wisdom, desirable qualities of mind or character, physical health, or general competence esp. by providing a course of normal study or instructions; provide or assist in providing with knowledge or wisdom, moral balance, or physical condition esp. by means of a formal education."

Out of all this morass of words, one two-letter word (no, not a four-letter word) is the key to the whole thing.

Almost every other word quoted here is open for argument. Let's take them one by one, starting with develop. What is develop? To grow, to increase, to add to. All these and more, but to grow in which direction? Which information to add to?

Knowledge is simple. Everyone knows what knowledge is; it's when one knows something. The only question—what knowledge to feed whom?

Wisdom is a toughie. What is wisdom? What is wise to one is foolish to another.

Desirable qualities falls into the same category. What is desirable to one is not desirable to another.

Physical health can generally be agreed upon, even by liberals and conservatives, to a degree anyway.

Have you discovered the key word, dear reader? By now, you should have, by the process of elimination.

No? Still don't have it? Ready? The word is up. Yes, I said up.

Who can say that up is not up? Who can argue that up is not up any more than they can argue with Newton's law of gravity?

Let he who would argue that up is not up jump out of a tree and see which way he will fall. Prove Newton wrong and we will arbitrate the word up.

Now that we have settled once and for all that the word up is not arbitrary, why is it the key word?

First, it is because it is not arbitrary. I'm sorry, dear liberal, but here we have ourselves an absolute. Yes, an absolute! (Some will argue that up is relative, depending on where you are. Not so. Using your present position as reference, benchmark, or starting point, up is still up!)

Taking this absolute, let us examine education per se, in the light of Mr. Norman O. Brown's thinking. Mr. Brown says that for "his kind of salvation" to be achieved, humanity has to annul the civilization it has created—not merely the civilization we have today, but all civilization (destroy history; "don't hang on to yesterday") ... in order to make the long descent (down, the opposite of up) backward into animal innocence.

Mr. Brown is convinced of the conclusion of this, coupled with a "reversion to infantile sexuality is the ultimate mission and secret destiny of the human race."

So there it is, folks, broken down to its simplest basic. Black or white, up or down is the choice—not whether we want a better education for our children, for what is better, and who is to define better and choose which is better?

Where we are now, to use the liberal's favorite word, is irrelevant. Even the liberals will agree that we are neither at the beginning of education, nor at the end of it. We are somewhere in between.

So now the question is, where do we go from here, up or down? Do we go down the gutter with Eldridge Cleaver for a step in the regression that Mr. Brown speaks of ... or do we go up—up to the divine heaven (we've always referred to heaven as being up) hoped for by all Christians and promised us by the Bible.

It is clear what the consensus of even the liberal press is concerning which direction these books and methods are taking us. This is surmised from the editorial of the *New York Times*, quoted earlier in this article, "In the end ... the insensate pursuit to shock, carried from one excess to a more abysmal one, is bound to achieve its own antidote and total boredom. When there is no lower depth to descend to ..." Descend to ...? In...the end ...?

Is that what we have come to? Are we merely on the defensive, fighting rearguard battles to stave off the inevitable? Have we already accepted Norman O. Brown's concept of destiny?

Is that why it is more important to be relevant than reasonable? To become familiar with Eldridge Cleaver's tactics in order to make the choice and carry out, execute, either to cope with him or join him instead of learning the principles of George Washington and the absolutes of the Bible to fight back the tide of immorality?

Instead of asking, what is truth, wouldn't it be more relevant for the now generation to ask, What is sanity? For out of sanity comes truth, and out of truth comes sanity.

Even if this were true, that the Bible had been written by a man or men (mortally inspired and constructed), wouldn't it still be just a choice of philosophies? How many skeptics, for how many centuries, including a Pulitzer Prize winning scholar of civilizations and anthropology, by his own admission spent the major portion of his life convinced that he was an atheist. When asked, in the interview for his Pulitzer Prize, what philosophy made the most sense to him out of all the knowledge that he had researched, he answered, "The philosophy of the carpenter of Nazareth, Jesus Christ."

Many have tried in many ways to discredit it ... to destroy it. And yet it stands.

When I was a boy growing up in the hills of West Virginia, to me, religion and Jesus were colloquial. They were peripheral in my little village, embodied in the weather-beaten, gnarled little form of my aging uncle standing behind the homemade pulpit of rough boards in the little rough board church built by him and his brothers on his father's farm.

When he pointed his work-hardened Pentecostal finger at me from behind that rough board pulpit and told me I was going to hell unless I mended my ways, I trembled in fear. The belief that someday I would walk the paved streets of the great city of Charleston, where reality and relevance prevailed gave me a feeling of comfort. Well, I made it to Charleston, and I admit that I felt more secure, sheltered from the hellfire and brimstone of my uncle and the other primitive thinkers of my backward surroundings.

Then I joined the navy to see the world. And I did experience a goodly portion of it, including the worldly Big Apple, New York, and the glitter of Hollywood.

Coming back home to Charleston, getting married and starting a business exposed me to a closer, more personal view of the world. The more I grew both personally and in friends and acquaintances, the more the perspective toward religion amazed me.

In my opinion, I ran the scale from the ignorance of my uncle, who narrow-mindedly thought all hocus-pocus was real, up to the reality of life in Charleston, then on to New York, and finally topped off my education and therefore gained my liberation from superstition and other primitive thoughts that were like shackles holding me down.

But then, as my relationships with people broadened, I began to run into belief in the same Jesus that I thought was my uncle's personal pipe dream.

I thought at first that it was confined to unlearned fundamentalists, but I gradually and surprisingly worked my way up the scale of the educational, social, and financial levels, finding people at all levels professing the same simple belief in the same Jesus. I began to look again at religion. (By now, I had begun to call it Christianity to differentiate from the other Great Religions of the world that I had also studied.)

I finally reached the peak of all three levels that Charleston had to offer, some of them quite wealthy and well traveled. The ones nearest the pinnacle had the same basic concept of Jesus and Christianity that my uncle had told me about.

The climbing of the scale was culminated by the statement of the Pulitzer Prize winner who had devoted a lifetime to studying civilizations, and therefore people and philosophies, when he said, "The man who makes more sense to me out of all this is Jesus Christ."

The man saying this had covered the world, near and far, with close scrutiny, and was world renowned for his expertise.

The liberal media refers to the word fundamentalist as if it were a dirty word. The term is applied to people who take the Bible literally. Not taking it literally means deleting or changing some of the contents, does it not? I ask you, dear reader, is that not a form of censorship?

If you like this book, you will want to read another book written from the point of view of one of the protesters: *Protester Voices: The 1974 Textbook Tea Party*, by Karl Priest.

[1] The author called Mel Gabler mid-February 1982 to obtain some research material for the writing of this book. Mr. Gabler informed him that the Japanese were sending television reporters to his home for an interview because Japan now had the same problem in their country's textbooks as Kanawha County had in 1974.

www.ingramcontent.com/pod-product-compliance
Lightning Source LLC
LaVergne TN
LVHW021220080526
838199LV00084B/4297

* 9 7 9 8 8 8 7 7 5 3 3 0 0 *